CANDID
NEW YORK

CANDID
NEW YORK

THE PIONEERING PHOTOGRAPHY
OF GEORGE BRADFORD BRAINERD

ERIK HESSELBERG

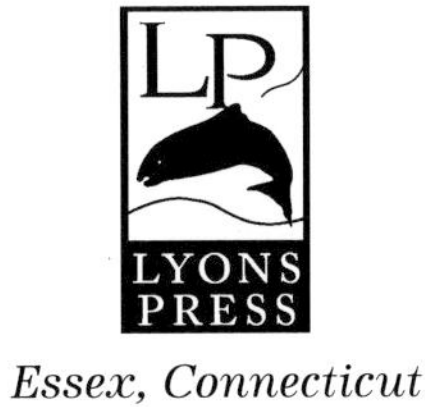

LYONS
PRESS

Essex, Connecticut

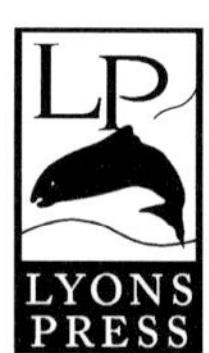

An imprint of The Globe Pequot Publishing Group, Inc.
64 South Main Street
Essex, Connecticut 6426
www.globepequot.com

British Library Cataloguing in Publication Information available

Library of Congress Cataloging-in-Publication Data available
ISBN 9781493090549 (hardback : alk. paper)
ISBN 9781493090716 (electronic)

♾️ The paper used in this publication meets the minimum requirements of American National Standard for Information Sciences—Permanence of Paper for Printed Library Materials, ANSI/NISO Z39.48-1992.

CONTENTS

New York is not a picturesque city, like London or Paris. . . . It has no great antiquity, and has, therefore, little regard for what is old. In London or Paris you may see some relics of past centuries; these are reverenced and preserved as long as they endure. But New York is a series of experiments, and every thing which has lived its life and played its part is held to be dead, and is buried, and over it grows a new world.

—*Harper's Weekly*, 1869

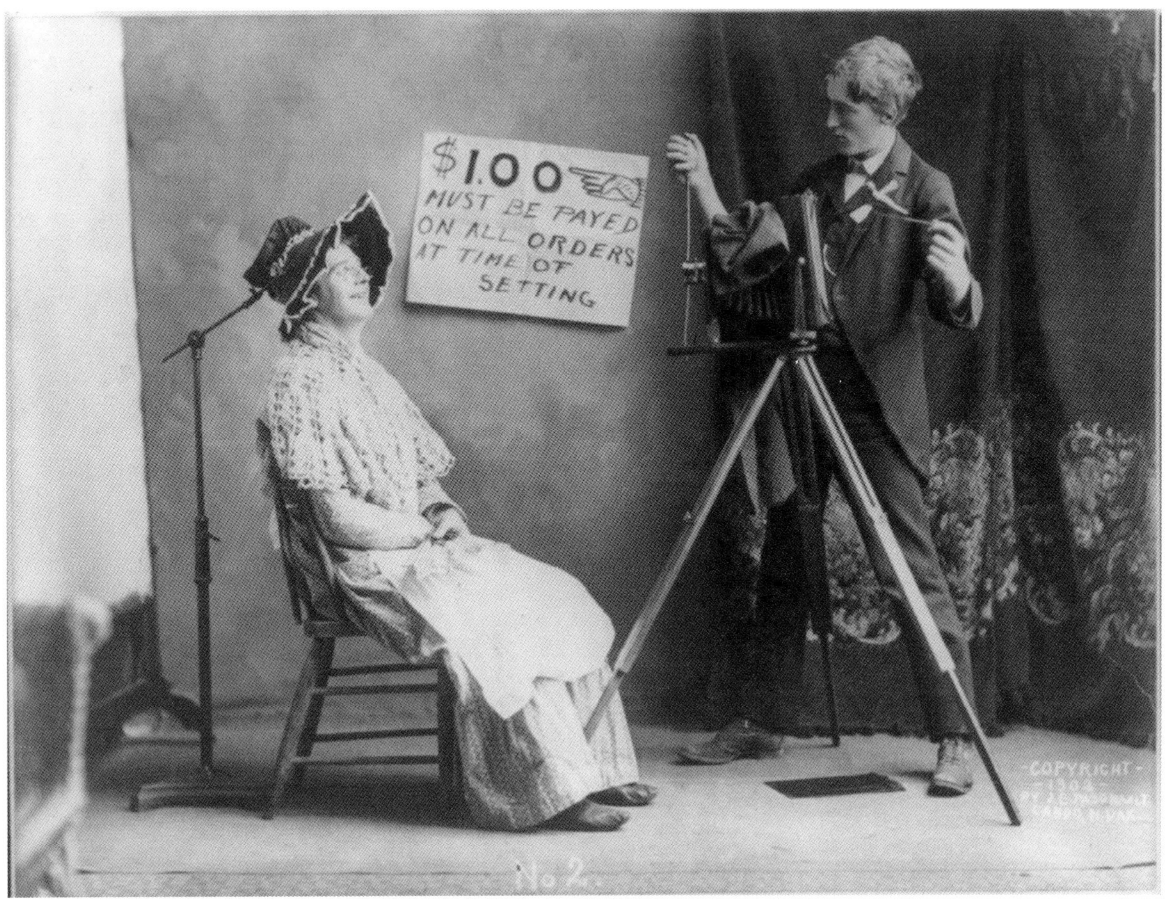

The Man of the Crowd

" **I** am a passionate lover of the snapshot," the great Austrian-American street photographer Lisette Model once remarked, "because of all photographic images it comes closest to the truth." The snapshot— it's part of our collective consciousness. And yet, the use of the word for an informal image taken quickly with a hand-held camera is rather recent. Many would date it to around 1888, when a former bank clerk from Upstate New York introduced to the world a compact box camera known as the "Kodak," a word its inventor, George Eastman, admitted meant nothing but could be pronounced in almost any language. The Kodak retailed for about $25—far less than most photographic cameras at the time. But the best part was that it came preloaded with 100 shots and when they were taken you shipped the entire camera back to Eastman's factory in Rochester, New York, where workers developed the photos and mailed them back to you along with your reloaded camera. "You press the button, we do the rest," the Kodak slogan rang.

George Eastman *was* a marketing genius who helped bring picture-taking to the masses with his inexpensive, easy-to-use-Kodak and Brownie cameras, but he is not the "father of the snapshot," as is often claimed. Nor was the Kodak Number One, US Patent No. 388,850, awarded on September 4, 1888, the first commercially produced handheld camera. That honor goes to William Schmid and his "Patent Detective Camera," which dates to 1883. And Schmid's camera was far from being unique. It was virtually an exact copy of a box-form camera patented the previous year by a well-known analytical chemist in London, Thomas Bolas. Bolas called his invention a "Detective Camera," as it was designed to aid police in investigations. The name stuck, and soon all hand cameras would be referred to in this way, much to the dismay of serious amateurs who would now be put in the category of Peeping Toms.

You won't find George Bradford Brainerd's name in any of the histories of photography. And yet there is every reason to believe that it was this 19th-century engineer with the Brooklyn Water Department, not Eastman nor even Bolas, who produced the first handheld photographic camera in existence—laying the groundwork for a new era of candid picture-taking. Brainerd, whose patrician lineage stretched back to the *Mayflower* Pilgrims, had been tinkering with photographic cameras since he was 12 years old. Later, the Brooklyn engineer, who worked with the Water Department in the 1870s and 1880s as its deputy purveyor of water,

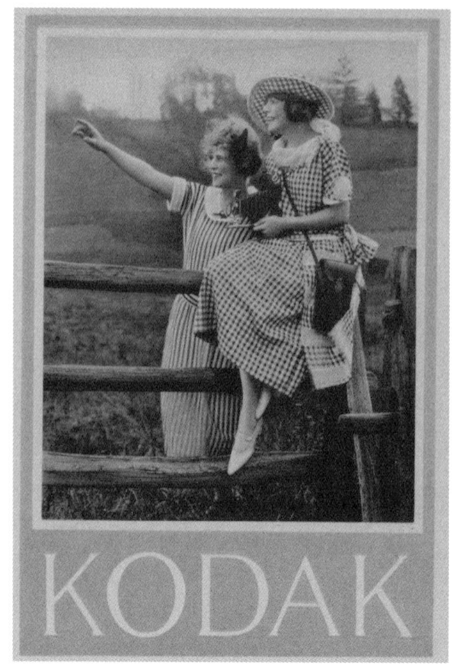

George Eastman brought picture-taking to the masses in the late 19th and early 20th century with his inexpensive, easy-to-use-Kodak and Brownie cameras. (The first Kodak was introduced in 1888.) However, his were not the first commercially produced handheld cameras. That honor goes to George Bradford Brainerd, who was employing "hand" cameras of his own make as early as 1875.

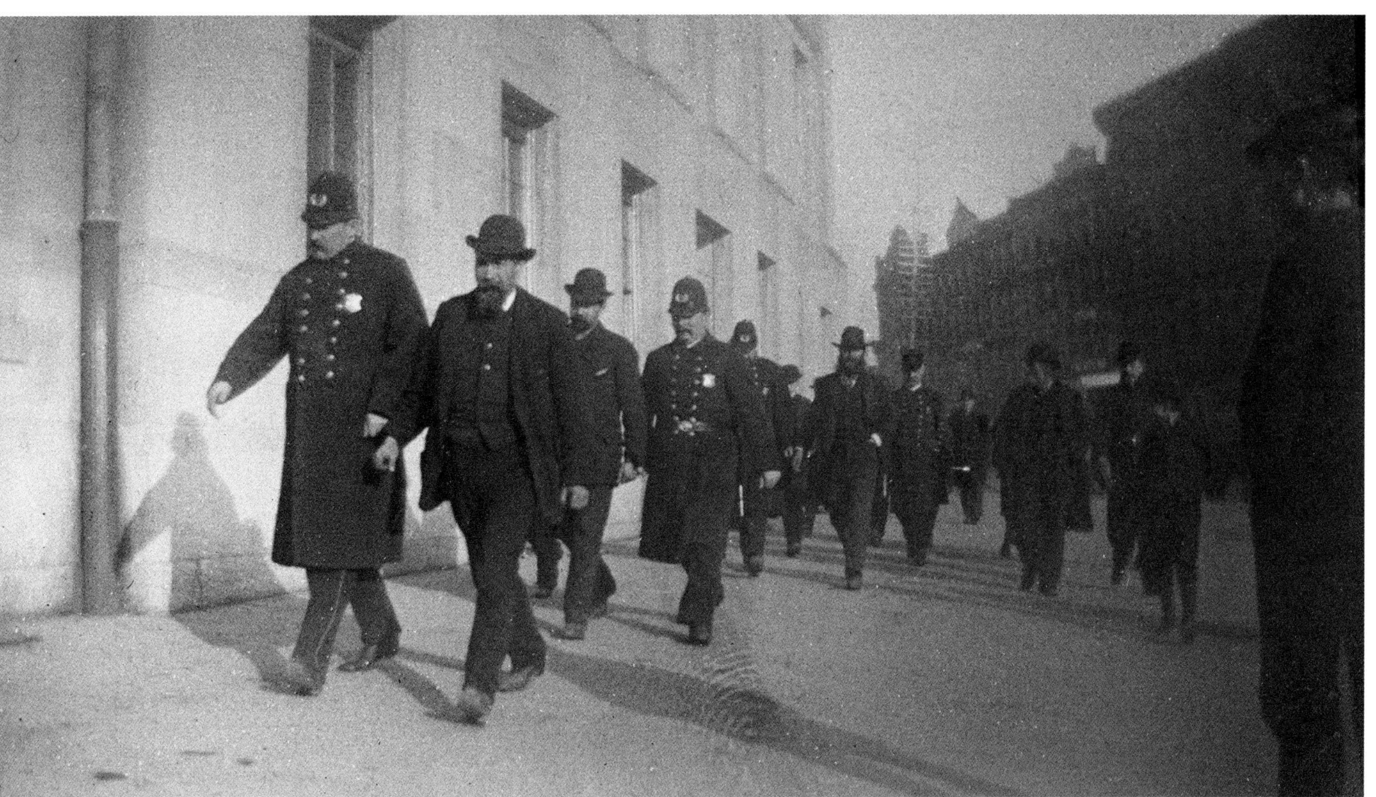

fashioned what he called a "slide-box," as it consisted of two boxes, one sliding into the other. Taking 3¼ by 4¼ inch plates, it had many features of the modern camera, such as a plate reservoir or "magazine," allowing six or eight exposures to be made before reloading, and a viewfinder for waist-level focusing. A perfected model resembling a twin-reflex camera had the viewing lens focused by the same mechanism as the taking lens. But the most important feature was a mechanical "snap shutter," permitting exposures of up to 1/250 of a second. This, along with more sensitive film emulsions, which Brainerd prepared himself, allowed the photographer to freeze motion as early as 1875—several years before the Englishman Eadweard Muybridge made his famous sequence of pictures of the trotting horse *Occident* galloping on a California racetrack.

Brainerd would create a wide range of hand-held and spy or "detective" cameras long before the

Prisoners escorted to court, Brooklyn, 1875. This image is remarkable for two reasons: First, Brainerd has managed to freeze movement as early as 1875, half a dozen years before anyone else, with the exception of Eadweard Muybridge. More significantly is that the Brainerd picture, what we now refer to as a "Perp Walk," may record a famous murder trial, one that rocked Brooklyn in 1875, when an Irishman, John McGuire, was sentenced to life in prison for killing two Black men in a Brooklyn park following a scuffle after a dance. Brainerd's photograph was taken just about the time McGuire and two associates were being tried in Brooklyn. The picture clearly shows three handcuffed men being led to court, surrounded by other officers, just the sort of show of force one would expect for a high-profile murder trial.

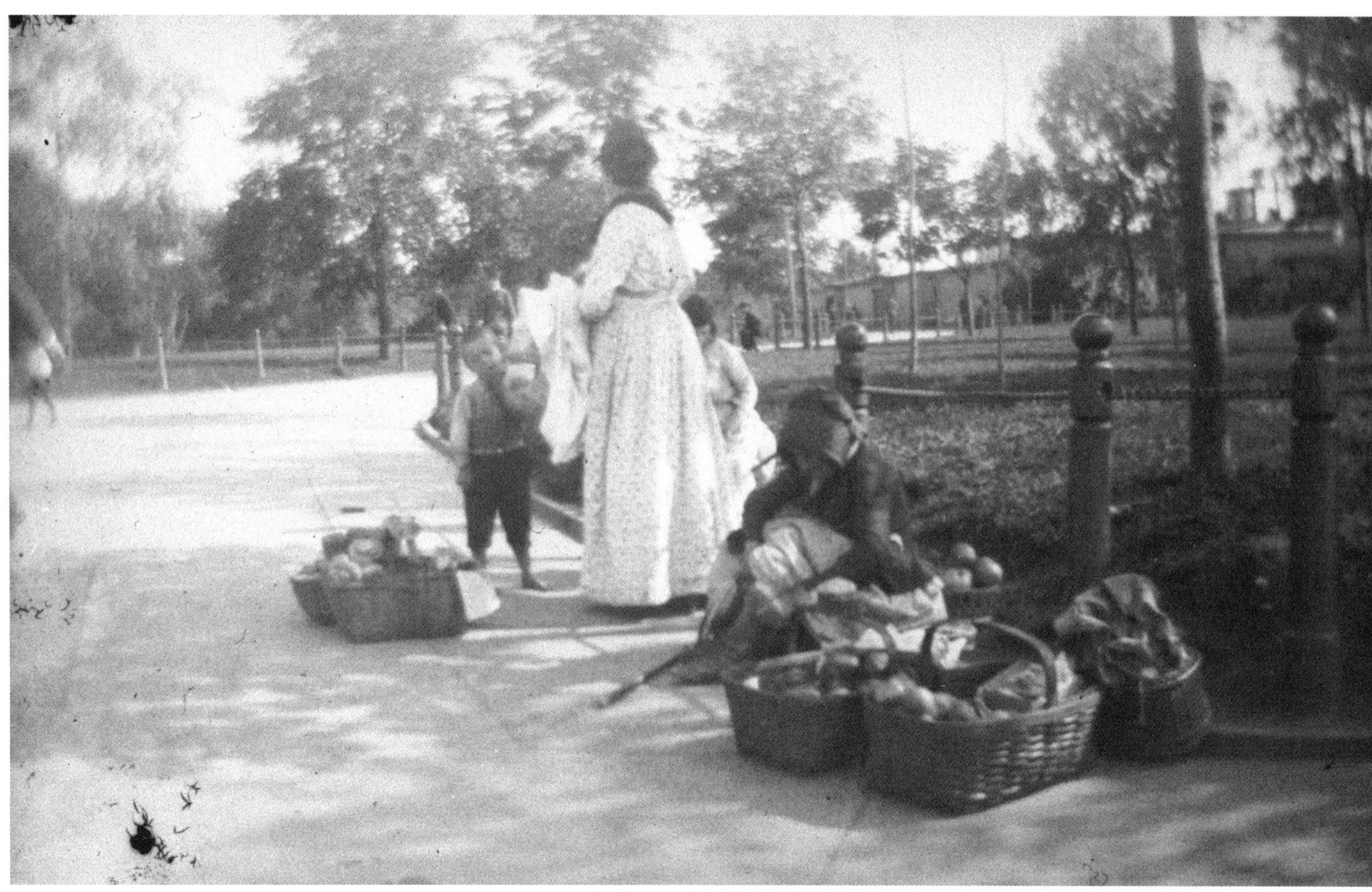

Apple seller in Battery Park in Lower Manhattan, late 1870s. George Bradford Brainerd Photograph Collection, Brooklyn Public Library/Center for Brooklyn History.

technology existed in the marketplace. But he never sought recognition for any of his inventions (only one of his cameras was ever patented), sharing his discoveries merely with other dedicated amateurs like himself who founded Brooklyn's first photography society. More than anything Brainerd loved picture-making. Breaking away from the romantic conventions of painting, which guided most photographers of the day, Brainerd used his camera to record the kinds of commonplace scenes that were seldom documented, offering a rare glimpse of urban life in the Victorian era. He would produce a total of 2,500 images during his brief 17-year career—a vast documentation of the urban landscape—dams and mills, bridges and train depots, engine houses and pumping stations—but also, starting in the late 1870s, images of city dwellers and street scenes. It is these latter pictures, many depicting long extinct Victorian

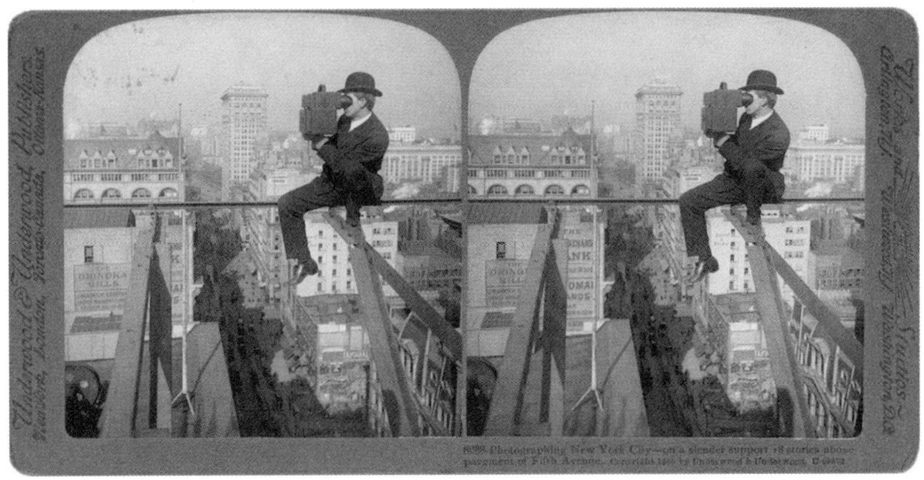

street types—apple peddlers, flower vendors, street musicians, dockworkers, artisans, and laborers—that are perhaps the most astonishing. Indeed, such a camera record is unknown in American photography at that period, making Brainerd not only a pioneering inventor, but also, it appears, New York's first street photographer.

Unposed street photographs of one sort or another had been made since the 1850s; the relatively small negatives of the stereographic camera allowed the use of short focal-length lenses that gave adequate exposure at snapshot speeds, which more or less stopped normal street action if the photographer kept his distance. If, however, the photographer wished to capture the character of the streets and something of the subject's quality of life, he posed the photograph. This was the technique used by the French photographer Charles Nègre in the 1850s, and the Scottish photographer John Thompson, who documented London street life in the 1870s. Meanwhile, Brainerd, revolutionary for the time, used instantaneous, snapshot photography to capture spontaneous, unrehearsed action.

It's worth noting that most of Brainerd's subjects didn't know they were being photographed. The Brooklyn engineer was the first to employ what came to be known as the spy or detective camera, allowing the photographer to sneak in for a shot without the subject's knowledge.

Dual-lens stereographic cameras such as the one pictured above, which used short focal-length lenses, produced some of the first "instantaneous" images, provided the photographer did not get too close to his subject. However, if the picture-taker wished to capture more of the character of the street, he had to pose his subjects. The was the technique employed in the 1870s by the French street photographer Charles Nègre.

Such clandestine cameras were often disguised to look like something other than what they were—a book, a bag, a briefcase, even a basket of flowers. An especially popular model was worn under a vest, "letting the lens wink through a deceiving button." Brainerd camouflaged his camera to look like a book or a brown paper package. The viewfinder was rudimentary and served mainly to aim rather than compose. Thus, horizons are often tilted and figures radically cropped at the edge of the frame—a style that would influence French Impressionist painter Edgar Degas, who was deeply interested in photography. It's this snapshot aesthetic that we see in Brainerd's street scenes that make his photographs appear so modern though they were taken 150 years ago.

The photographer's love of motion and delight in freezing action also drew him to pleasure grounds like Coney Island, where his keen eye captured bathers frolicking in the waves and little boys and girls playing in the sand. Winter brought Brainerd to New York's Central Park and Brooklyn's Prospect Park to photograph skaters gliding over the ice and boys sledding down hills. His ubiquitous camera also recorded what are probably the first action shots ever produced of ladies playing tennis, the fashionable new sport that had just arrived in New York from England. Victorians are rarely seen smiling, but Brainerd managed to snap a picture of a young woman in a fur coat squealing with delight as she is whisked across the ice in a special chair with runners. The role of women was changing and with it what was considered proper behavior for ladies in public. There was a new looseness and relaxation in the air. And George Brainerd was there to capture those changes.

Without reference to its artistic quality, Brainerd's photographic record of Gilded Age Brooklyn and New York would be important by virtue of its sensitivity as an ethnographic study. And yet, the photographer was unknown for half a century. Even today, few have heard his name outside a handful of specialists. One problem is

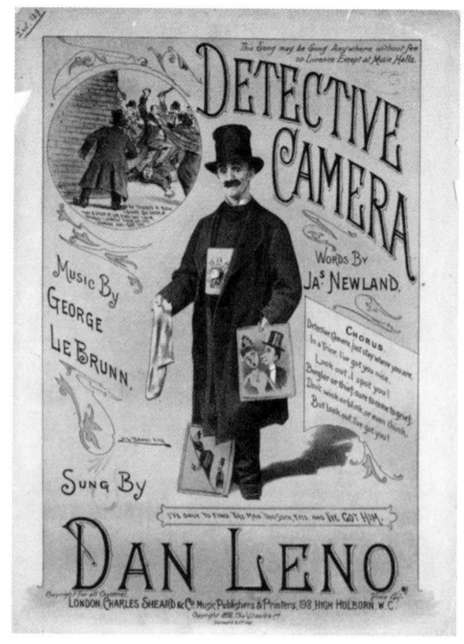

So called "detective" cameras were so ubiquitous in the 1890s there was even song poking fun at the fad, made popular by the English music hall star Dan Leno: "Don't wink or blink, or even think, but just stay where you are/I'll introduce myself to you—Detective camera," went the rollicking tune. The name "detective" stemmed from the fact that the first models were intended for police use.

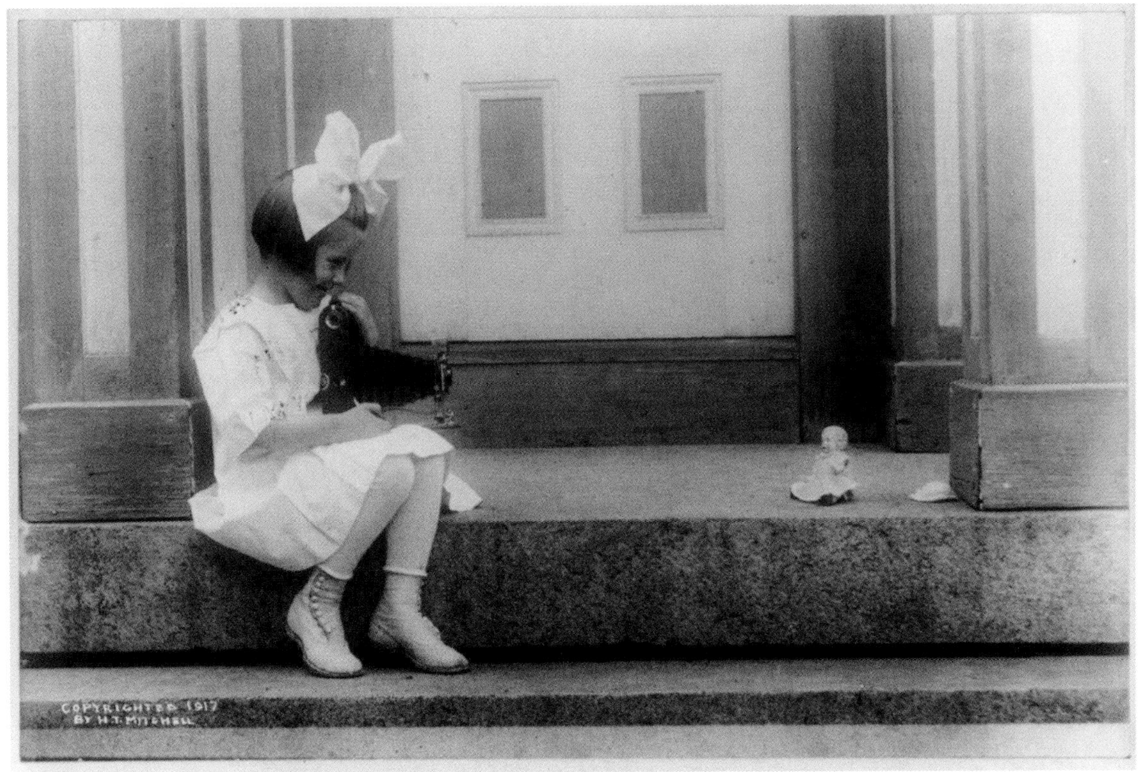

that Brainerd, despite his prolific output, left behind not a single print—not even contact prints. One wonders whether Brainerd would have wanted his work to be seen at all. Was he embarrassed by the fact that he had used subterfuge to obtain his best pictures? Such surreptitious photography carried the taint of the voyeur, with the new "snap-shooters" appearing to peer into others' private affairs for their own devilish pleasure. In Germany, then called Prussia, a ban was even considered on the use of such detective cameras, which would be dubbed *Zabur apparat* or "witch's machine." "We now have snapshots," a member of the Prussian state assembly warned. "This process will allow portraits to be stolen, and it may be that extraordinary precautions will need to be taken, and perhaps in the end we shall have to wear masks."

That Brainerd is known at all is almost entirely due to an Estonian-born aristocrat and engineer who had once worked on the 2,000-kilometer Murmansk to Moscow railway. Hermann de Wetter, whose full name was Hermann

A whimsical Kodak promotional image from the early 1900s designed to show that the camera, in this case an early bellows model, was so simple even a child could operate it.

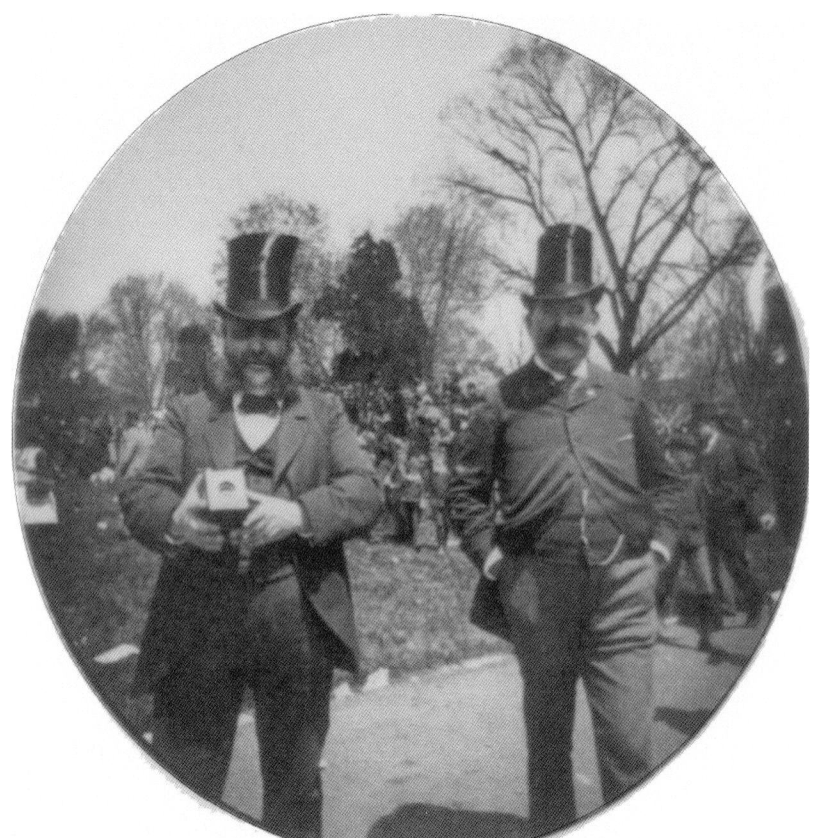

Two prosperous gentlemen, one with an early handheld camera, out for a photographic excursion on the "White House," grounds. Though immensely popular, such mobile cameras were not universally appreciated. In Germany, for instance, a ban was even considered on the use of such detective cameras, which were dubbed *Zabur apparat* or "witch's machine."

Ferdinand Friedrich von Wetter-Rosenthal, had been a civil engineer for the prominent construction firm of Holbrook, Cabot & Rollins, which also built the New York subway system. However, like so many during the Great Depression, de Wetter lost his job after the stock market crash of October 28, 1929, and the former engineer, who had "built a railroad and made it run," was himself asking his brother if he "could spare a dime." Fortunately, de Wetter was not without skills. While in Moscow, he had taught himself photography and was an accomplished portraitist. This, along with his patrician pedigree, made him attractive to the directors of the Brooklyn Museum, which in 1934, hired de Wetter as a staff photographer and head of their newly created photography department. It was during a survey of the museum's holdings that de Wetter stumbled upon a large collection of glass negatives from an unknown 19th-century photographer that for years had been sitting in the museum's damp basement.

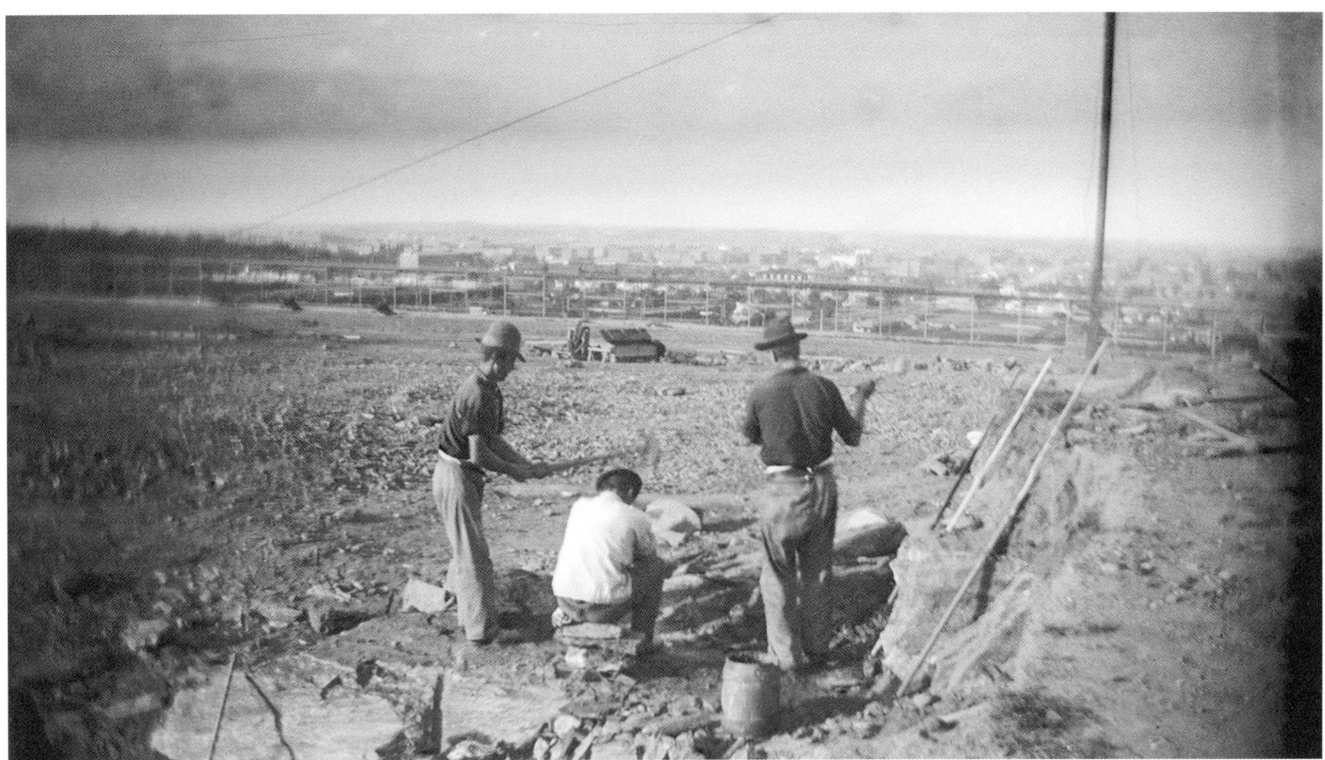

It's something of a mystery how the Brainerd negatives, more than 2,500 at the time of their discovery, ended up at the Brooklyn Museum. Some of the plates may have been donated by a family member soon after the photographer's death in 1887. However, the bulk of the collection, some 2,000 plates, arrived through a random discovery, when some years before World War I, boxes of Brainerd's negatives were found in an empty house on Gates Avenue in Brooklyn's Bedford-Stuyvesant neighborhood. Before de Wetter, no one had ever considered exhibiting the work. It's likely no one even looked at the fragile glass plates, many of which were still wrapped in old newspapers.

For a museum to make a serious commitment to photography at the time was almost inconceivable, let alone the work of an unknown amateur. Only a few years before, the Museum of Modern Art's acquisition of a painting by Cézanne had raised eyebrows. The notion that photography deserved serious attention was, in the words of the great curator John Szarkowski, "simply unintelligible

Though himself a member of the silk-stocking set, George Brainerd had a keen appreciation for work and the working-class, whose toils he often photographed. Quarry workers, such as those seen above, had a special place in his heart, as his father, Diodate Brainerd, owned granite quarries in Haddam Neck, Connecticut, where George was born in 1845.

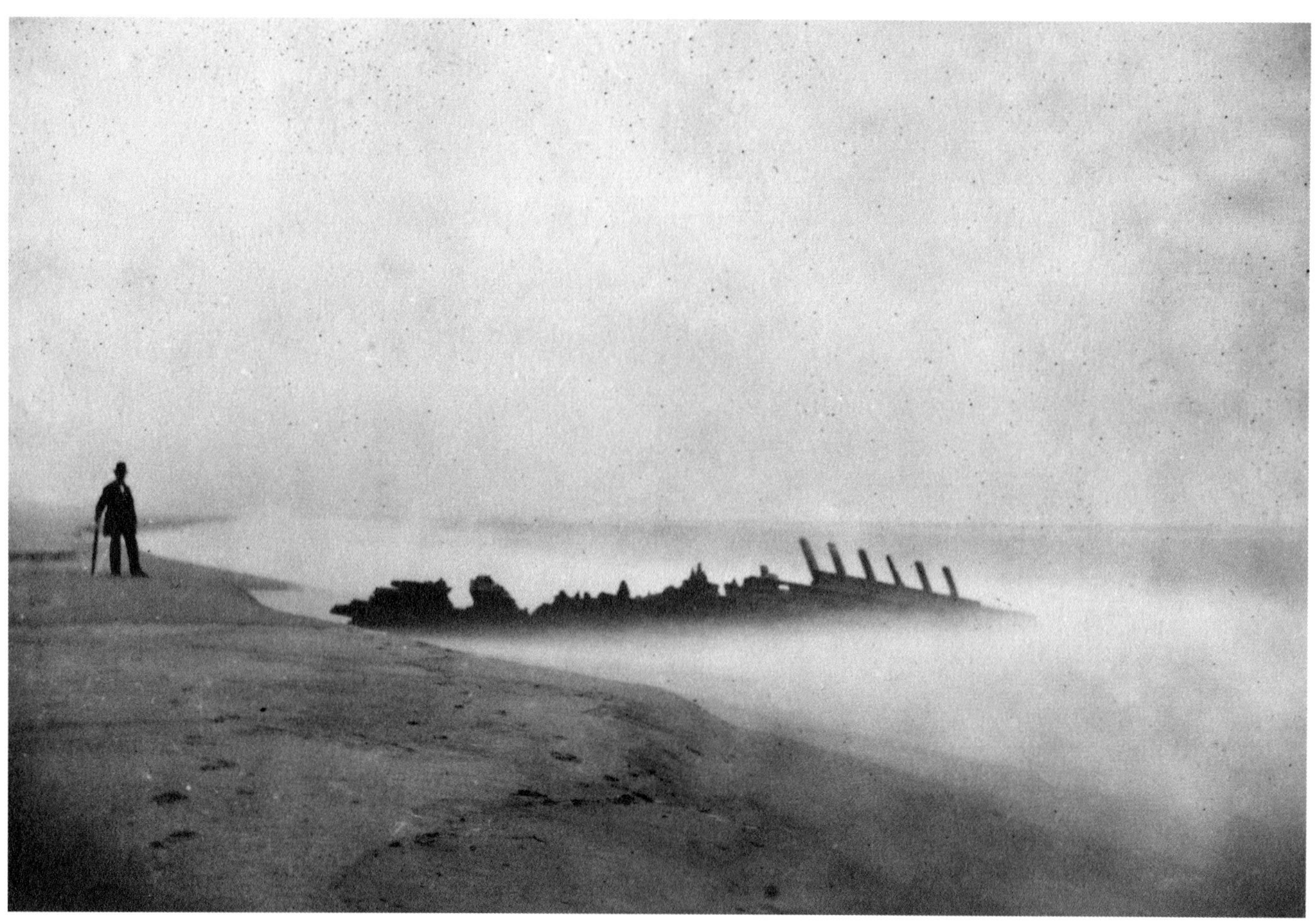

to the leaders of most art museums." But de Wetter was far-sighted. It was the onetime engineer who started the Brooklyn Museum's photography collection, acquiring the relatively unknown works of Walker Evans, André Kertesz, Lázló Moholy-Nagy, Man Ray, and Charles Sheeler. De Wetter was also a close friend of Berenice Abbott, the gifted documentary photographer who had studied with Man Ray and had just returned from Paris to begin her landmark study of New York, "Changing New York," which would be funded by Roosevelt's Works Project Administration, or WPA.

In New York, Abbott could not stop talking about a French street photographer she had met at Man Ray's studio and even photographed a few days before he died. This was Eugène Atget, whose prints and negatives she would

Wreck on Amagansett Beach, Brighton, 1875. An eerie, early morning image using the wet-plate process with a relatively long exposure. George Bradford Brainerd Photograph Collection, Brooklyn Public Library/ Center for Brooklyn History.

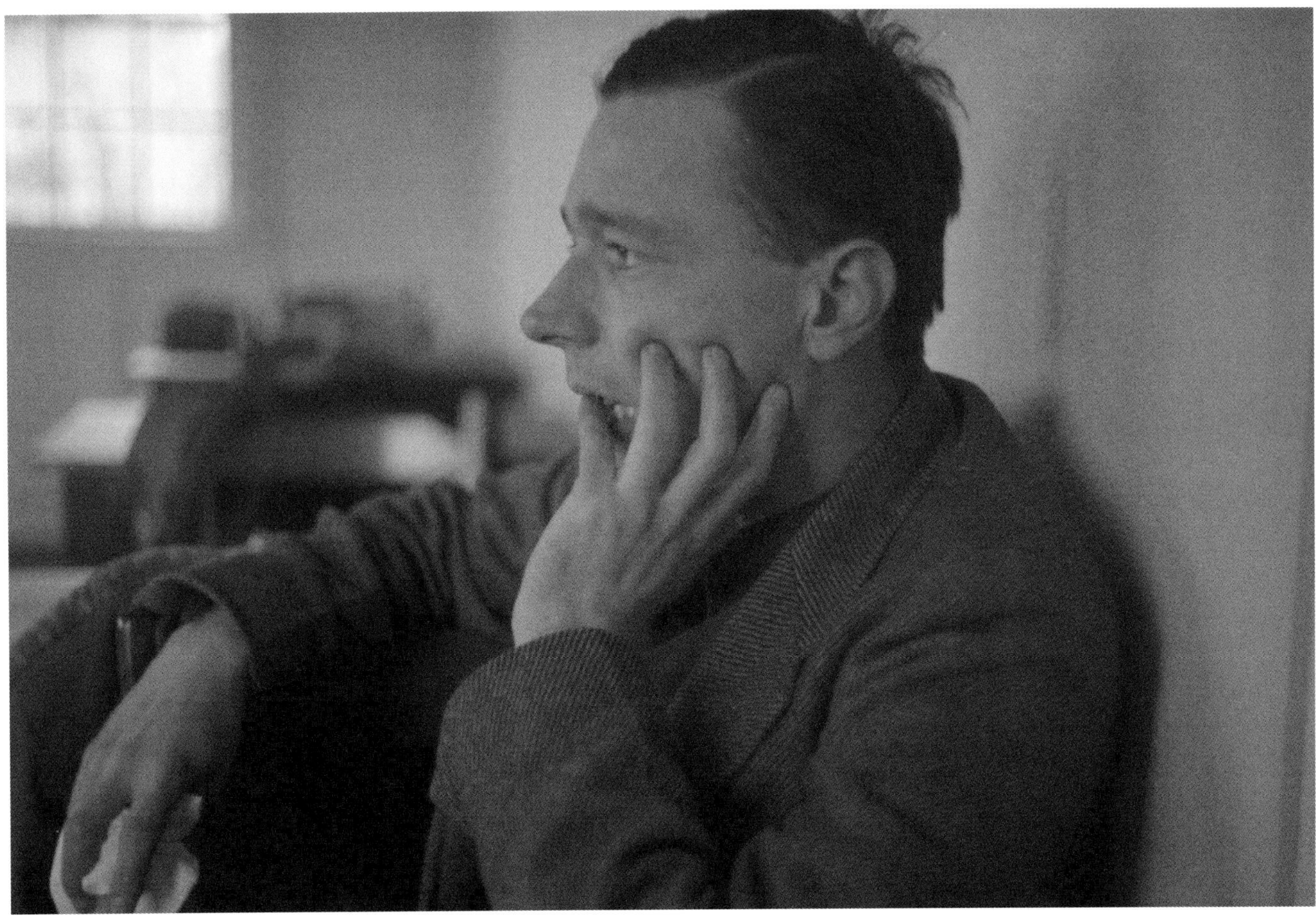

acquire after Atget's passing in 1927. Like George Brainerd, Atget worked quietly out of the spotlight. And yet, his visual catalogue of Paris, with its purity and intensity of vision, would be considered the benchmark against which later photography measured itself.

Whatever his inspiration, de Wetter knew he had a treasure in Brainerd. With funds from the Federal Arts Project, he had the glass negatives carefully cleaned, and modern prints produced and matted. No less than five exhibitions of Brainerd's work would be held between 1937 and 1940. "The two earliest exhibitions in May of 1937 and September of 1939 were of such immense interest that the museum decided to install a permanent display of George Brainerd's prints in December of 1939," wrote Julie C. Moffat, in

Hermann de Wetter, the Brooklyn Museum's first Curator of Photography in the 1930s, was also among the first museum directors to acquire photography, such as the work of the social documentary photographer, Walker Evans, pictured above. Brainerd's style, with its focus on unsentimental, everyday scenes, anticipates Evans as well as Berenice Abbott, whose work de Wetter also admired.

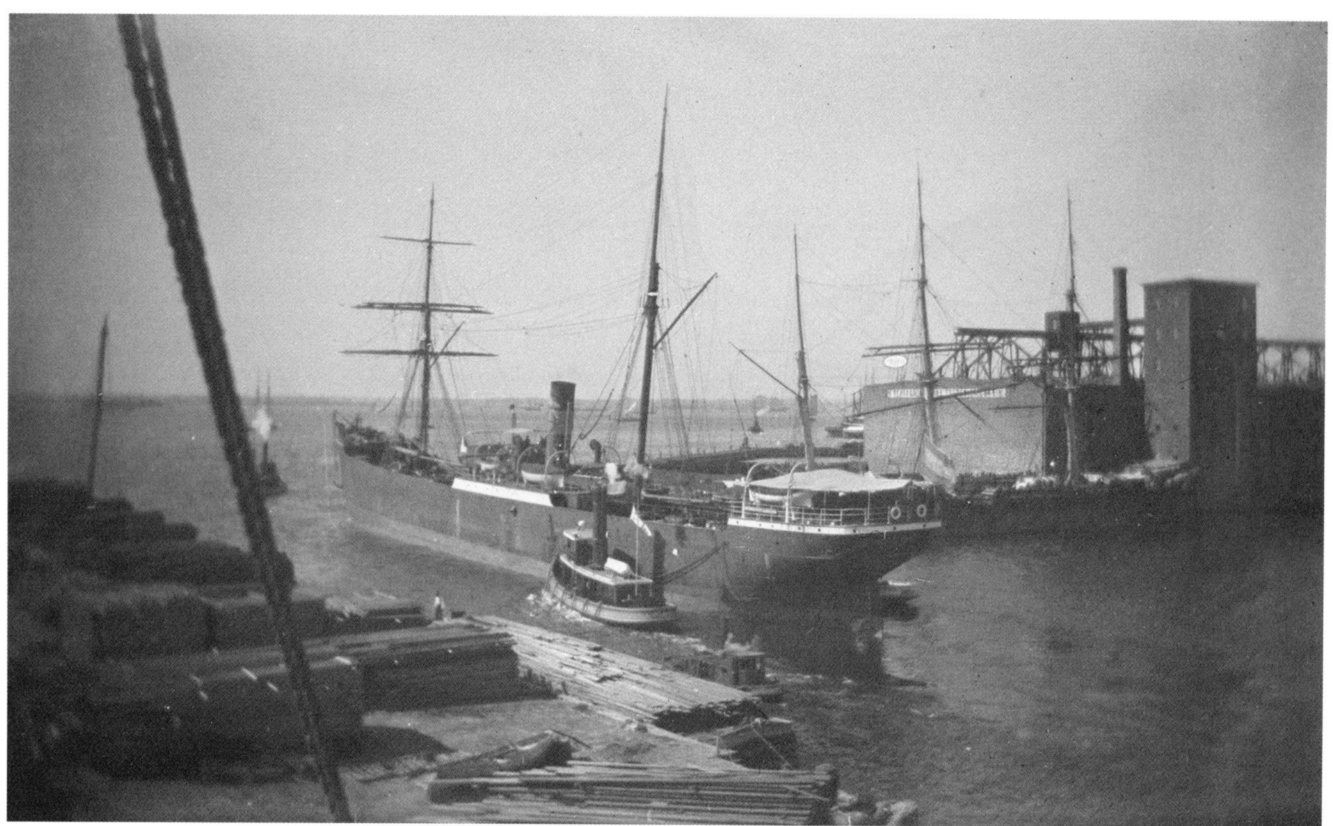

her 1994 unpublished master's thesis on Brainerd. "Every few months the prints were changed in order to show the extent of Brainerd's photography of sixty-seven different communities. Surprisingly, the department received more than four requests each day to view Brainerd's images." Then, with the death of de Wetter around 1950, the Brooklyn Museum decided that photography was not art and gave most of what it had to the Brooklyn Public Library. Once again, George Brainerd slipped into obscurity.

Erie Basin, Red Hook, 1870s. Puffing little steam tugs were the workhorses of the waterfront, towing ocean-going vessels as well as barges and canal boats up to the docks where their cargos were discharged. Brainerd took this "instantaneous" image using one of his handheld cameras. George Bradford Brainerd Photograph Collection, Brooklyn Public Library/Center for Brooklyn History.

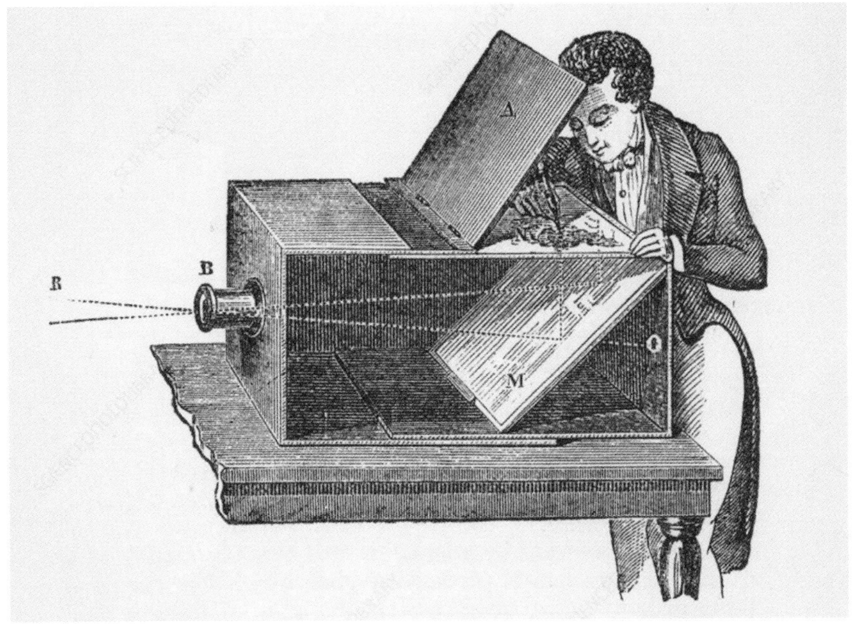

Camera obscura came from the Latin "camerae obscurae," meaning "dark room." The camera obscura was based on the principal that rays of light passing through a small hole in a dark room form an image where they strike a surface, resulting in an inverted (upside down) and reversed (left to right) view of the outside. Though the phenomenon was known since the Renaissance, camera obscuras, such as the one shown, were not actually built until the early 1800s.

"Photograph: a picture painted by the sun without instruction in art."

—Ambrose Bierce

There's a story that the famous Civil War photographer Mathew Brady (1822–1896) was blamed for the Northern defeat at the first battle of Bull Run, because raw recruits, seeing his mammoth view camera and barrel lens looming above the battlefield, mistook it for a rapid-fire steam gun and took to their heels. Still, Brady's apparatus was more portable than the camera's progenitor, which in the Renaissance was as big as a room; in fact, it was a room, something called the *camera obscura*, or "dark room," described in 1586, by the Italian, Daniele Barbaro:

> Close all the shutters and doors until no light enters the camera except through the lens and opposite hold a sheet of paper which you move forward and backwards until the scene appears in sharpest detail. There on the paper you will see the whole view as it really is, with its distances, its colors

and shadows and motion, the clouds, the water twinkling, the birds flying. By holding the paper steady, you can trace the whole perspective with a pen, shade it and delicately color it from nature.

However, capturing the transient image of the camera obscura to make it everlasting turned out to be very difficult.

The first person to try this was Thomas Wedgwood, son of the famous British potter, who around 1800, attempted to make permanent the sun's projection on a media of white leather moistened with a solution of silver nitrate. But his "sun prints," as he called them, darkened when exposed to light and Wedgwood was compelled to display his handiwork almost furtively by candlelight. The Frenchman Joseph Nicéphore Niépce had better luck. A tireless tinkerer who with his brother Claude had invented the first internal combustion engine, Niepce became fascinated with the camera obscura and in 1827 produced the iconic "View from the Window at Le Gras," history's first permanent photograph. Niepce used pewter plates coated with light-sensitive asphalt, known as bitumen of Judea, dissolved in lavender oil. Still his heliographs were quite indistinct.

Far more successful was Louis-Jacques-Mandé Daguerre, a French scenic artist and showman most famous until then as the proprietor of the Diorama, a popular Parisian spectacle featuring theatrical painting and lighting effects. Daguerre had been in partnership with Niepce until the latter died in 1833. After, he realized the necessity of developing a new process. His procedure was to coat a copper plate with a thin layer of silver. The plate was then carefully cleaned with nitric acid and buffed and polished to reach a mirrorlike finish. After, the polished side was exposed to iodine vapor in the dark to make it light sensitive. The plate was finally exposed in a camera obscura and developed with mercury vapor and fixed in a bath of hyposulphite of soda. The daguerreotype, as it was known, became the dominant photographic process up until the American Civil War.

Daguerreotypes are cherished for their eerie clarity, the mirrorlike plates exhibiting an almost three-dimensional quality. Unfortunately, achieving such detail required agonizingly long exposure times, from 15 minutes to a half-hour, depending on lighting. To steady their subjects and avoid motion blur, early photographic studios stocked all manner of props, including chairs fitted with iron neck collars. It was all too much for serene Ralph Waldo Emerson who feared he might twitch before the merciless lens: "Were you ever Daguerreotyped, O immortal man?" he wrote in 1841. "And in your zeal not to blur the image, did you keep every finger in its place with such energy that your hands became clenched as for fight or despair, and in your resolution to keep your face still, did you feel every muscle becoming every moment more rigid: the brows contracted into a Tartarean frown, and the eyes fixed as only they are fixed in a fit, in madness, or in death?"

To Emerson and others' great relief, a new photographic process came along, which among other advantages, dramatically reduced exposure times. This was the wet-collodion or wet-plate process, introduced in 1851, by the English sculptor, Frederick Scott Archer. Collodion is a nitrocellulose lacquer made by dissolving gun cotton in a mixture of alcohol and ether. Archer added potassium iodide to the collodion and coated a glass plate with it. Then in subdued light, he dipped the plate in a solution of silver nitrate. He exposed the plate while wet in the camera, hence the name "wet plate." It was developed in pyrogallic acid, fixed in hyposulphite of soda, washed, and dried. All these operations had to be done rapidly (from 10–15 minutes) before the collodion dried after which it was useless. Photographers thus could never be very far from a darkroom and a tent, or a wagon was needed for processing in the field.

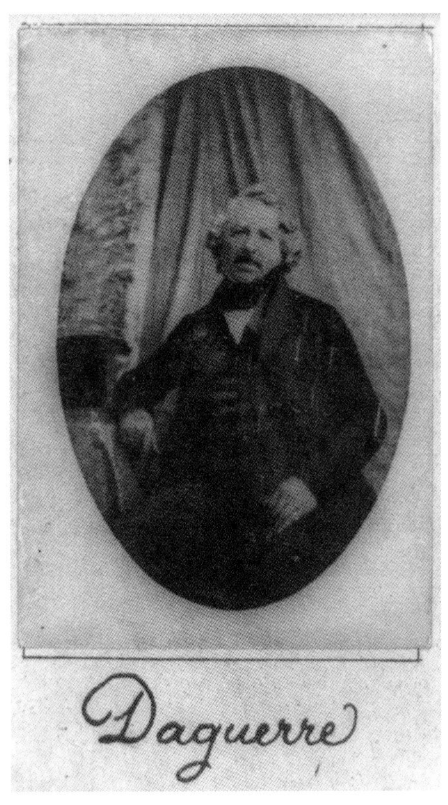

Before getting into photography, Frenchman Louis-Jacques-Mandé Daguerre had been a scenic artist and showman, well known as the proprietor of the Diorama, a popular Parisian spectacle featuring theatrical painting and lighting effects. Daguerre had been in partnership with Joseph Nicéphore Niépce until the latter died in 1833. After, Daguerre realized the necessity of developing a new process, which came to be known as the "daguerreotype."

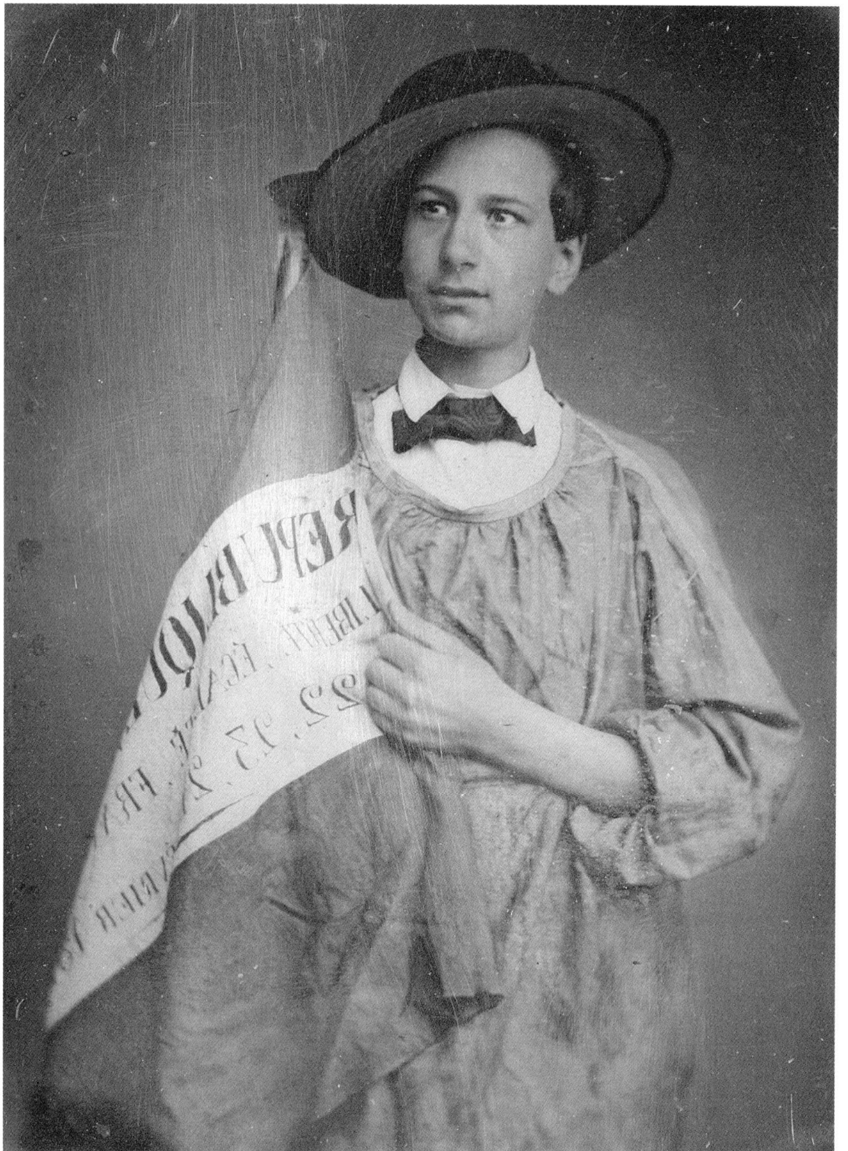

Daguerreotypes are cherished for their eerie clarity, like the one at left, from the 1840s. Unfortunately, achieving such detail required agonizingly long exposure times, from 15 minutes to a half-hour, depending on lighting. This required subjects to sit motionless for long periods of time, and various props were employed to keep sitters still and avoid motion blur.

While wet collodion did reduce exposure times, the apparatus was still quite bulky. Indeed, like the dinosaur before extinction, photographic cameras in the wet-plate era seemed to wax to their greatest proportions before making an exit. At this time photographers did not use enlargers for printing. Prints were made by contact printing, and to obtain prints of three sizes, the photographer would bring along three different cameras, the largest taking 20 × 16-inch plates. Frederick S. Dellenbaugh, one of the photographers attached to John Wesley Powell's expedition to the Grand

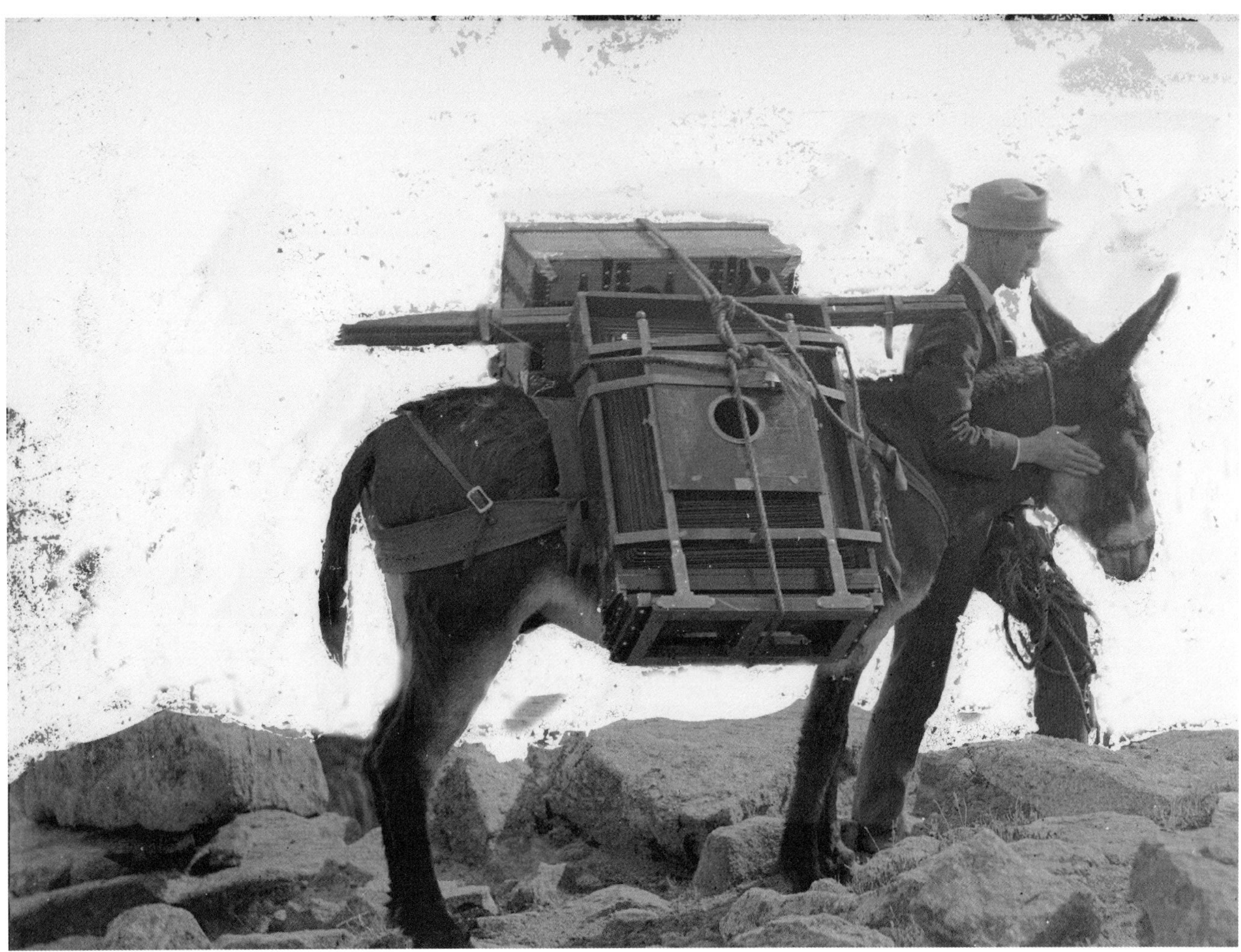

Canyon in 1871, gives us a picture of the agonies of having to haul such cumbersome equipment up the sides of mountains to expose a few plates:

> The camera in its strong box was a heavy load to carry up the rocks, but it was nothing to the chemical and plate holder box, which in turn was featherweight compared to the imitation hand organ which served for a darkroom. This box was the special sorrow of the expedition, as it had to be dragged up the heights from 500 to 3000 feet.

The idea of a camera that could be held in the hand during exposure had little relevance until the introduction of the gelatin dry plate made the "instantaneous"

During the wet collodion era, the apparatus was still quite bulky, and photographic equipment was often hauled up mountainsides by packhorse. At this time, photographers did not use enlargers for printing. Prints were made by contact printing, and to obtain prints of three sizes, the photographer would bring along three different cameras, the largest taking 20 x 16-inch plates.

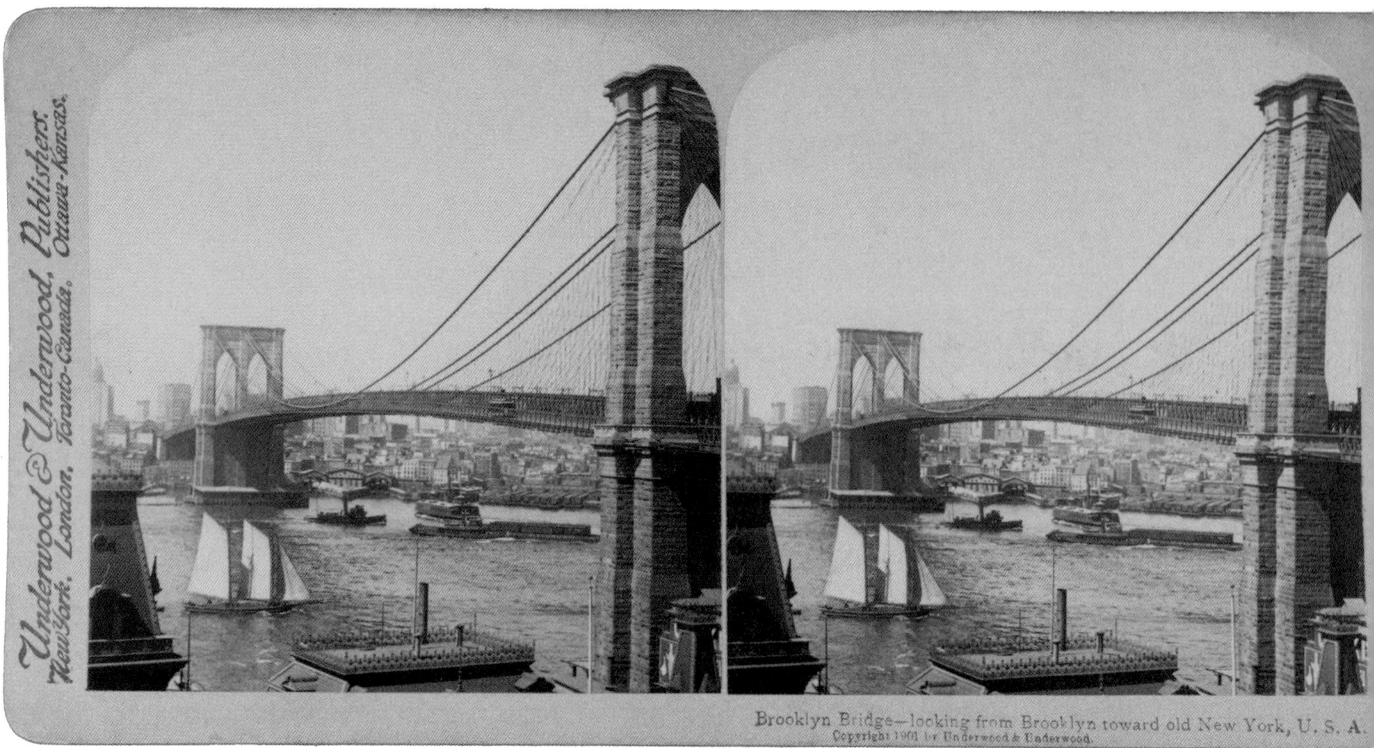

Brooklyn Bridge—looking from Brooklyn toward old New York, U. S. A.
Copyright 1901 by Underwood & Underwood.

exposure fully practical. The new process, which revolutionized photography, came about not because its inventor, a London medical man, found anything troublesome about the wet collodion method, but because he could not tolerate the pungent odor of ether in the hot glass house where he did his processing. Richard Leach Maddox was already well known for his photomicrography, capturing minute organisms under the microscope, when he set about searching for a new emulsion to replace smelly collodion. Around 1871, Maddox tried gelatin used in candy-making to which he added cadmium bromide in solution and silver nitrate; these chemicals reacted to form silver bromide crystals suspended in the gelatin. This emulsion was flowed on glass and allowed to dry, hence the term, "dry plate."

It took several years to refine Maddox's odorless dry process to a workable technique. In 1878, Charles Harper Bennett found that heating the gelatin silver emulsion to harden it also made it much more sensitive. Photographers were now able to use commercial dry plates off the

Stereographic cards, such as the one above, were originally produced using the wet-plate process, although they would later employ more portable dry plates, which would be commercially produced in the early 1880s.

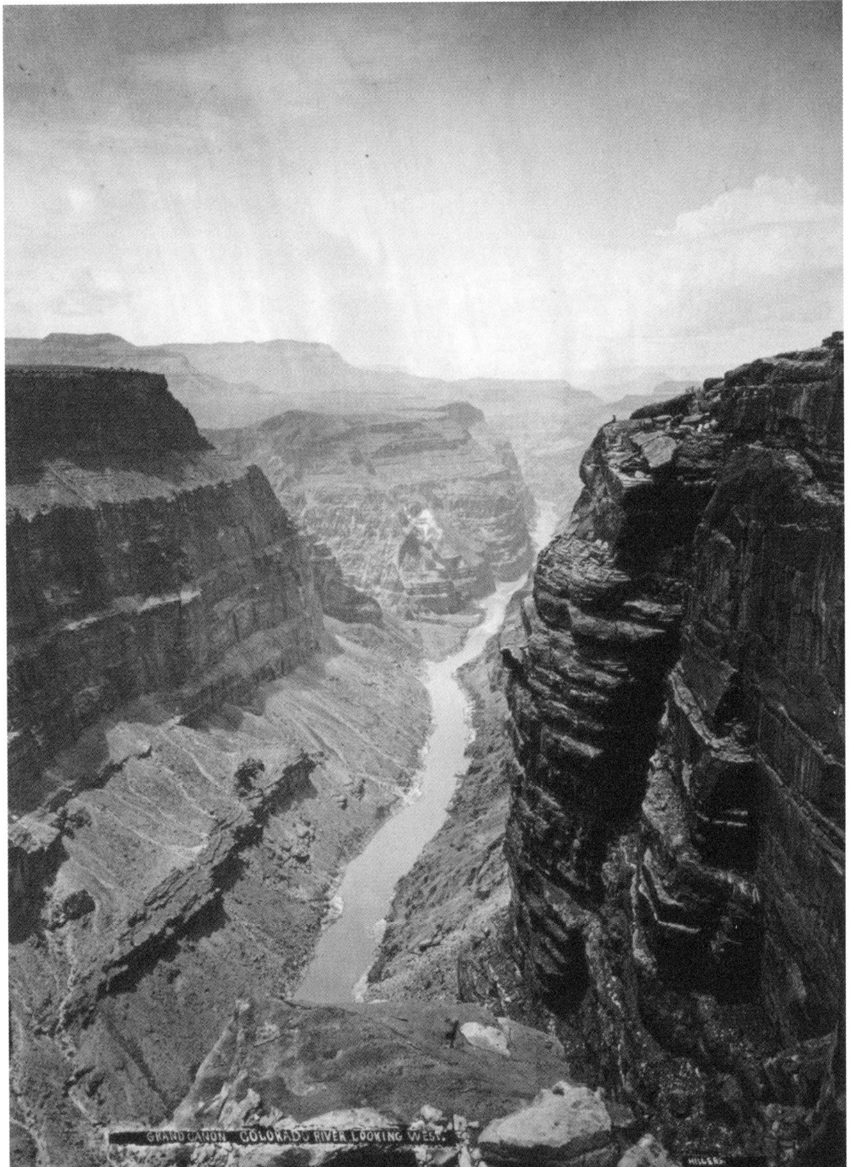

To obtain this level of detail, the photographer probably employed 20 x 16- inch plates. Much smaller dry plates, which could be exposed and developed at a later time, revolutionized picture-taking and made possible the debut of the portable hand camera.

shelf instead of having to prepare their own emulsions in a mobile darkroom. Negatives did not have to be developed immediately. Most importantly, lightweight gelatin dry plates permitted exposures of fractions of a second, making possible the debut of the hand camera.

And yet, even before such dry plates were commercially available, George Brainerd of Brooklyn was using handheld cameras he built himself to capture colorful street life in Brooklyn and Lower Manhattan. Even today, no one is quite sure how he did this.

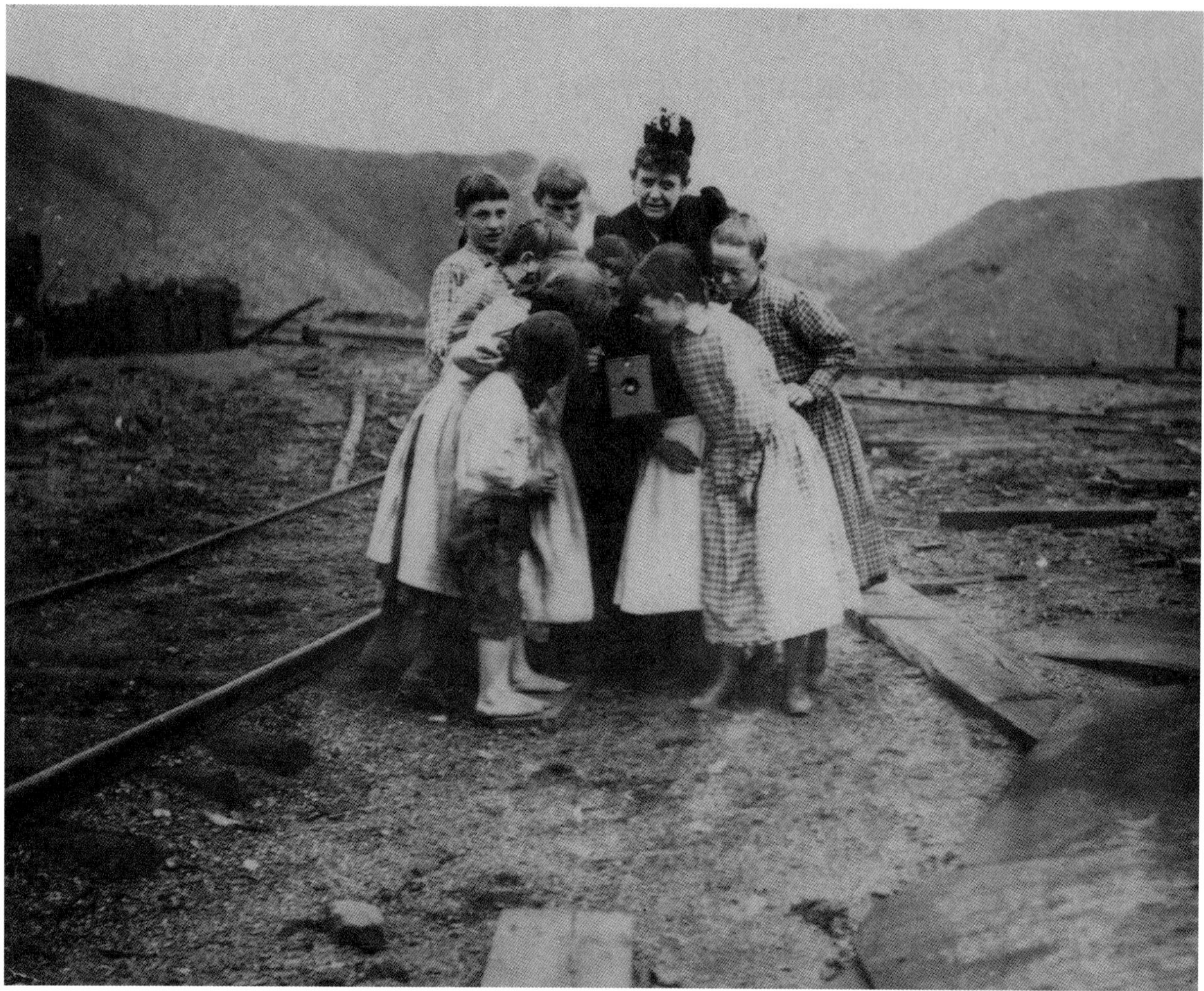

"I really believe there are things nobody would see if I didn't photograph them."
—Diane Arbus

One of the first glass negatives selected for printing by Hermann de Wetter was a Brainerd plate entitled "The Soap Fat Man." It was a reminder of a vanished industry. "Soap making during the 1800s was dirty business," the Brooklyn Library would write of the Brainerd image, taken in 1877 or 1878. "It required two key ingredients: rendered animal fat and lye, a caustic substance traditionally made from wood ashes." Before industrialization, many Brooklynites made their own soap

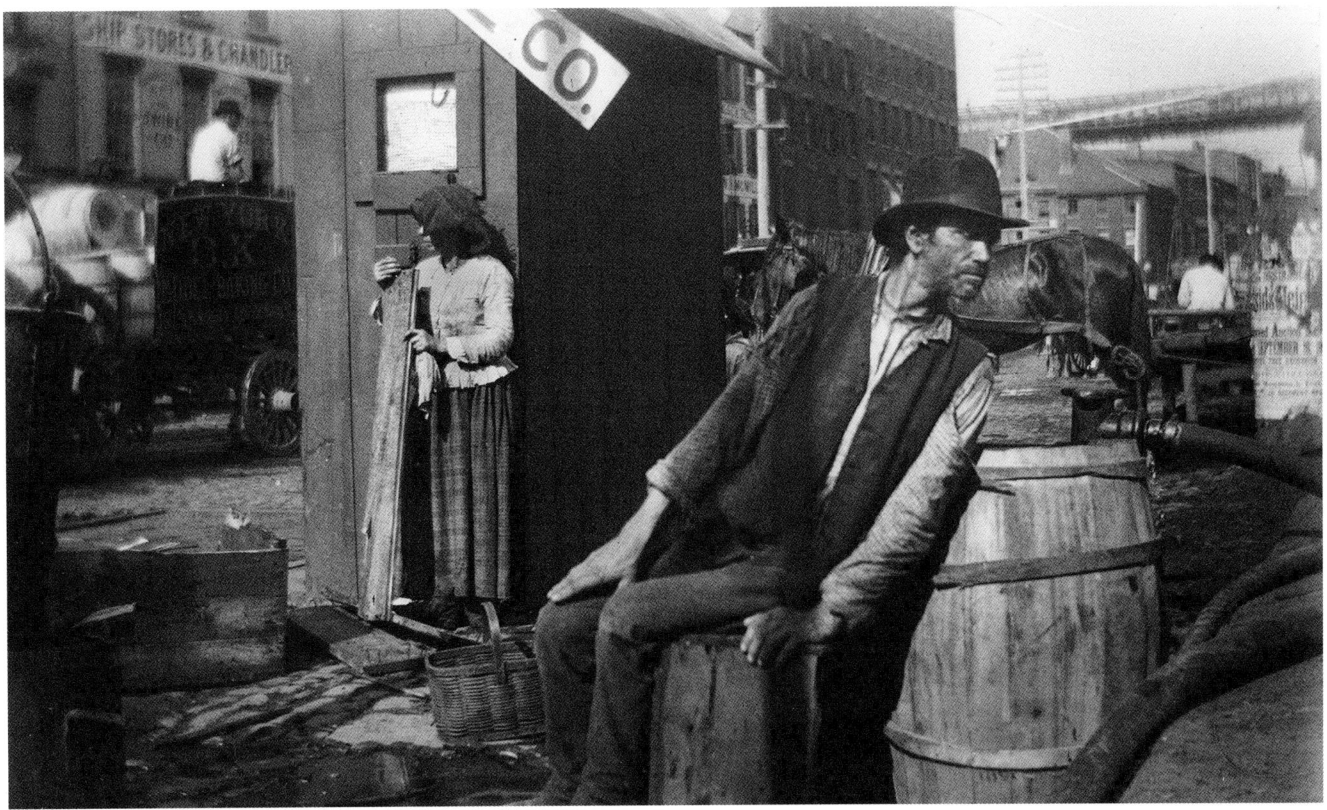

using accumulated cooking fat and grease from the home. By the late 19th century, soap production was carried on at an industrial scale, and companies such as Kirkman & Sons in Brooklyn hired workers, known as "soap fat men," to perform the dirty job of collecting fat waste from homes, hotels, and butchers across the borough and beyond.

With his love of street folk, Brainerd thought he would make a record of a neighborhood soap fat collector, a Chinese American, who was easily spotted with his ragged, dirty clothes, and trademark tin pail cinched to his back. Brainerd made several tries before getting an image he found satisfactory. Though taken relatively early in his career, "The Soap Fat Man" is one of his most powerful images. Although taken on the fly without a steadying tripod, Brainerd captures the almost balletic grace with which the worker glides down some steps in Brooklyn's Prospect Park, all the while balancing a pail of greasy waste on his back. The soap fat man, whose face is hidden, has one leg

Longshoreman, Brooklyn, 1878. Brainerd's "spy camera," a box-form apparatus disguised to look like a book, allowed him to move in quite close without drawing attention to himself. This image of a longshoreman in Brooklyn's rough and tumble waterfront district might have been snatched from the pages of Dickens or Thackeray. What *is* the grizzled, old dockworker peering at? And what of the lass? She appears to be guarding the door of an outhouse, but we can't be sure. George Bradford Brainerd Photograph Collection, Brooklyn Public Library/Center for Brooklyn History.

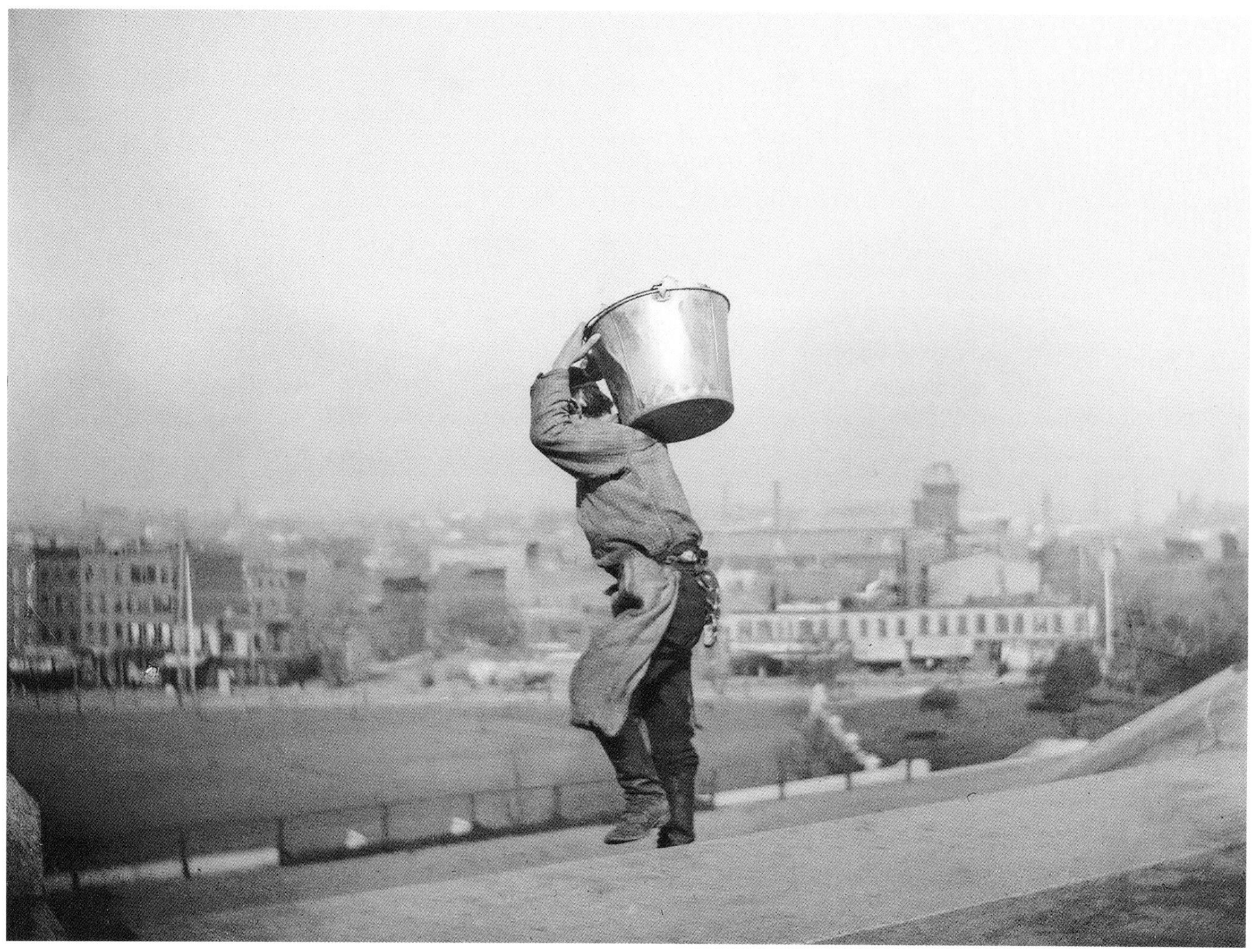

lifted, directing the viewer's attention to a booted foot, which is supple like a dancer's slipper. It's that foot, so delicately poised in the air, which excited Brainerd. Developing the image, he would later say, represented one of the "happiest moments in his life," as he finally caught his subject "walking with his foot off the ground."

Though a chronicler of crowds, George Brainerd was not *of* the crowd. Indeed, Brainerd's upbringing in the bosom of Brooklyn wealth and refinement could not have been further from the street folk whose daily struggles he sought to document.

Born in 1845 in Haddam Neck, Connecticut, George Bradford Brainerd was the fourth child of Diodate Brainerd (1808–1879), a wealthy merchant, and Rebecca Bradford

The Soap Fat Man, Brooklyn, 1877. Brainerd often singled out "The Soap Fat Man" as his first successful "instantaneous" snapshot, because he managed to capture his subject, "walking with his foot off the ground." From other plates we know Brainerd had conquered action as early as 1873. The Soap Fat Man has the monumental quality of a Margaret Bourke-White. Such sharpness and detail are remarkable for this early date, an indication of just how advanced Brainerd's camera skills were. George Bradford Brainerd Photograph Collection, Brooklyn Public Library/Center for Brooklyn History.

(1803–1858), eighth descendant of Governor William Bradford who founded the Plymouth Colony. At the time of
George's birth, Diodate was engaged in quarrying feldspar
and granite in mines opened by his great-grandfather, Deacon Ezra Brainerd, who shipped the Haddam stone as far as
New Orleans. Haddam Neck granite also went into early seacoast defenses like Fort Adams in Newport, Rhode Island,
and Fort Hamilton in Brooklyn. However, by the 1850s
small Connecticut quarries were facing stiff competition
from larger operations at Yonkers, just north of Manhattan,
and Diodate was casting about for other ventures. Robert
Fulton's steam ferry linking New York City with Brooklyn across the East River sparked an era of unprecedented
growth in Brooklyn. This prompted many old New England
merchant families like the Pierreponts and Lows to remove
to Brooklyn Heights, where from opulent waterfront mansions they could glimpse the spars and masts of their fleets
anchored in New York Harbor. Diodate had already begun
investing in Brooklyn real estate, buying lots as speculation.
In 1847, when George was two, he moved the family to
Clinton Hill, a fashionable neighborhood just up from the
Brooklyn Navy Yard.

Brooklyn was a hub of manufacturing with a busy port
whose shipping in tonnage would soon exceed its rival
across the East River. Sugar refining was its largest single
industry, but the city was also a center of ironworks, nota-
bly Greenpoint where the ironclad battleship *Monitor*, of
Civil War fame, was launched. The waterfront fairly bris-
tled with wharves, in back of which stood slaughterhouses,
breweries, and factories turning out hats, clocks, cigars,
insulated wiring, packaged coffee, and even teddy bears.
All these industries required manpower, and waves of Irish
immigrants escaping famine and Germans fleeing the dis-
ruption of a failed revolution poured into the city, and by
1855 nearly half of Brooklyn's 250,000 inhabitants were foreign born. By 1880, the population would swell to close to
600,000, making it the third largest city in the United States.

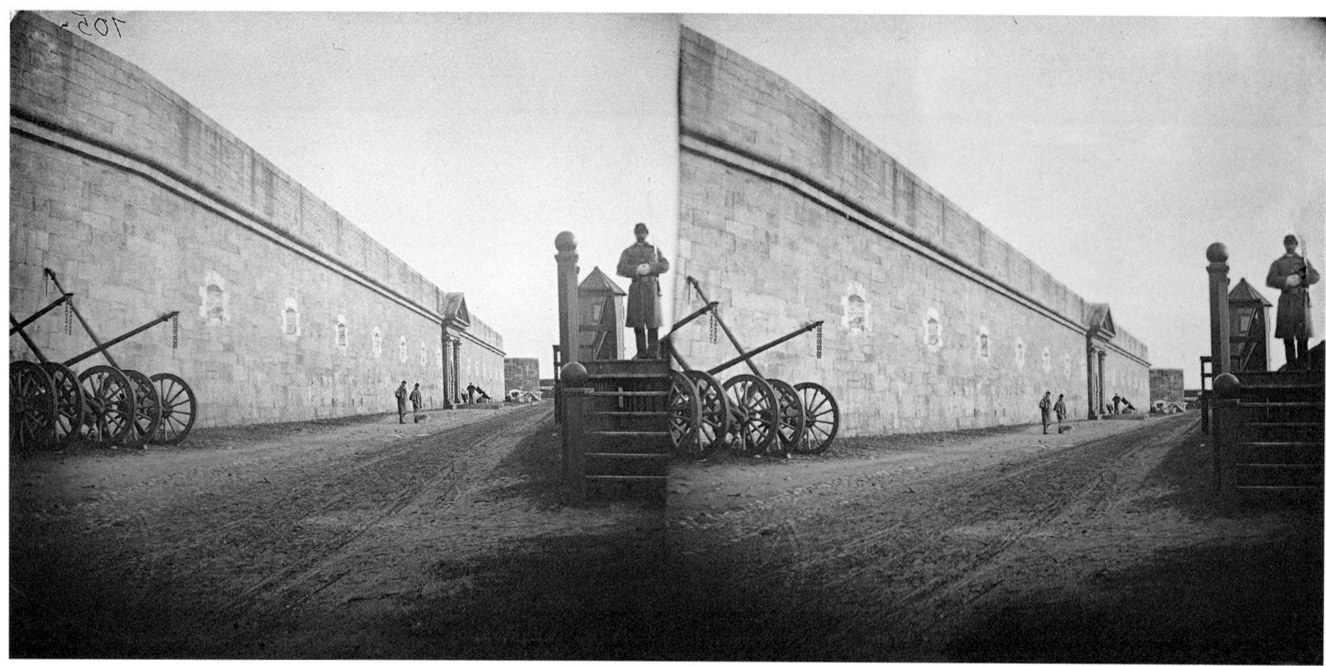

As a member of Brooklyn's elite, young George's early education consisted of French primary schools as well as tutors, from whom he was instructed in languages as well as geology and mineralogy, the latter encouraged by his father from his quarrying days in Haddam Neck, where the family still maintained a summer house. Like a young Audubon, Brainerd also taught himself taxidermy, amassing a large collection of stuffed birds that would eventually number 400 species. He also maintained an herbarium, and would become an expert on ferns and mosses, in later years asked to lecture on the subject. As for photography, Brainerd is said to have built his first camera at the age of 12 using a cigar box and lenses from old opera glasses. With this primitive apparatus, he managed to produce a few crude ambrotypes, a wet-plate process in which a positive is made on glass. Even at that young age, his interest went beyond the captured image to the mechanism of the camera itself, and the possibilities offered by the new technology. This obsession with the workings of things led him to study engineering, and at just 16, Brainerd entered Rensselaer Polytechnic Institute in Troy, New York, graduating

At the time of George's birth in Haddam Neck Connecticut, Diodate Brainerd was engaged in quarrying feldspar and granite in mines opened by his great-grandfather, Deacon Erza Brainerd, who shipped Haddam stone as far as New Orleans. Haddam Neck granite also went into early seacoast defenses like Fort Hamilton in Brooklyn pictured here, which is probably why Brainerd chose to photograph the fort in the late 1870s.

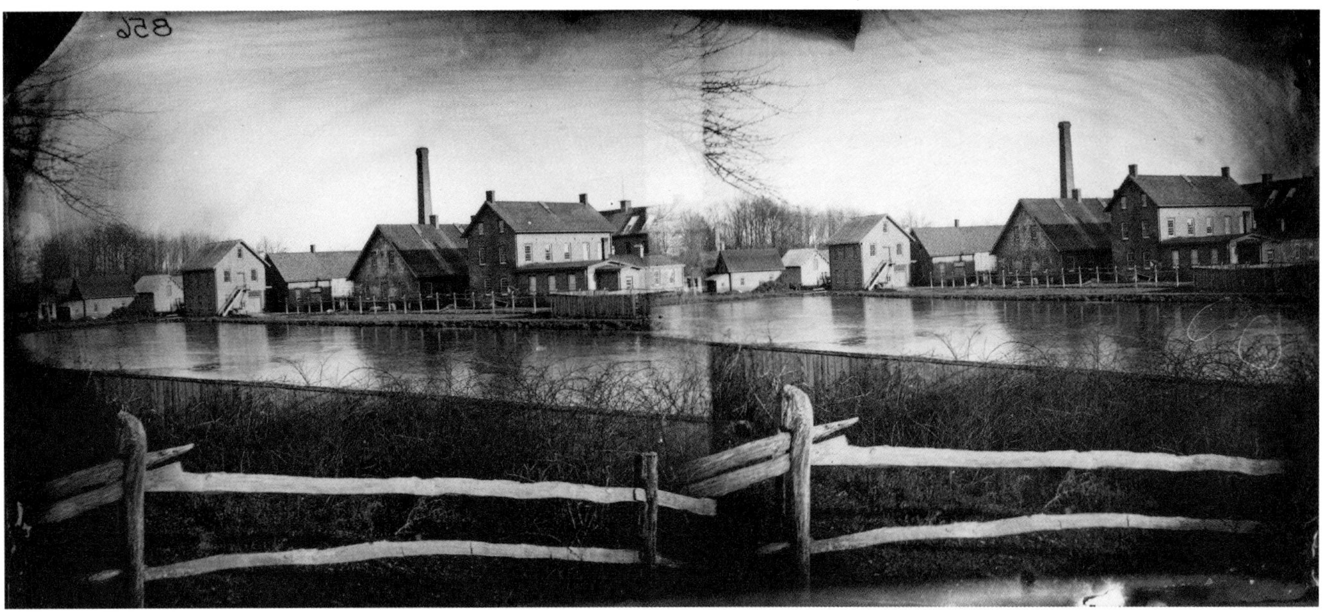

Dye factory, Staten Island. Stereoscopic slide, 1874. Just as Brainerd documented the latest engineering marvels in the city, so too was he eager to record the many outmoded industries he saw in his travels, industries that were fast disappearing, such as this dye works on Staten Island. George Bradford Brainerd Photograph Collection, Brooklyn Public Library/Center for Brooklyn History.

with a four-year degree in civil engineering. His first job after college was with the Atlantic Dock Company in Red Hook—work that would plunge the young engineer into the very heart of the torrent of progress.

"Men are shouting, steam whistles are screaming, and great derricks are groaning as they slowly hoist bales and boxes from the hold of some great ship and then swing them around to be deposited on the dock," the *Brooklyn Daily Eagle* wrote in 1881 of Brooklyn's docks in Red Hook, where workmen moved, stored, and inventoried freight arriving from all over the world. Another report from 1873 noted: "The docks are covered with long rows of barrels of sugar and molasses while the ground is almost sticky with the spilled sweets. Through the low doors of the warehouses, you catch glimpses of piles of boxes, tiers of hogsheads and bales of goods."

The Atlantic Docks was the brainchild of Colonel Daniel Richards, who in 1839 began to develop the Brooklyn harbor shoreline by erecting a contained set of docks, warehouses, and a basin for deep water ships in the area presently known as Red Hook and South Brooklyn. The company was chartered by New York State in 1840 and

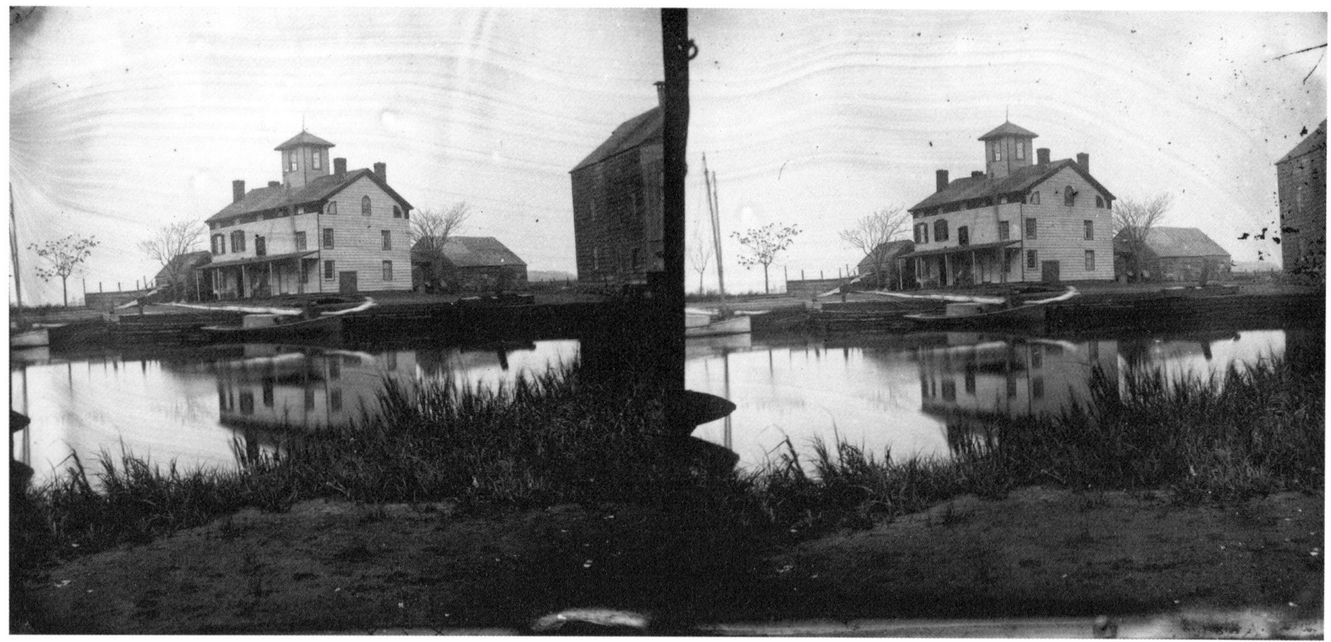

began excavation and construction, capitalized at $1 million. Later, William Beard and two brothers, Jeremiah P. Robinson and George Robinson, began work on a second basin, some 100 acres in extent, named the "Erie," as it was initially designed to process wheat coming downriver on barges and ships from the Erie Canal. While grain was a principal cargo, lumber, iron, coffee, raw cotton, leather, foodstuffs, and countless other products also arrived on the docks. There were even live animals, such as Latin-American and African monkeys, parrots, and reptiles imported by dealers for sale to zoos, museums, and private collectors. Dockworkers would be charged with finding the animals in the case of their escape, although some men, like "old Joe the veteran stevedore," offered a blunt "No thanks, not for me," when asked to recover a large snake, probably a python, destined for the Smithsonian Institution that had slithered out of the hold of a South American ship docked in 1868.

Brainerd was probably tapped for his expertise with high pressure steam engines. His college thesis bears the weighty title: *A discussion of the review of the high-pressure engine of Messrs. Starbuck.* In addition to strong arms and

Grain mill at Forbel's Landing, Brooklyn, 1874. George Bradford Brainerd Photograph Collection, Brooklyn Public Library/Center for Brooklyn History.

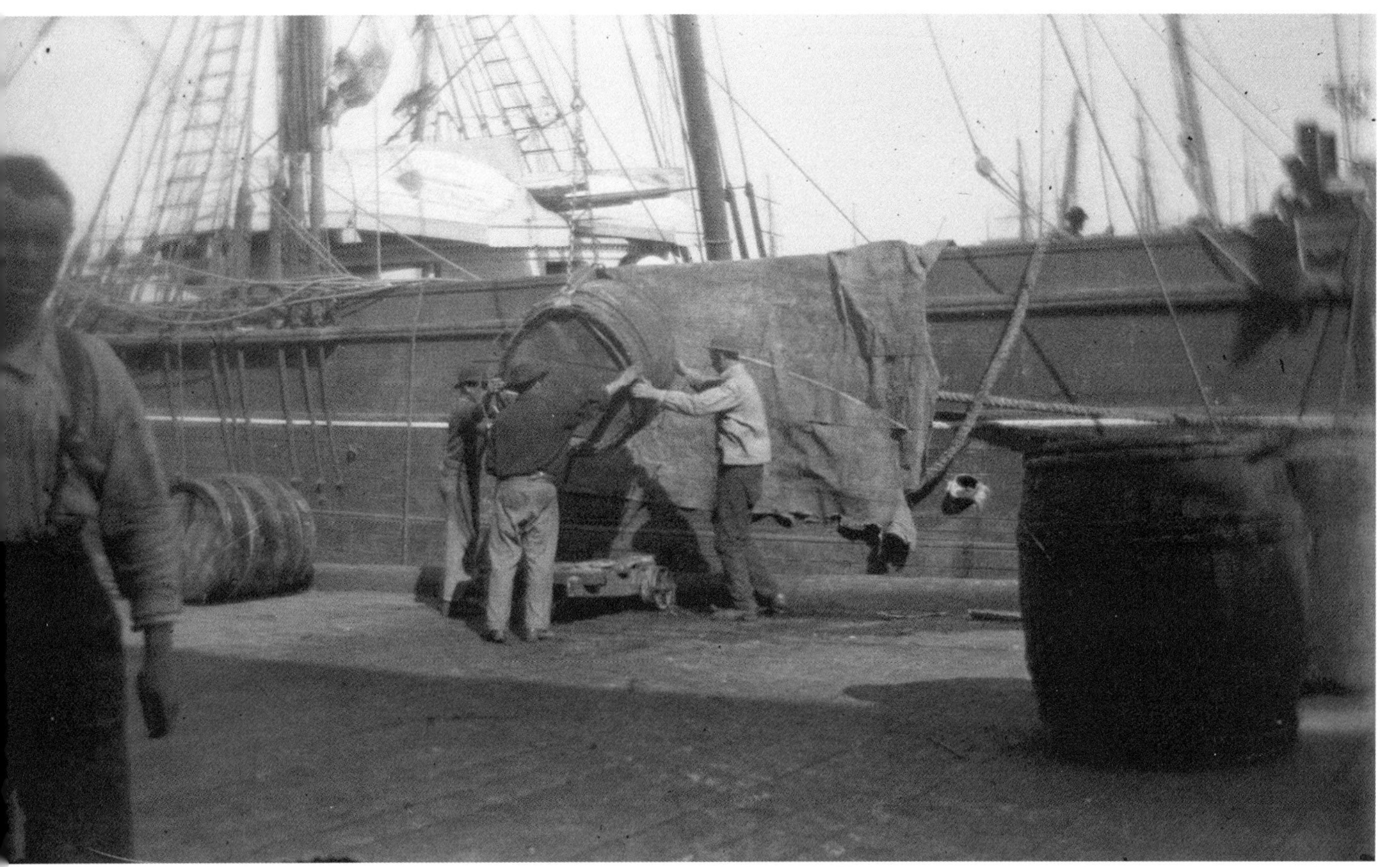

backs, steam power was needed to drive the derricks as well as power the grain elevators which that the bushels and bushels of grain out of the barges high up into siloes to dry. The barges had been towed down the Hudson by huge side-wheel towboats and puffing little screw propeller tugs. Lashed together in groups called "strings," fifty to a hundred barges and canal boats were hauled downriver at a clip, the tows reaching back a quarter of a mile from the stern of the leaders to the sterns of the last boats.

In Brooklyn, the grain barges were home to entire families and in late fall, as the canals began to freeze, from 500 to 700 canal boats assembled in Erie Basin for the winter with 2,000 to 3,000 people living on board. They were a colorful lot, the barge folk, with their wash hanging on deck, while the women gathered in the tiny cabins below to crochet or sew, and the men played fiddle or squeezed out a tune on an accordion. "The sitting or living room was

Atlantic Docks, Brooklyn, 1870s. Brainerd often worked his photography into his busy schedule, snapping pictures while on breaks. As Brooklyn's Deputy Water Purveyor, Brainerd was responsible for provisioning ships with fresh drinking water, a process Brainerd documented here with longshoremen loading casks of water into the hold of a ship. The photographer took some care with the composition, drawing our attention to the workers steadying their load, framed by a strong foreground figure and more barrels in deep shadow to the right. George Bradford Brainerd Photograph Collection, Brooklyn Public Library/Center for Brooklyn History.

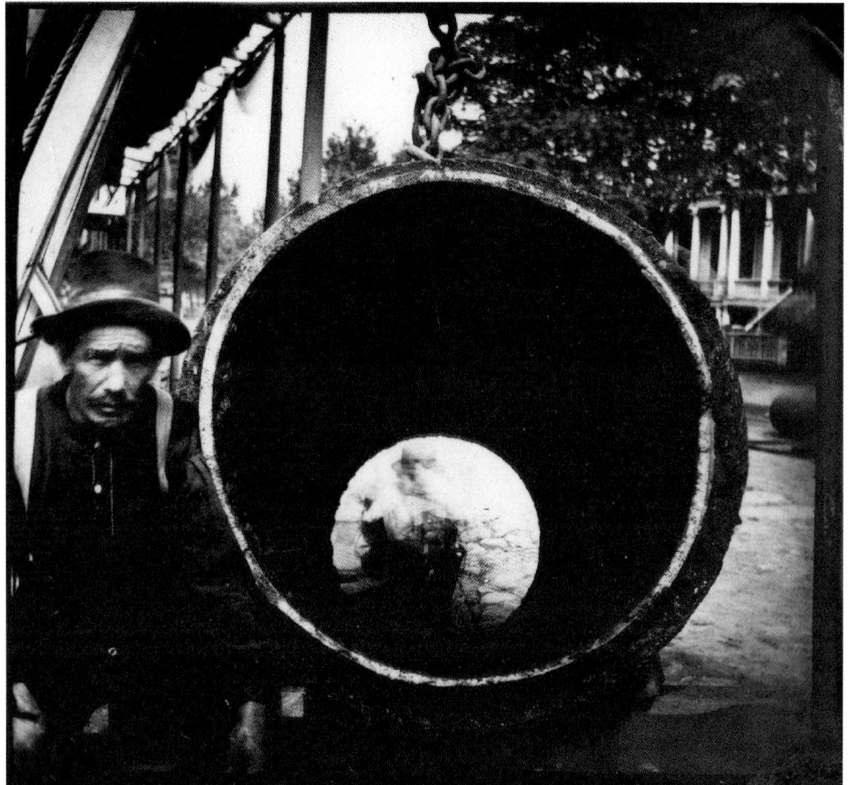

Thirty-six-inch main, Brooklyn, 1874. As a water department engineer, Brainerd diligently recorded many public works projects like the laying of miles and miles of new water pipe under Brooklyn streets. In this stereoscopic print, Brainerd enlisted the participation of a laborer for scale, who by his dress is possibly an Italian immigrant, as Italians were beginning to join the Irish as well as African Americans at the bottom of the social rung. George Bradford Brainerd Photograph Collection, Brooklyn Public Library/Center for Brooklyn History.

about ten feet long and eight feet wide," a visitor to one of the barges wrote in the 1890s. "The floor was covered with the same kind of oilcloth as that on the stairs; the furniture consisted of a bureau, two chairs, one rocking chair, of a green painted cottage bedroom suite, a round walnut table, and one extra brown chair. The woodwork was grained, and the ceiling and walls painted white. Two long closets, one for dishes and one for clothes, were built in one side of the wall; also a half dozen drawers. The walls were plentifully decorated with highly colored chromos, and these two texts: 'Give us this day our daily bread.' 'Thou shalt not kill.' In that crowded abode, a man, a woman, a girl of fourteen, a boy of twelve and a baby two years old lived, as the woman said, 'year in and year out.'"

It was a world in which George Brainerd felt very much at home. Though a member of the silk-stocking set, the Brooklyn engineer never strayed too far from his roots on the Connecticut River in Haddam Neck, to which family

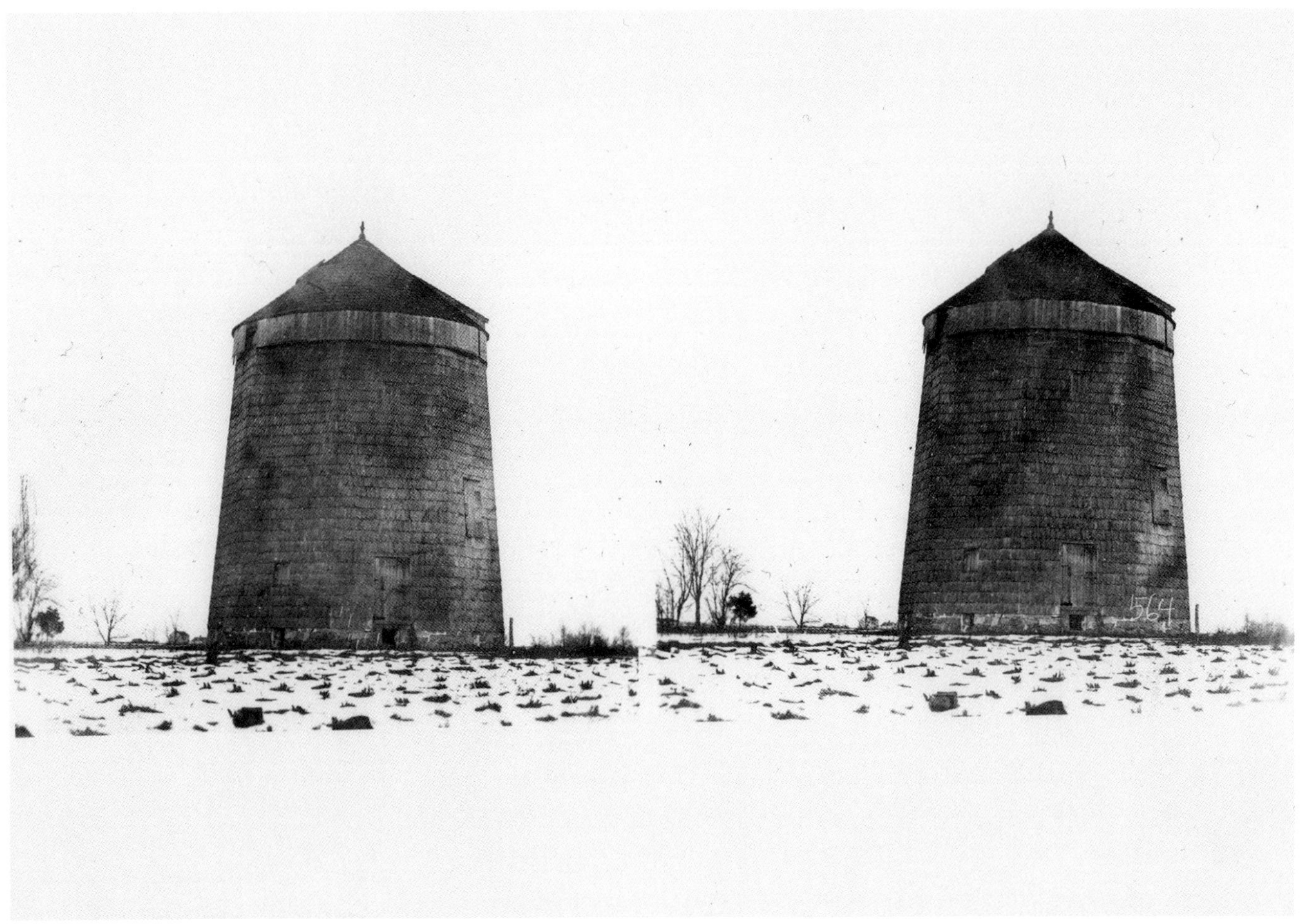

returned each summer on the steamboat, dwelling for a time in their ancient chestnut-beamed homes on Quarry Hill. The high bluff above the water was the principal lookout and sunset resort for villagers who liked to gather in the afternoon when the hills of "Old Haddam" on the west bank glowed pink and orange and the river was a silver ribbon running through the valley below. In the middle of the river was Haddam Island, famous for its shad fishery in the spring and shady grove of blackberry fields and luxuriant bathing ground on the western shore. Some of Brainerd's earliest photography, when he picked up his camera in the early 1870s, would be to document traditional Connecticut River industries like shad fishing, stone quarrying, charcoal-making, timbering, and the picturesque cutting of saltmarsh hay in the brackish tidal marshes at the wide river's mouth.

Old Vanderveer Mill, Flatbush, 1875. The first mill ever constructed on Long Island, the old Vanderveer mill, was built in 1805 by enslaved Africans. The mill was being used as a grain silo when Brainerd photographed it. The monumental structure, built of oak and shingled with cypress with a stone base, was four stories high—"tall enough back then to see all the way to the ocean." It boasted 24-foot sails that caught the wind to grind grain 24 hours a day for farmers who came from all over the island. George Bradford Brainerd Photograph Collection, Brooklyn Public Library/Center for Brooklyn History.

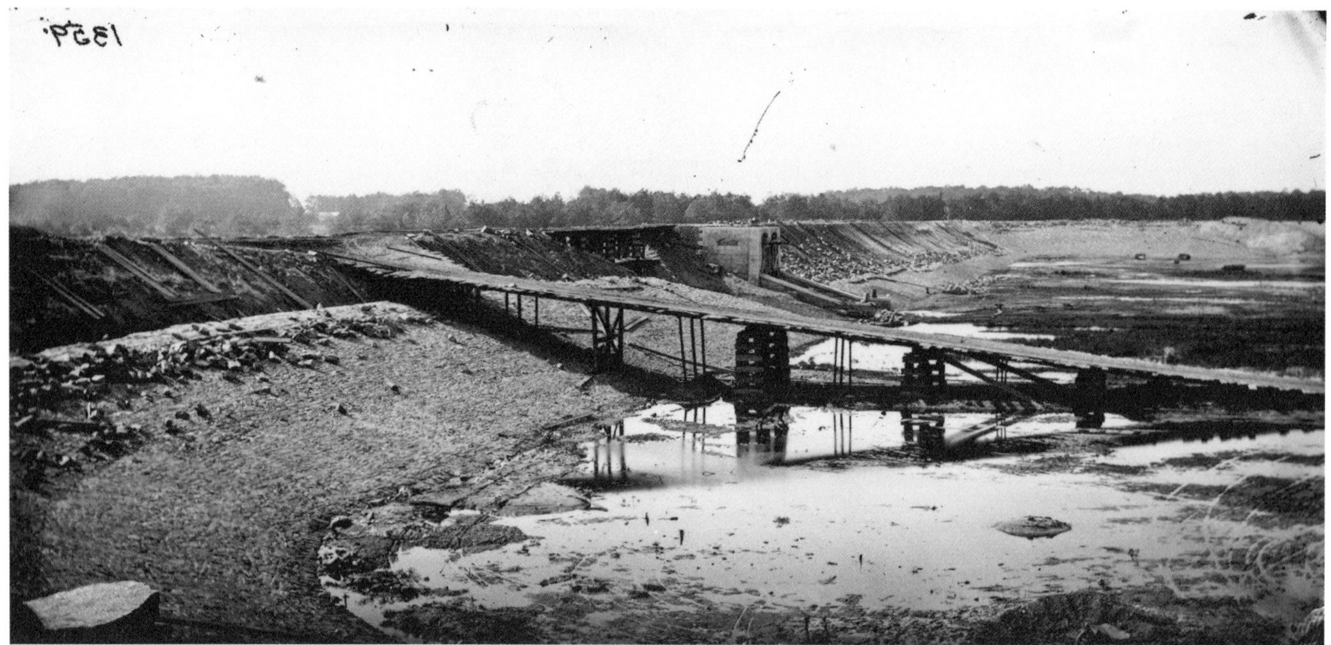

Later, Brainerd would venture far out on Long Island to photograph outmoded industries like gristmills, fish oil factories, clay beds, sand pits, and the iconic Dutch-style windmills, with their great sails silhouetted against the sky. Along the way, he documented one-room schools, churches, and rural street scenes, constructing a portrait of the countryside that was disappearing. This was decades before the practice of "survey photography," in which amateur picture-takers were encouraged to pay close attention to ancient customs that still lingered in remote villages. "Photography is an art of observation," the great photographer Walker Evans once said. "It's about finding something interesting in an ordinary place." Like Evans, Brainerd knew instinctively that the quality of a photograph lay in the language of vision, which is learned by chance, not system. With cameras he built himself, Brainerd was defining a new aesthetic, one that found beauty in the unspectacular and everyday. It was a mining of the mundane, a sifting of the routine, in search of scenes, which, as a result of familiarity, remained submerged beneath absentminded attention.

New storage reservoir, Brooklyn, 1874. Brainerd produced dozens of images of Brooklyn's water works, probably to illustrate a book he penned on the subject. George Bradford Brainerd Photograph Collection, Brooklyn Public Library/Center for Brooklyn History.

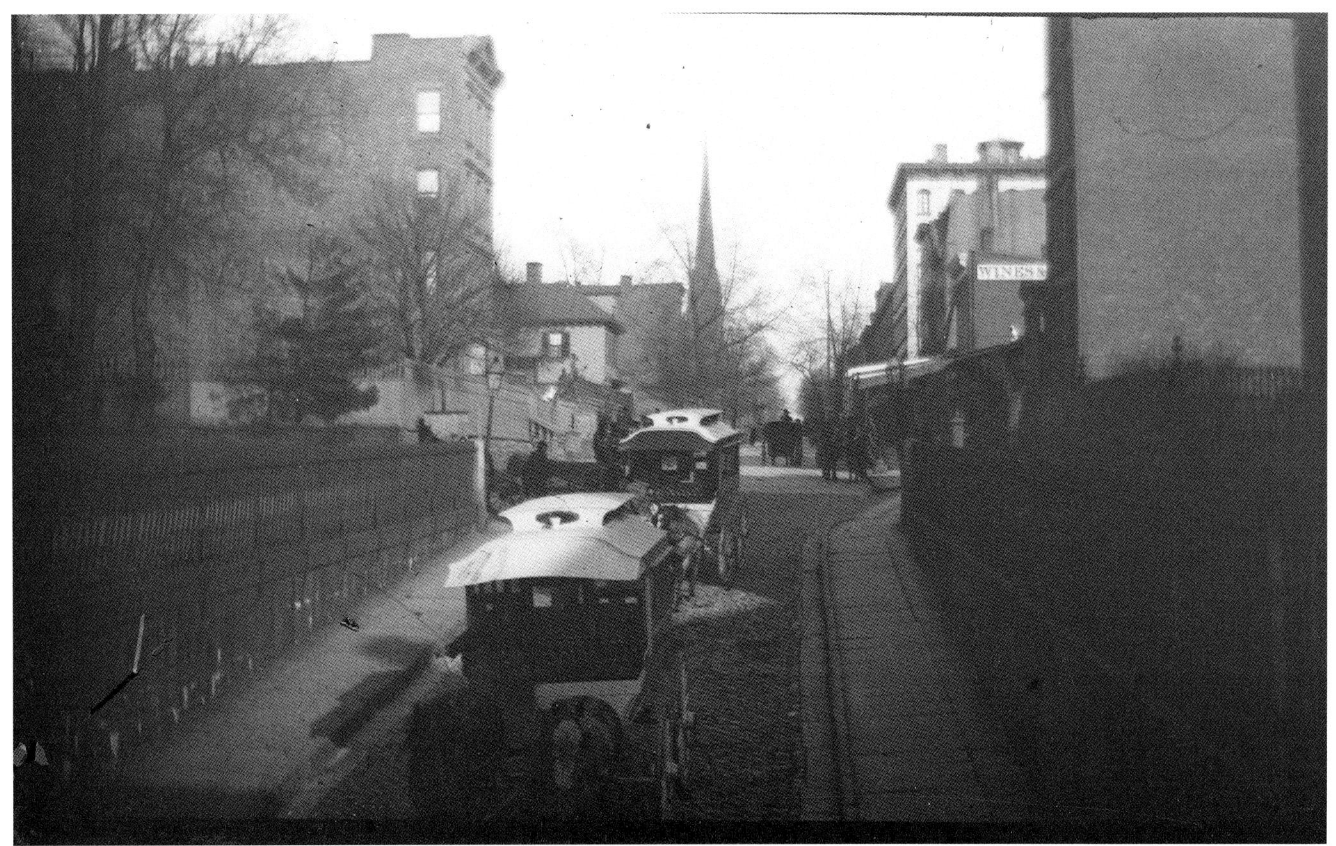

"Photography is a reality so subtle that it becomes more real than reality."

—Alfred Stieglitz

In 1869, Brainerd took a job with the Brooklyn Water Department, where he rose quickly to deputy purveyor of water. Supplying Brooklyn's rapidly growing population with clean drinking water was a principal task, but ships needed water too. This is where Brainerd came in. As deputy purveyor, Brainerd oversaw the provisioning of ships with drinking water for their long sea voyages. This led Brainerd to study languages, so he might communicate with foreign captains. It was not too many years after Melville's *Moby Dick*, in which Ishmael's ship the *Pequod* represented a sort of symbolic microcosm of the American melting pot, comprising sailors from all over

Horse-drawn trolleys queue up near the waterfront in Brooklyn, circa 1878. Brainerd used this new form of transportation to crisscross the city for his job as the city's deputy purveyor of water.

the world—African, Native American, Malay, white New Englanders, and even a Zoroastrian "Parsi"—united in a common purpose. Similarly, the Brooklyn waterfront was a polyglot nation, and Brainerd, an ethnographer of sorts, set out to learn the more exotic tongues spoken in this dockside Babel.

Streetcars were now common in the city, the open-air conveyances running on rails pulled by horses on the cobblestone streets. While this mass transportation transformed urban mobility, horse-drawn trolleys were notoriously slow, especially on Brooklyn's crowded thoroughfares. Brainerd put his extra time to good use. Like a modern subway commuter, Brainerd put his face in a book, mostly language books, and in just a few months, is said to have gained a working knowledge of 12 languages. He also began to ponder the problems of photography, and ways to make the camera more portable, just as Eastman would do many years later. Photography in the early days was a costly hobby, accessible mainly to the well-to-do. A tight budget during his college days is probably the reason Brainerd put down his camera in those years. But now a personal estate of $12,000 (equivalent to around $300,000 today) combined with a yearly salary of $2,000 (around $50,000 now) enabled Brainerd to indulge in his passion. For the young civil engineer, the new medium would become an important tool to document Brooklyn's ever-expanding water works, with its impressive, elevated reservoirs and pumping stations, and the miles and miles of pipe that was being laid nearly every day.

Brainerd's arrival in the water department coincided with the city's push to expand its water supply to meet the needs of Brooklyn's exploding population. Unlike Manhattan, which was able to tap the substantial flows of the Croton River, just north of the city, Brooklyn was forced to look eastward to a series of ponds and streams in Jamaica and Nassau County. This water was carried in a 12-mile-long masonry conduit called the Ridgewood Aqueduct, to a pumping station at Atlantic Avenue and Chestnut Street.

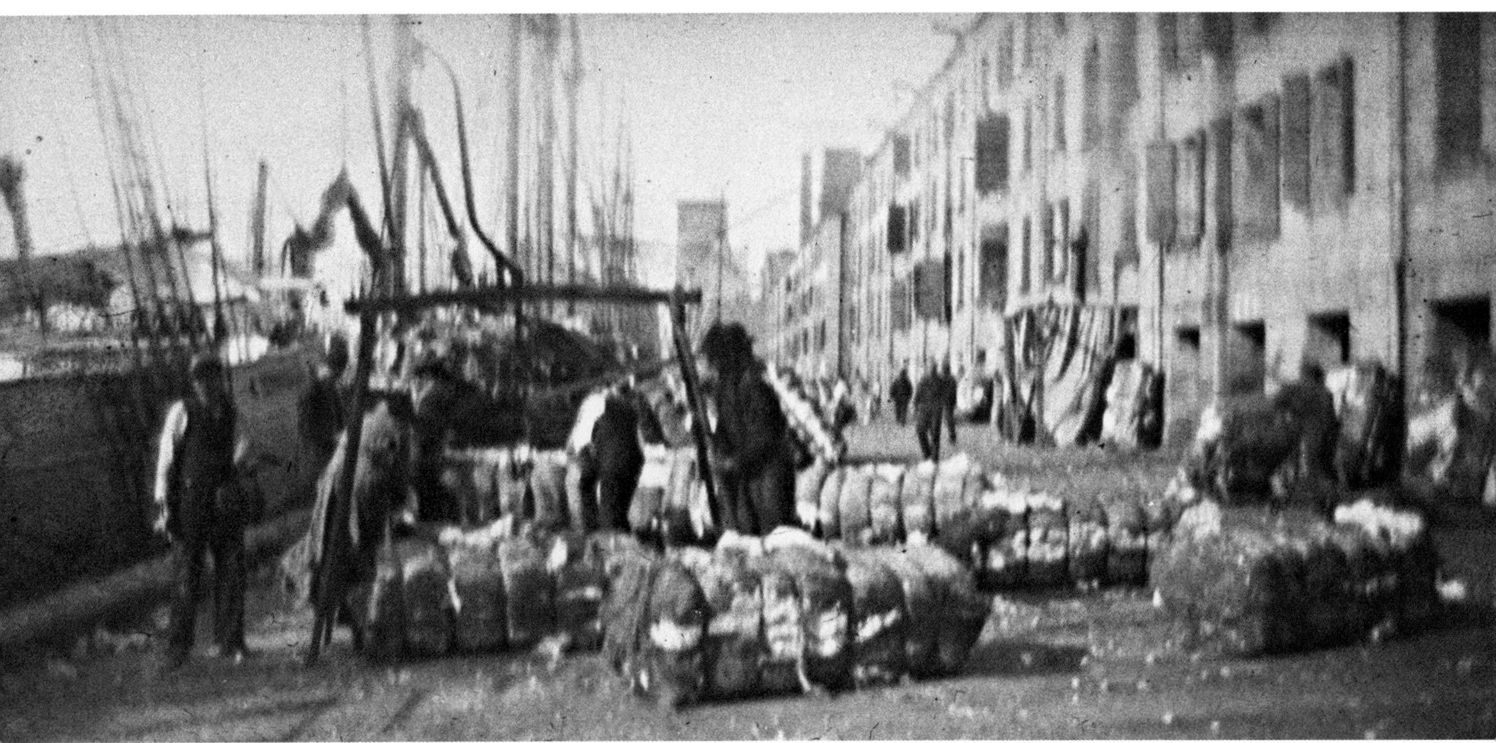

There, steam-powered pumps, each with a capacity of 14 million gallons per day, forced the water up through a reinforced tube into the high reservoir from which it was distributed. However, as Brooklyn's population continued to surge, the city was forced to dig additional supply wells farther out on Long Island, which brought it into conflict with farmers and oystermen who claimed the wells were lowering the water table and threatening their livelihoods. Brooklyn's ongoing water troubles were one of the main reasons it would merge with New York in 1898 to become one of the Five Boroughs.

Brainerd's first use of photography, as previously mentioned, was to document the city's impressive water works, probably to accompany a pamphlet he penned with the lofty title: *The Water Works of Brooklyn: A Historical Descriptive Account of the Construction of the Works, and the Quantity, Quality and Cost of the Supply.* Brainerd begins his story with an orotund flourish: "An abundant supply of pure and wholesome water is one of the first requirements of a

Cotton bales, Atlantic Docks, Brooklyn, 1870s. In the 1870s, sharecroppers, small farmers, and plantation owners in the American South were producing more cotton than they had before the Civil War; and just as before, the dirty brown bales were heaved onto the docks at Red Hook, where George Brainerd was waiting with his camera. George Bradford Brainerd Photograph Collection, Brooklyn Public Library/Center for Brooklyn History.

growing city . . . how a city procures this supply usually constitutes one of the most important and expensive branches of the public works. . . . The question soon is asked: whence does the water come and how is it conveyed?"

Brainerd was still using the wet collodion process for his landscape photography, assisted by another of Brooklyn's first amateurs, Naojh Taylor, and probably Wallace Goold Levison. "The process required Brainerd to carry a portable darkroom with him at all times, probably in the form of a tent," writes Julie Moffat, in her thesis on Brainerd. "Despite the burdensome equipment and the difficulty of working with wet collodion, Brainerd persisted. Quickly establishing himself as a capable and clever amateur, his photographic pursuits took off with drive." Brainerd took over 1,500 exposures in the decade of the 1870s, using three different plate sizes, which he carefully numbered in the top left corner of each plate.

There is a noticeable absence of people in Brainerd's early work, except for the occasional intrusion of a figure for scale. One exception is an image, identified in the parlance of the civil engineer, as "Thirty-Six Inch Main," showing a huge concrete conduit before it went in the ground. It was taken with a stereographic camera, which produces side-by-side images, varying slightly, resulting from their slightly different vantage points. In the image on the right, one begins to see emerging from the shadows, the deeply tanned face of an immigrant laborer. He wears a jaunty hat and baggy dark shirt with suspenders. It was a portend of things to come.

Photography, when Brainerd picked up his camera in the early 1870s, was still caught up in the debate over whether it was an art or a science; and if the former, could its products stand beside the great works of pencil and brush. Perhaps this is why so many leading picture-takers after the Civil War packed up their bags and headed West, where their mammoth view cameras and huge glass plates would record in the fullest detail the monumental

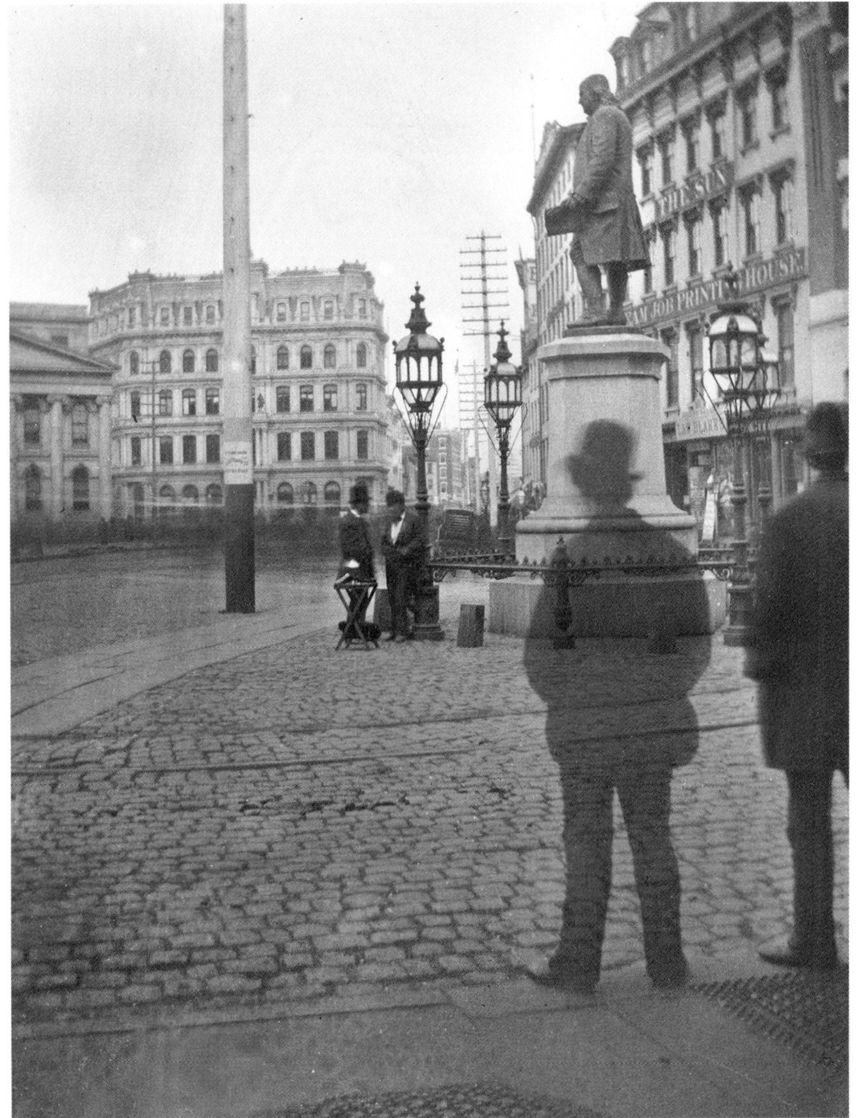

Franklin Square, New York City, 1878. An enchanting view of Victorian New York is preserved in this lovely image showing a broad expanse of cobblestones studded with gas lamps near the statue of Benjamin Franklin, opposite City Hall Park, at the intersection of Park Row and the Brooklyn Bridge approach. Some ghosting is seen, a result of the longer exposure required with the wet-plate process, which could be five or six seconds to several minutes. George Bradford Brainerd Photograph Collection, Brooklyn Public Library/Center for Brooklyn History.

scenery of America's remote interior. Few, if any, were drawn to urban environments, which in the words of Lewis Mumford, were increasingly tinged with "the visible smut of early industrialization." Moreover, the long exposures on which wet-plate photography relied were a discouragement, making it virtually impossible to record movement, giving city streets a bleak, deserted look, with the throngs of pedestrians reduced to mere ghosts.

Still, a few grasped the potential of street scenes. As early as the 1840s, the Englishman Henry Fox Talbot, inventor of the first practicable negative-positive process,

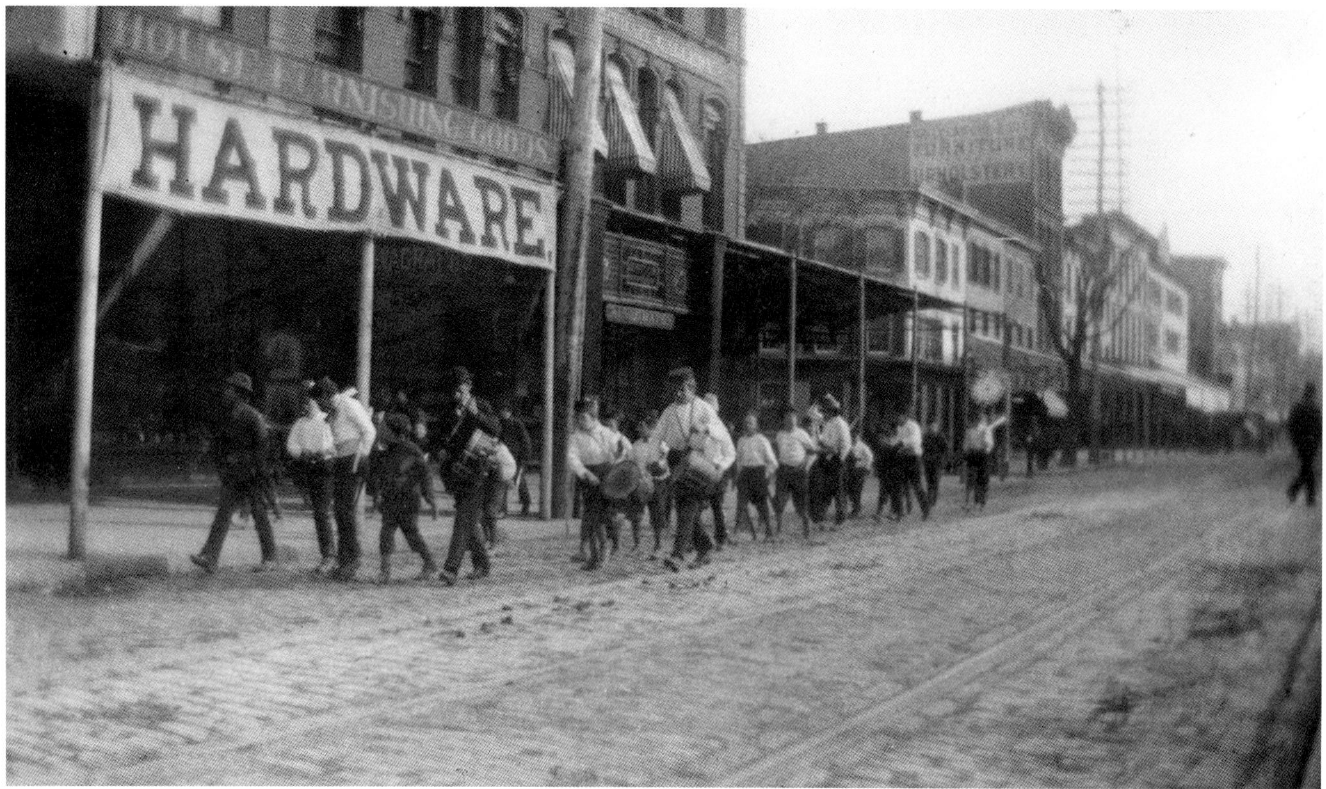

experimented with making motion in street photography visible. "If we proceed to the city," he wrote in 1846, "and attempt to take a picture of the moving multitude, we fail, for in a small fraction of a second, they changed their position so much, as to destroy the distinctness of the representation." For this reason, Talbot recommended arranging groups of persons who would need "to maintain absolute immobility for seconds at a time." This technique of staging scenes to create a simulated spontaneity was used to great effect by Charles Nègre, who beginning in the early 1850s photographed members of the Parisian proletariat—construction workers, hurdy-gurdy players, chimney sweeps, roofers, and stone masons—in their gritty urban milieu. Using faster lenses and the calotype process, Nègre was able to get his exposure time down to about three seconds. But it wasn't until the late 1850s, and the introduction of the stereoscopic camera, that action could be stopped with more or less regular assurance.

Columbia Street, Brooklyn, 1870s. Everyone loves a parade, none more than George Brainerd who often seized the opportunity to test his ability to capture motion. In this image from around 1878, the bustling waterfront area of Columbia Street, between Cobble Hill and Red Hook, pauses to allow a procession of boys with fifes and drums to pass, adding a bit of cheer to the day's drudgery. Brainerd probably chose his background first with the bold letters "HARDWARE," as a strong graphic element. He then waited patiently until his subjects moved into the frame. George Bradford Brainerd Photograph Collection, Brooklyn Public Library/Center for Brooklyn History.

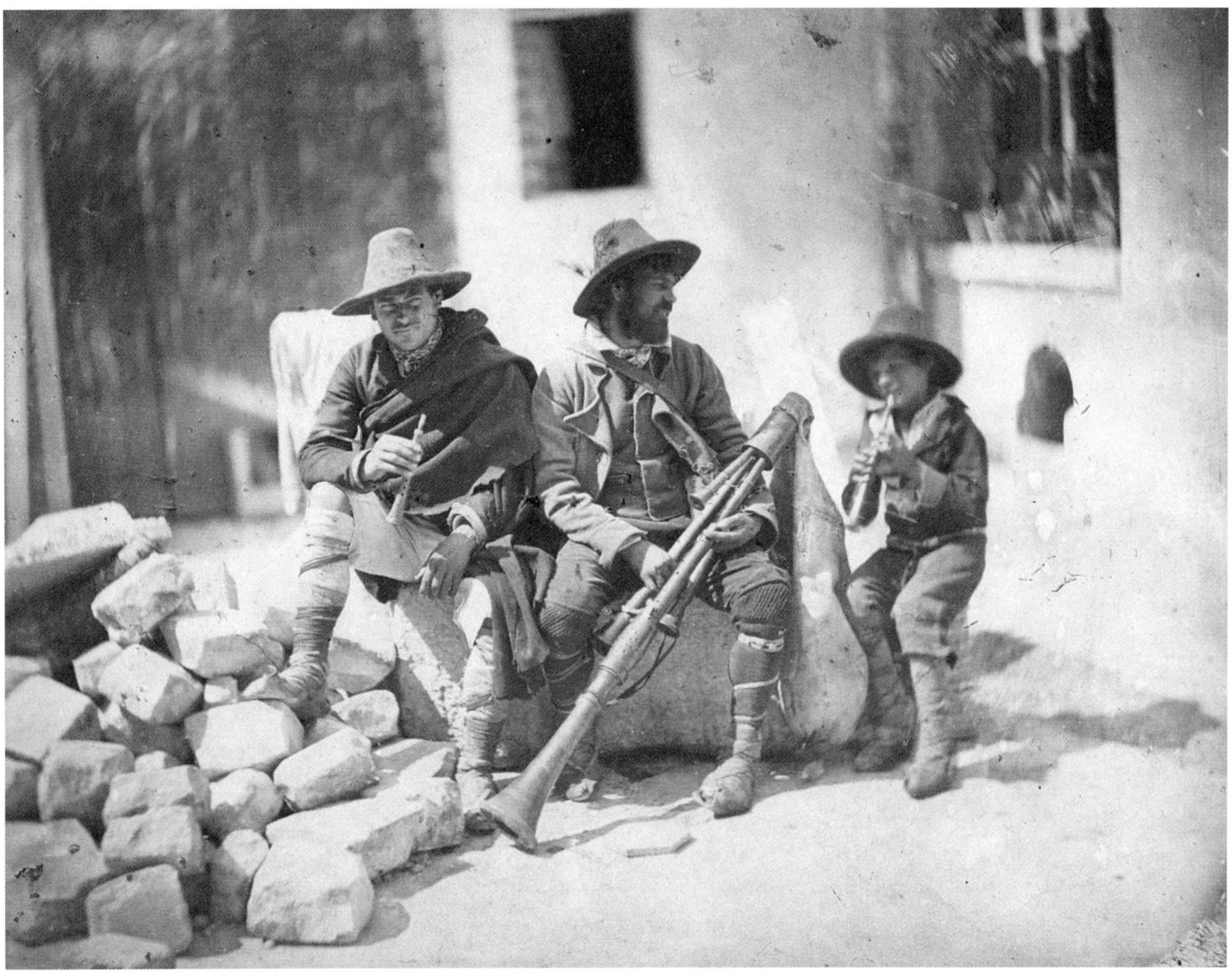

Stereoscopic photography is based on the principle that if two photographs are taken of a subject from viewpoints approximately equal in separation to the distance between the human eyes, the two pictures will merge into one three-dimensional image. Stereo pictures could be viewed using small handheld devices, offering the armchair traveler the vicarious thrill of a journey into distant and exotic lands. Less known is the fact that twin lens stereo cameras also made possible the first "instantaneous" pictures.

Generally, in the Victorian era the term was applied to any photograph that contained an element of movement, or which was taken with an exposure of less than one second. While very difficult to achieve, this was possible even in

The technique of staging scenes to create a simulated spontaneity was first used by the Frenchman Charles Nègre, whose image is seen above. In the early 1850s, Nègre, who was trained as a painter, began to photograph members of the Parisian proletariat—construction workers, hurdy-gurdy players, chimney sweeps, roofers, and stone masons—in their gritty urban milieu.

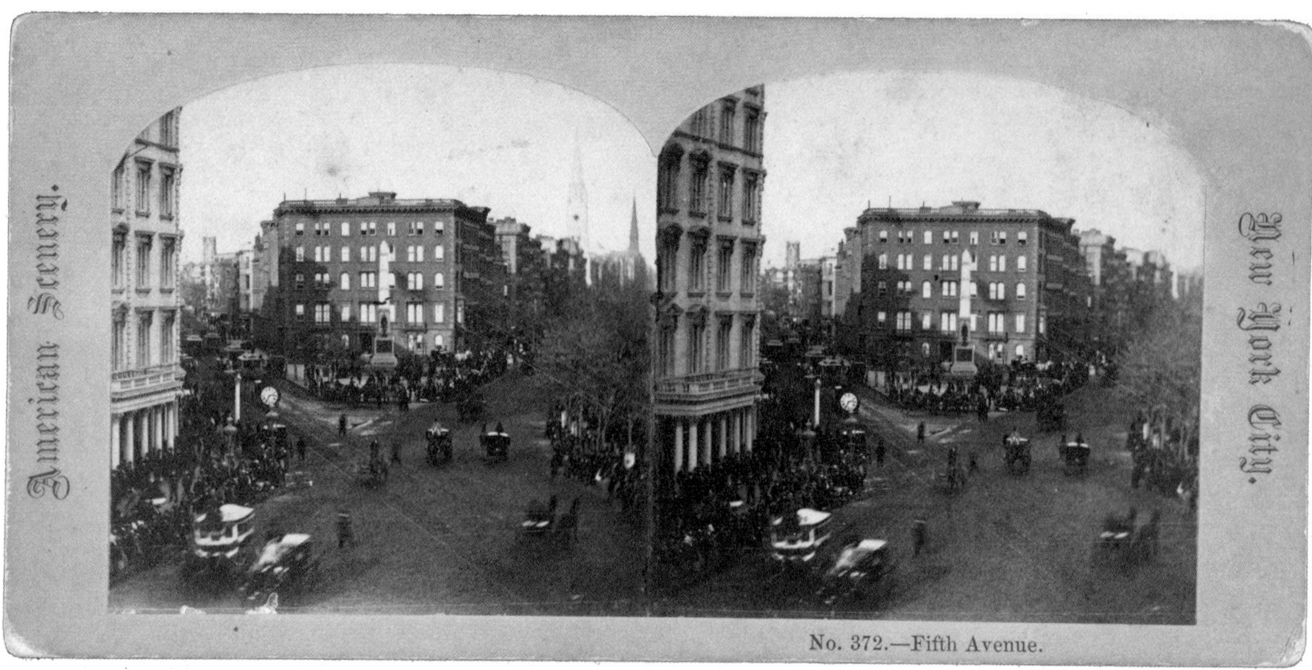

the wet-plate era using a modified emulsion and developer and a stereo camera fitted with a pair of wide-aperture, short focal length lenses. In 1859, George Washington Wilson photographed people walking on Princess Street in Edinburgh, and in the same year Edward Anthony made a remarkable series of instantaneous stereographs of traffic in New York, some of which were even taken on a rainy day. He sent the samples to Thomas Sutton, editor of the British magazine *Photographic Notes*, with a letter dated August 29, 1859, asking: "If you have any specimens of similar results obtained in Europe, we should be pleased to hear how they compare." Sutton answered in his magazine: "We can only say we know of no pictures, save two or three of [George Washington] Wilson's best, which could be put on comparison of with those [Mr. Anthony's] as sent."

Images like Anthony's "A Rainy Day on Broadway" and other stereo views capturing the urban hustle were popular with the public, helping to develop a taste for the metropolitan picturesque. Stereographic images of vibrant street life would also influence Impressionists like Degas, Monet, and Pissarro, but especially Gustave Caillebotte,

Stereo cameras, such as the one used for the above image of New York's Fifth Avenue, made possible the first "instantaneous" pictures. Generally, in the Victorian era the term was applied to any photograph that contained an element of movement, or that was taken with an exposure of less than one second. While difficult to achieve, this was possible using a modified emulsion and developer and a stereo camera fitted with a pair of wide-aperture, short focal length lenses.

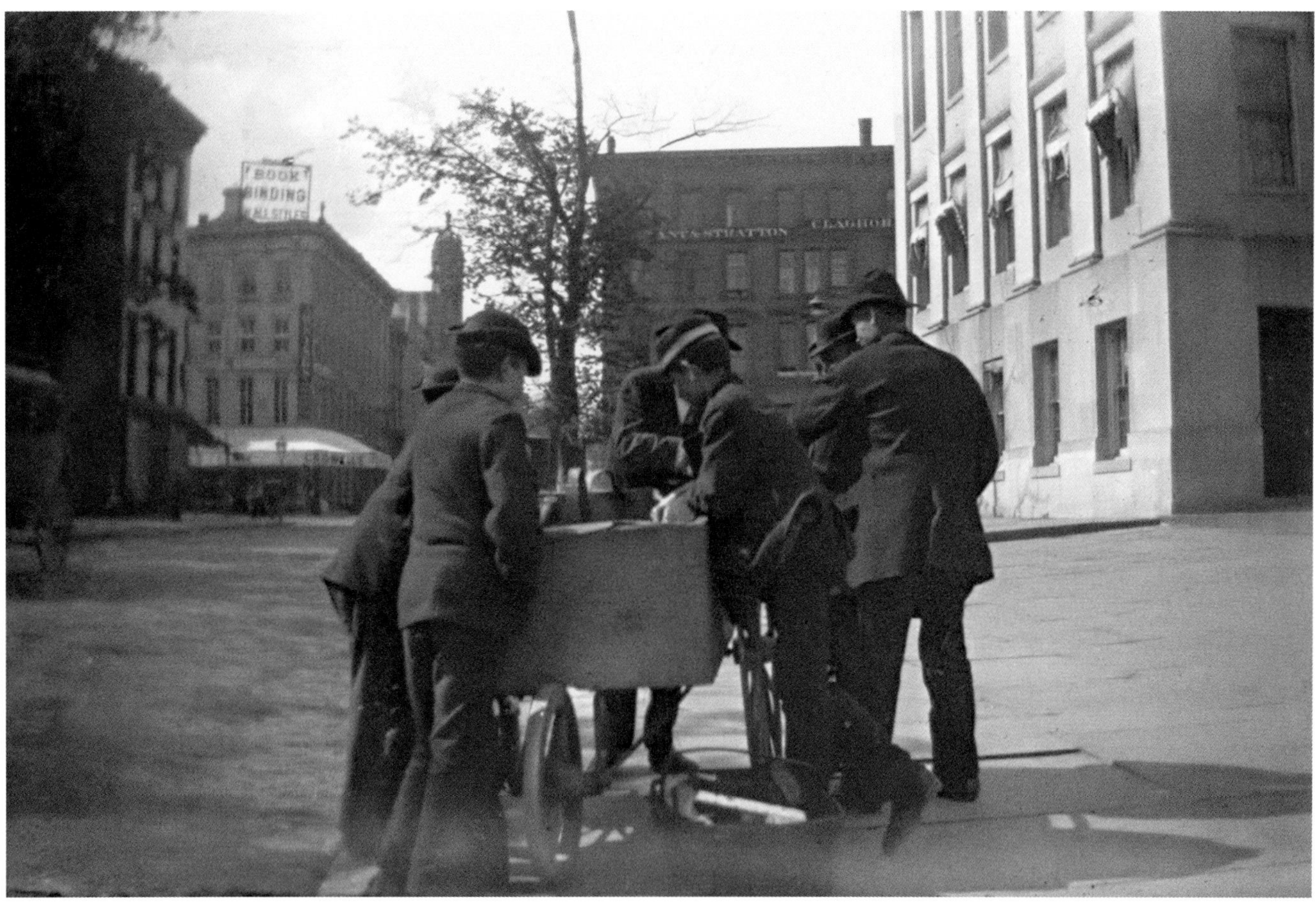

whose works, like the huge canvas, *Paris Street, Rainy Day*, from 1877, drew heavily on photography. Still, scholars tell us, it wasn't until the 1890s, with Jacob Riis and Lewis Hine, that documentary street photography was born. "It can be said that he [Riis] pioneered what we now term street photography," historian Rick Halpern wrote, "capturing the feel and texture of an urban canvas in an emotionally powerful and distinctive way in an era before rolled film and portable cameras."

Meanwhile, two decades before Riis and Hine, a new documentary style was being pioneered by a Brooklyn engineer who had taken upon himself to become a chronicler of life at the ground level.

The Pie Man, Brooklyn, late 1870s. The pie man was undoubtedly a well-known figure on the streets of Brooklyn, his delectable treats eagerly awaited. George Bradford Brainerd Photograph Collection, Brooklyn Public Library/Center for Brooklyn History.

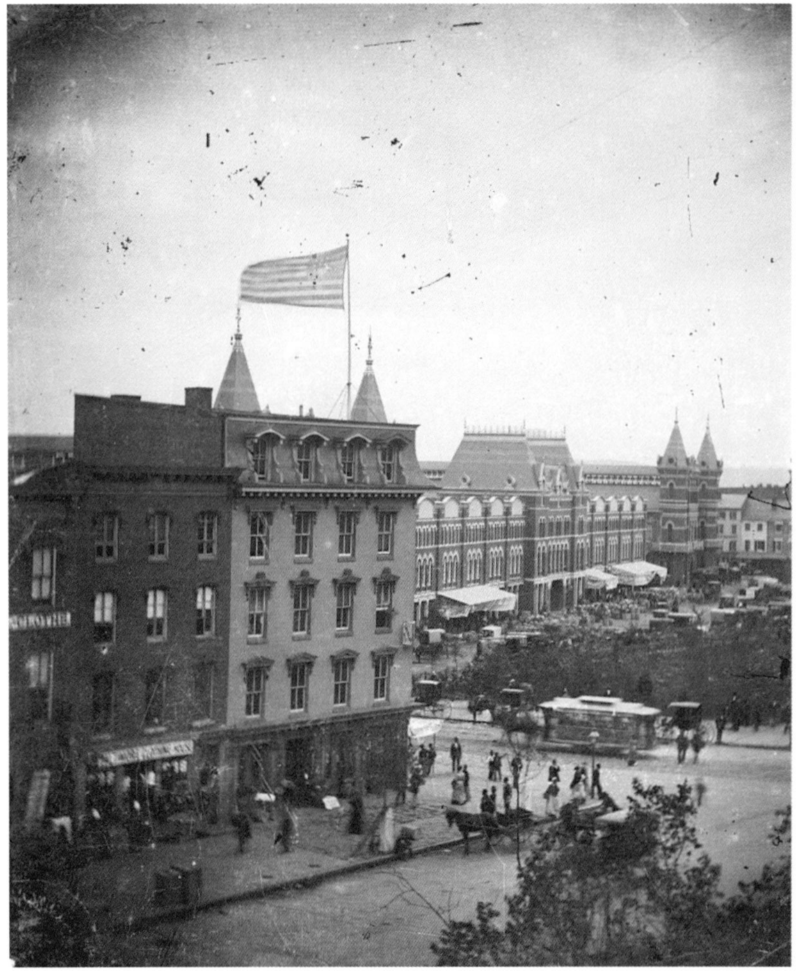

Edward Anthony's photographic studio on Broadway in New York City. Anthony (1819–1888), a cofounder of E. & H. T. Anthony & Company, was the brother of Henry T. Anthony and did business with the celebrated Civil War photographer Mathew Brady.

"If I could tell the story in words, I wouldn't need to lug around a camera."

—Lewis Hine

New York had been a center of photography almost from its inception with Daguerre in the 1830s. The French novelty would be introduced to America in 1839 by Samuel F. B. Morse, future inventor of the telegraph, then a painter of miniatures, who opened the first daguerreotype studio in the country on Broadway in New York City, where Mathew Brady later hung out his shingle. It was in New York too that some of the very first urban views were produced. This was in the 1850s, when Victor

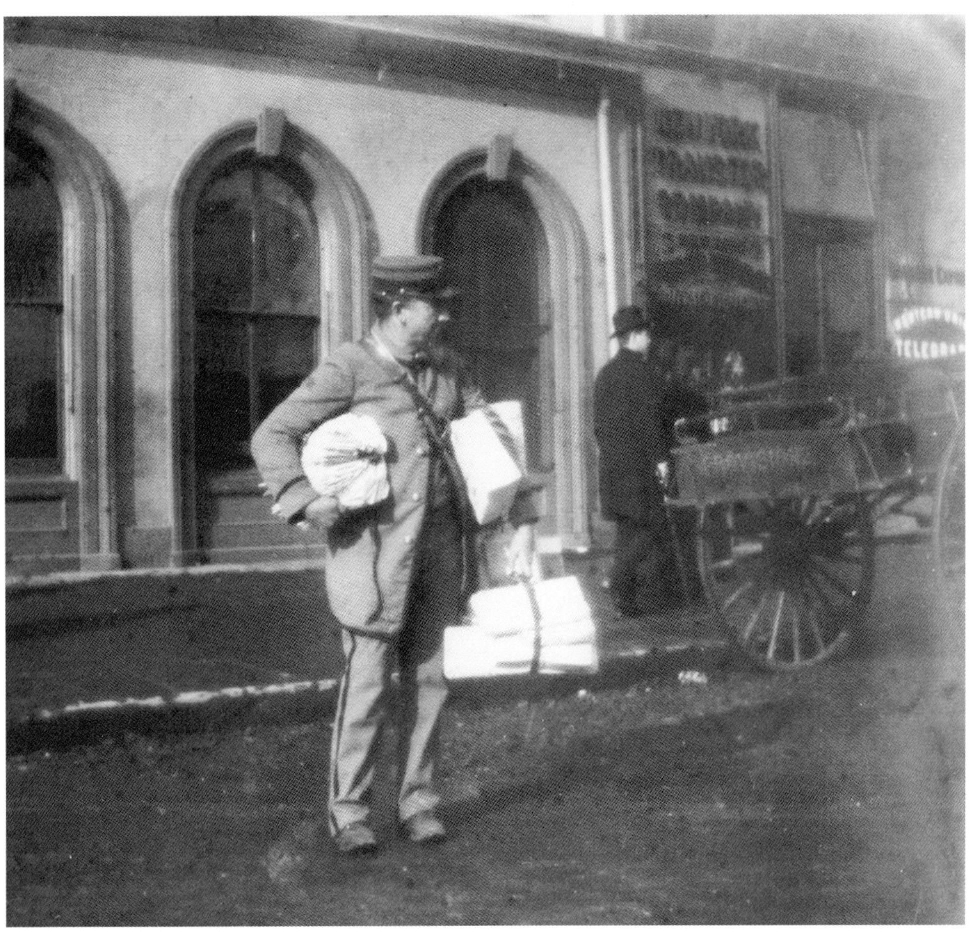

Christmas Letter Carrier, Brooklyn, 1873. One of Brainerd's earliest "instantaneous" images, "Christmas Letter Carrier," was photographed in 1873 using a handheld camera and dry plates of his own make. Note the pedestrian on the sidewalk, caught in mid-stride with no motion blur. George Bradford Brainerd Photograph Collection, Brooklyn Public Library/Center for Brooklyn History.

Prevost, a Frenchman who studied the calotype process with the photographer Gustave LeGray, began methodically photographing prominent city buildings and streets on sensitized wax paper. Other pioneering New York photographers were Anthony, a contemporary of Prevost's, Marcus Ormsbee, who worked just after the Civil War, and Joshua Beal, who was active in the early 1880s. However, except for Anthony, who used a stereo camera equipped with a fast lens, these early photographers were hampered by the cumbersome wet-plate apparatus, which, except in rare instances, could not record movement. George Brainerd would change all that.

Brainerd liked to say, "The Soap Fat Man," taken around 1877 or 1878, was his first successful "instantaneous" snapshot. However, it appears he was experimenting with hand cameras and faster dry plates of his own make several

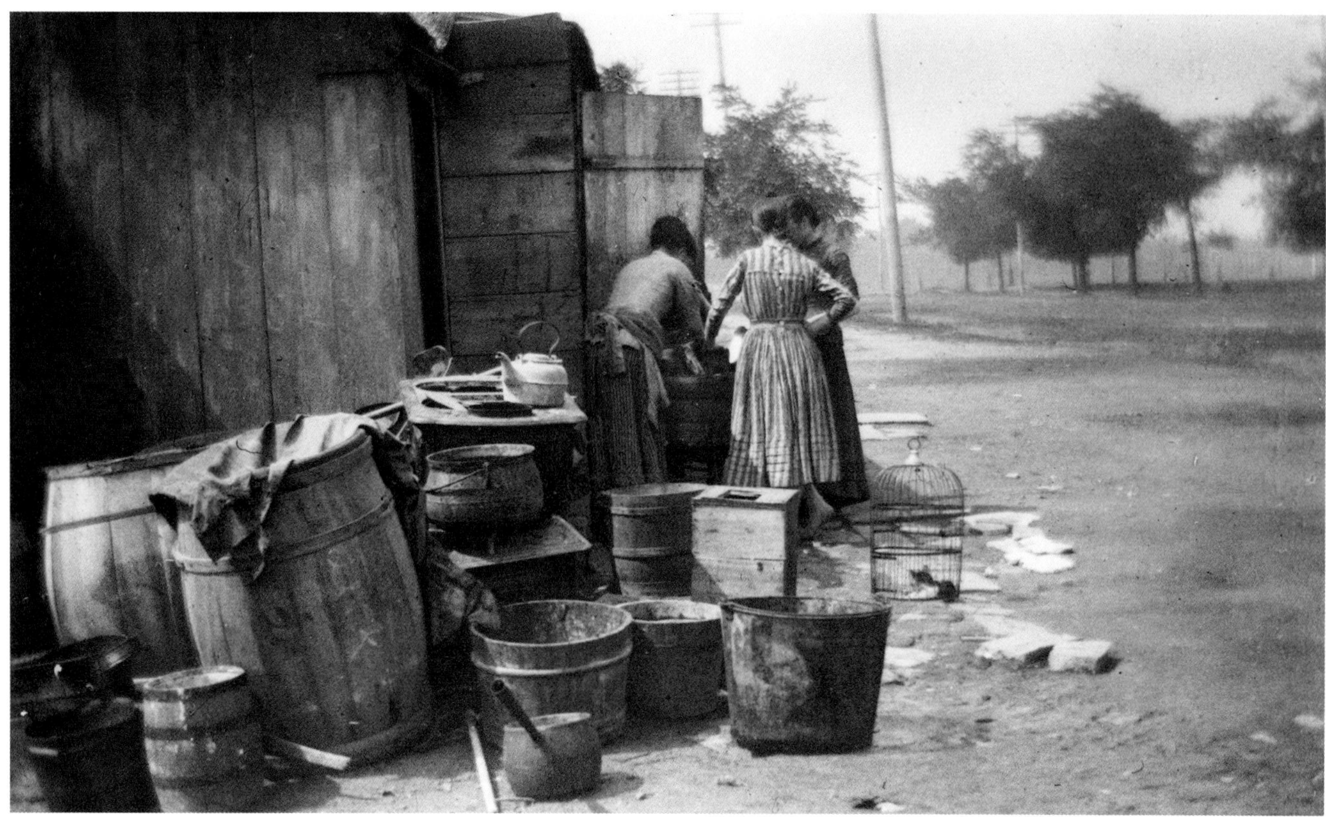

years earlier. An overlooked plate is the "Christmas Letter Carrier," depicting a portly mailman crossing the street with two enormous bundles under his arms. Although not one of Brainerd's best images, the glass negative is sharp enough to reveal the creases in the mailman's rumpled uniform. One might even detect a weary expression, suggesting a busy season. Most striking is a pedestrian on the sidewalk—a smartly dressed gentleman in a bowler hat, whose walking motion is frozen in mid-stride. Astonishingly, Brainerd had conquered action by 1873, the date of "Christmas Letter Carrier."

As noted earlier, Brainerd was among the first to employ so-called detective cameras, allowing subjects to be photographed without their knowledge much less permission. We are told he used the apparatus as early as 1876. That was the year of the great Centennial Exhibition in Philadelphia, the first official world's fair to be held in the United States, which also coincided with the centennial anniversary of

Fourth Avenue Shanties, Brooklyn, 1870s. "I hear America singing," wrote fellow Brooklynite, Walt Whitman, onetime editor of *The Brooklyn Daily Eagle,* where he often described the humble lives of immigrants, even paying a visit to Brooklyn's Irish Shanties. "The delicious singing of the mother, or of the young wife at work, or of the girl sewing or washing. Each singing what belongs to him or her and to no one else." George Bradford Brainerd Photograph Collection, Brooklyn Public Library/Center for Brooklyn History.

the Declaration of Independence's adoption in Philadelphia on July 4, 1776. Held in Fairmount Park along the Schuylkill River, "The 1876 International Exhibition of the Arts, Manufacturers, and Products of the Soil and Mine" showcased American ingenuity, innovation, and technology, subjects which were of keen interest to Brainerd, who, as a dedicated amateur photographer, hoped to record with the new medium. The only problem was the fair's directors had imposed a strict ban on photography for all but a select few, a prohibition that was vigorously enforced by police. Thus, Brainerd was obliged to employ a bit of subterfuge, as the *Brooklyn Daily Eagle* would later report:

> In 1876, the management of the Centennial Exhibition at Philadelphia, having given the exclusive right of securing photographs of the building and grounds to a single firm, it was almost impossible, on account of the vigilance of the police for amateurs to expose any plates on the premises. But Mr. Brainerd, by his inventive turn was able to disregard the rule with impunity. He designed a hidden camera with the box done up in brown paper, the whole having the appearance of a harmless budget. Not one of the guardians of the law looked at this bundle with suspicion, and Mr. Brainerd went about the grounds taking pictures of everything he liked and without the least fear of molestation.

Brainerd quickly realized that such camouflaged cameras were ideal for recording the spontaneous, unrehearsed action of the street—fulfilling the promise of photography to be a true representation of life. Later, when such surreptitious technology became widely available, there would be a backlash, with self-restrained Victorians voicing concerns over privacy and the lack of control over one's own image. Many worried indiscriminate "snap-shooters" would capture them in awkward, frozen poses, subjecting them to ridicule. Indeed, Walter D. Welford echoed such concerns in his 1890 manual, *The Hand Camera and How to Use It*, noting that whenever he showed up at a gathering with his portable box camera, his friends got fidgety, fearing they

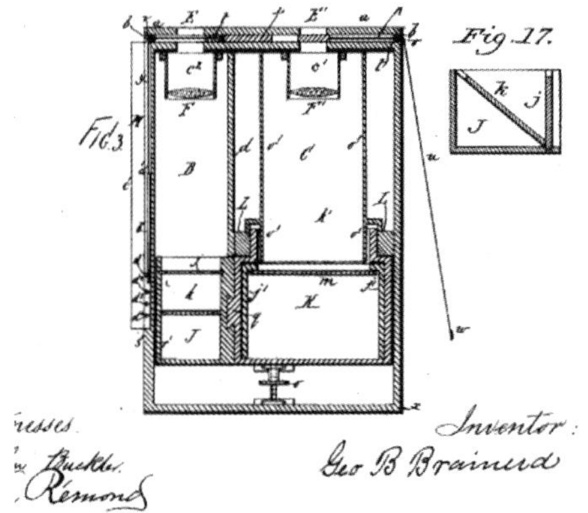

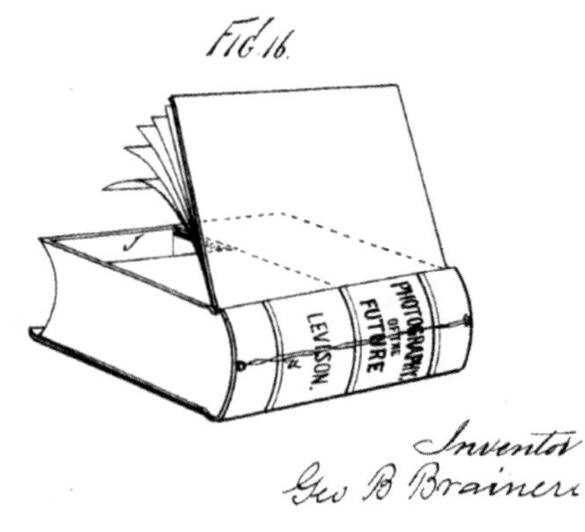

George Brainerd's "Detective" camera, for which he received a patent in 1885, although the device was in use a least a decade earlier. Brainerd's camera was camouflaged to look like a book. Its real novelty, however, was the twin-lens reflex system, with a waist-level rangefinder, designed to take pictures on the fly without the need for a steadying tripod.

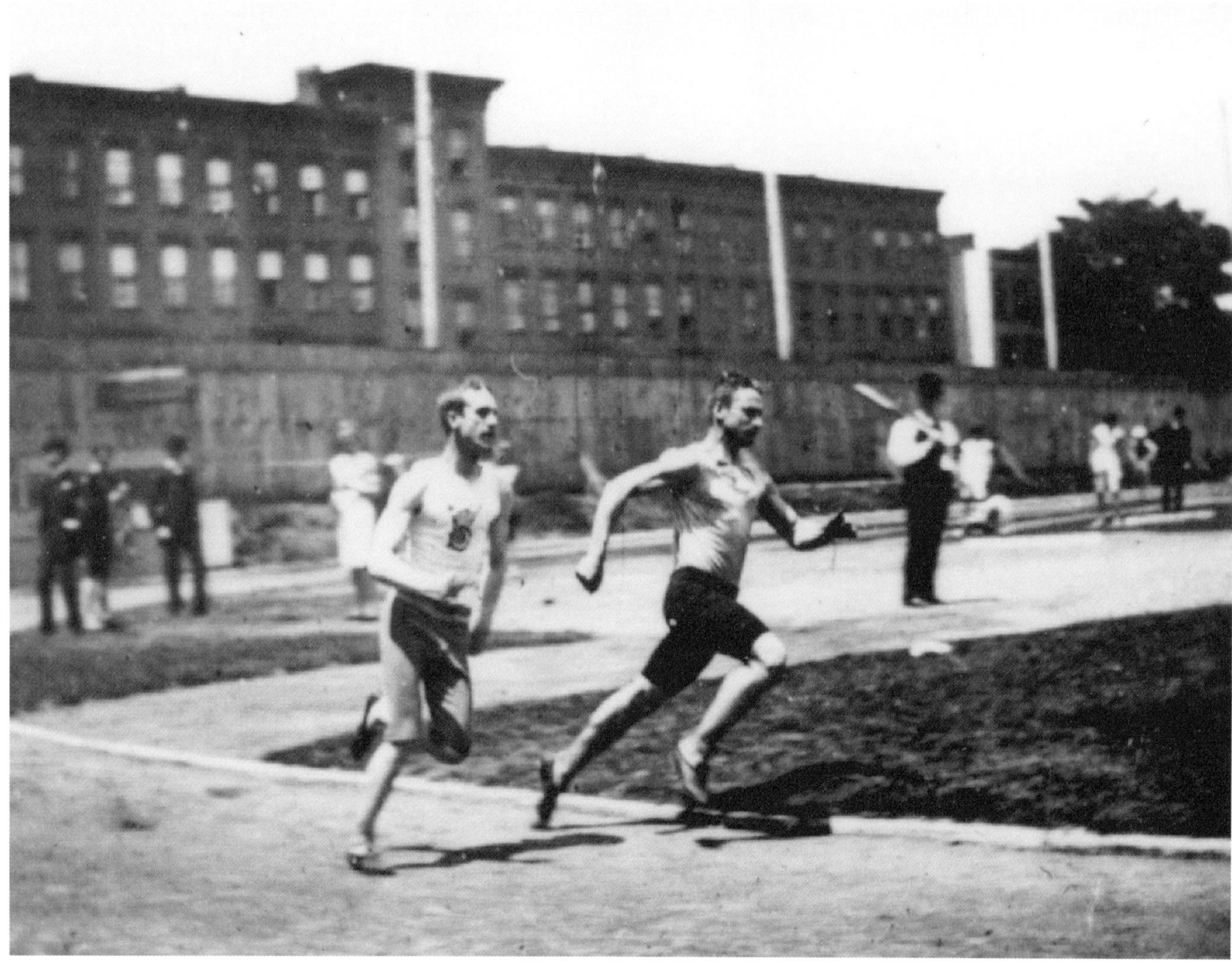

would be "taken when they don't know it." The same year the *Yonkers Statesman* ran the following item under the headline, "The Snapshot Again":

> Miriam: Did you take the picture of the young man on the mantel?
>
> Mildred: Yes.
>
> Miriam: Friend of yours, I suppose?
>
> Mildred: Well, he was before I took the picture.

It was probably this fear of committing a social faux pas that pushed Brainerd into the streets, where his subjects, itinerant merchants and laborers, were in no position to

One of George Brainerd's most remarkable action photos of runners sprinting on a New York track, snapped in the late 1870s. Brainerd was experimenting with improved handheld cameras and faster dry-plate technology, which drew him more and more to action scenes. He had developed his own emulsions, carefully working out the right combination of light-sensitive silver halides suspended in the gelatin binder to coat the glass plates. Brainerd would also devise a mechanical shutter that could click off exposures of at least 1/250 of a second.

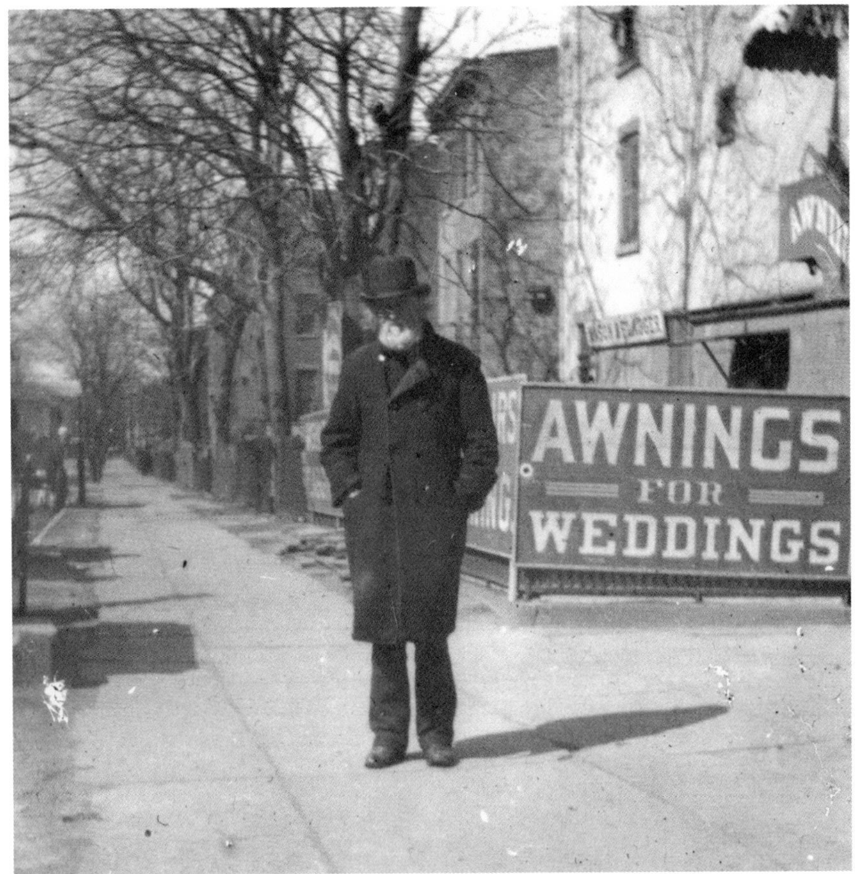

Old Letter Carrier, Brooklyn, 1875. Like the pioneering London journalist Henry Mayhew, author of *London Labour and the London Poor,* published in 1851, George Brainerd had a lifelong interest in documenting well-known street types and personalities in Brooklyn and New York City, hence this image entitled, "Old Letter Carrier." Indeed, for those who know his work, Brainerd's pictures of such vanished Victorian person-alities are among his most admired plates. George Bradford Brainerd Photograph Collection, Brooklyn Public Library/Center for Brooklyn History.

protest. Also, the job with the Brooklyn Water Department plunged the young engineer into new, unexplored regions that he could mine for material. Writers such as Edgar Allan Poe (1809–1849) and Charles Baudelaire (1821–1867) had already begun to explore the modern metropolis as a back-drop for their stories. Baudelaire was fascinated by one of Poe's short stories, "The Man of the Crowd," in which a con-valescent, sitting in the window of a London coffeehouse, becomes absorbed in the movement of the crowd outside and, after observing the various urban types and person-alities, is moved to follow one such representative back and forth through the bustling streets of the city. "This old man," Poe concludes at the end of his story, "is the type and the genius of deep crime. He refuses to be alone. He is the man of the crowd."

"The Man of the Crowd" began to define a new type of urban personality, the *flâneur*, or stroller, usually a

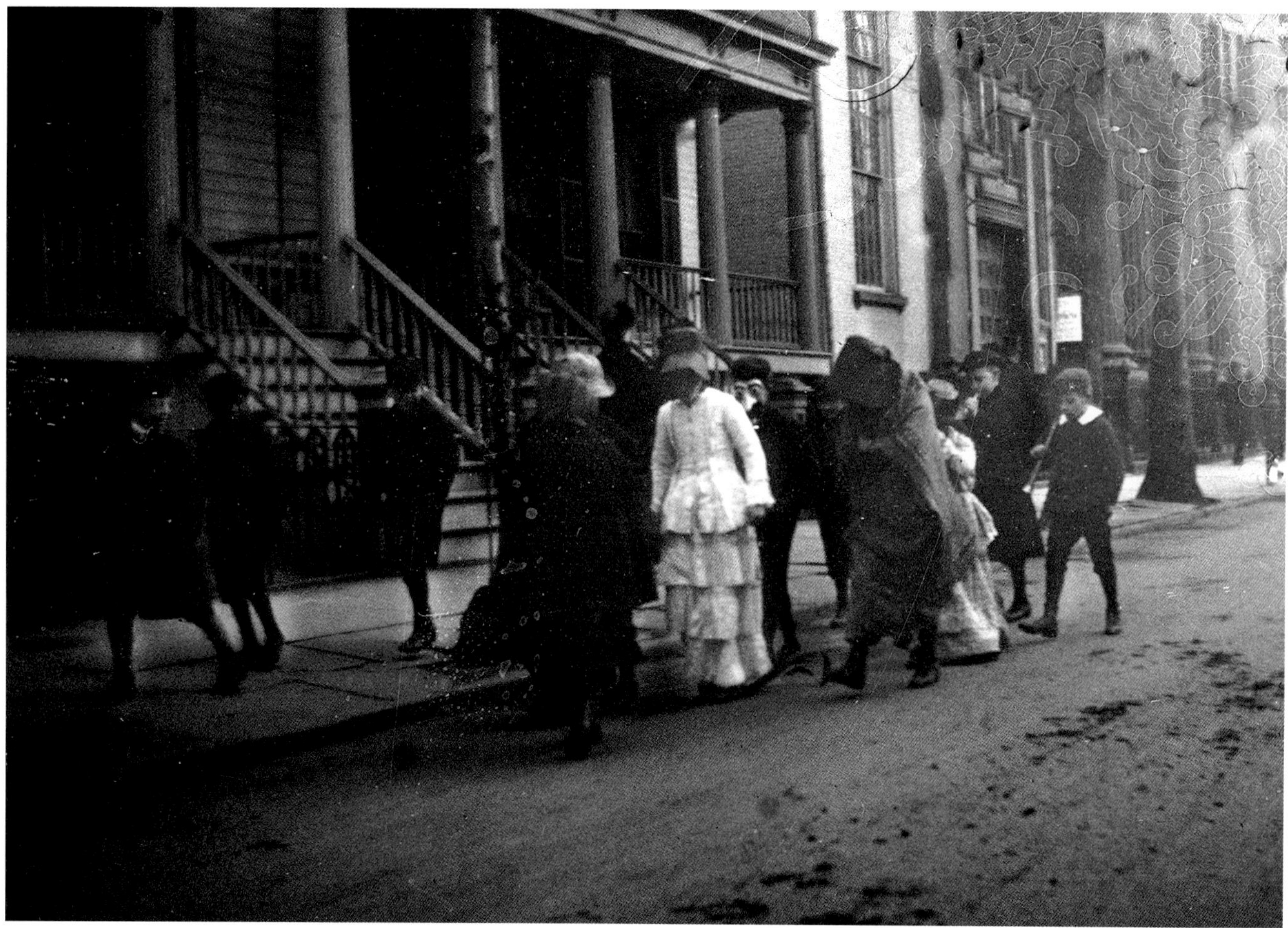

well-heeled gentleman who had the time to wander, observe, eavesdrop, drawing energy from the hustle and bustle. A man of means, Brainerd possessed some of the characteristics of the *flâneur*—tall and handsome, with an extravagant moustache and never without his bowler hat, black in winter, gray in summer. One imagines the dapper engineer with a Sherlock Holmes, "game's-afoot" spring in his step, as he weaves in and out of the throng, gusts tugging at his coattails, which billow up at a strategic moment to reveal a simple box camera, camouflaged to look like a book, ready to be deployed at a moment's notice. (Indeed, the word *snapshot* was hunter's parlance for a wild shot from the hip.)

There is also in Brainerd a Victorian obsession with collecting and cataloging. The engineer, it should be noted, was an eager botanist, a sufferer no less of what was known

Thanksgiving Day Parade along Columbia Street in Brooklyn around 1875. George Bradford Brainerd Photograph Collection, Brooklyn Public Library/Center for Brooklyn History.

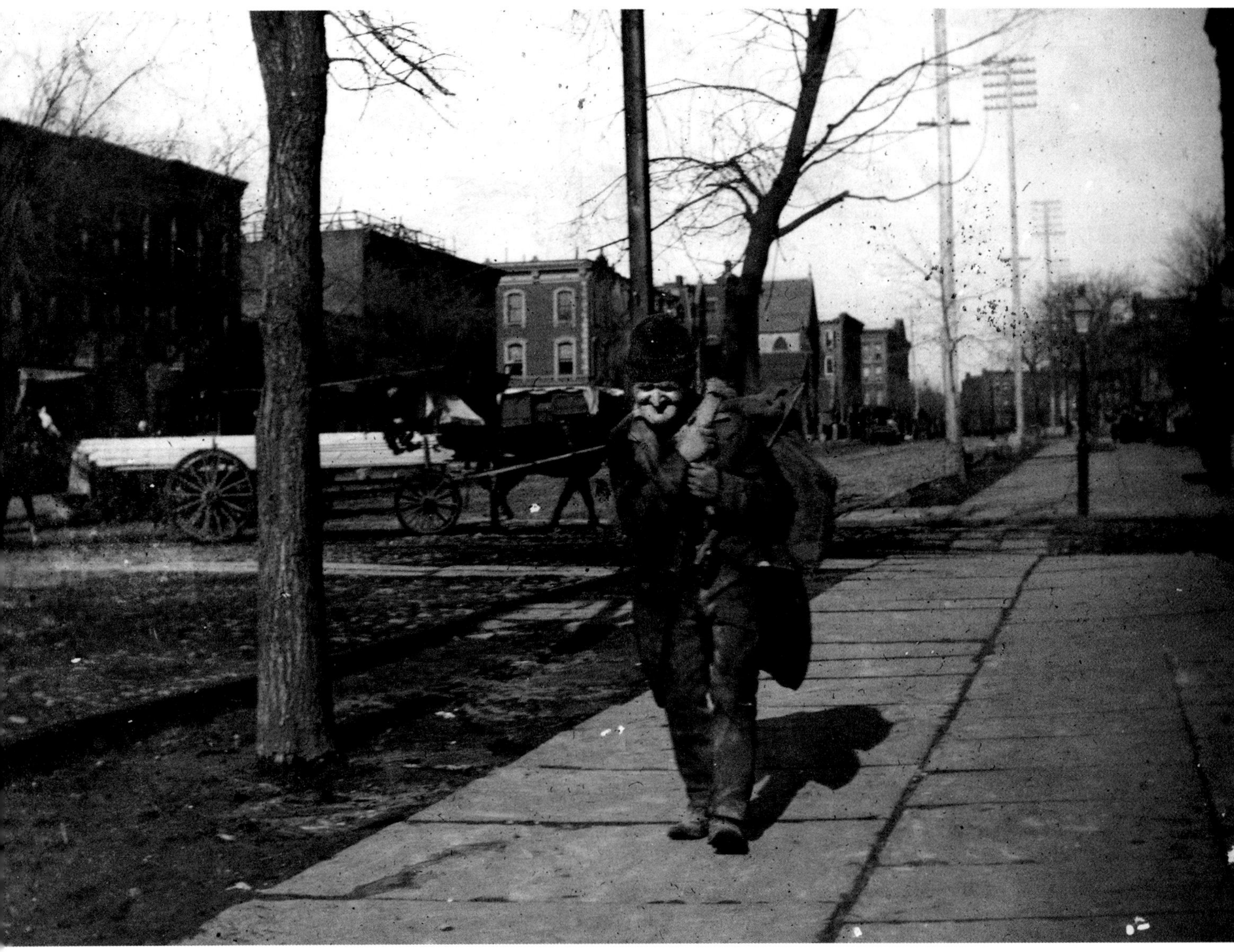

A beloved character, the Ragpicker, Brooklyn, 1870s. Dubbed "rag-and-bone men," these itinerant pickers combed the neighborhood for castoff items that might be of value—scraps of cloth and paper and even bits of broken glass that could be melted down and reused.

as *Pteridomania* or "fern fever." The word was coined in 1855 by Charles Kingsley in his book *Glaucus, or the Wonders of the Shore*: "Your daughters, perhaps, have been seized with the prevailing 'Pteridomania' . . . and wrangling over unpronounceable names of species (which seem different in each new Fern-book that they buy) . . . and yet you cannot deny that they find enjoyment in it, and are more active, more cheerful, more self-forgetful over it, than they would have been over novels and gossip, crochet and Berlin-wool."

This Victorian zeal for taxonomic classification spilled over into Brainerd's photography. In his best street pictures,

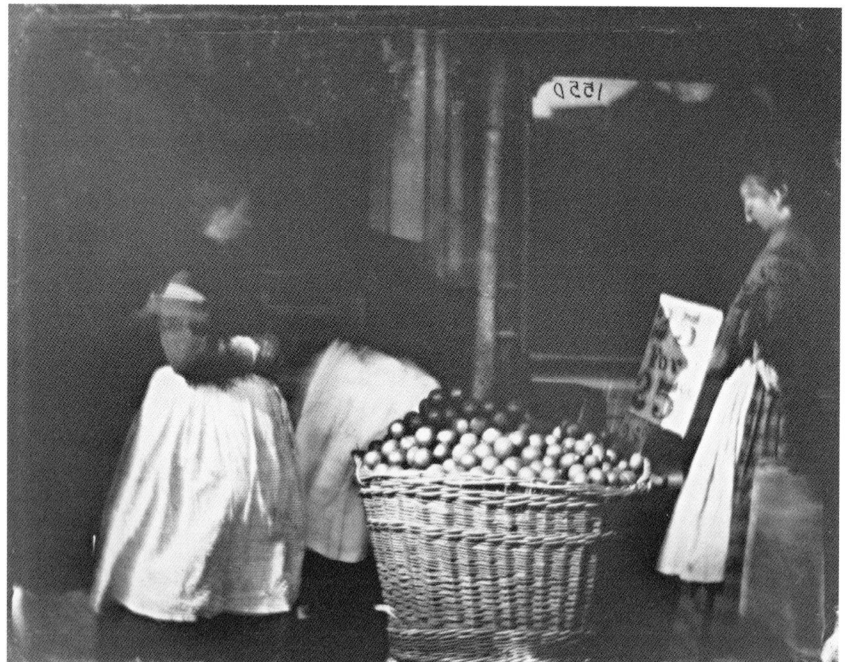

Apple stand, New York, 1870s. Apple peddlers were ubiquitous in New York during the 19th century, with fruit stands occupying virtually every street corner. Here we see Brainerd's painterly sense, his image evoking the deft brushwork of a Whistler, or even Robert Henri, the late 19th century founder of the so-called Ashcan School of painting.

we see a desire to record "types," to carry out a sort of an ethnographic mapping of the city. At no time were the sidewalks of Brooklyn and New York home to a richer cast of characters. Every corner, it seemed, had its flower lady, its apple peddler and shoeblack, its little knot of news-hawks. Here too was the chestnut seller, offering his roasted treats in rolled newspapers, and the candy man, with the squashed nose of a bare-knuckles prizefighter, doling out sweet confections with a hearty "Hallo!" Perhaps best of all were the street musicians, whose lively airs, mingling with the shouts of peddlers and rhythmic clip-clopping of horses' hooves on pavement, made for a cacophony of sound, which if not comforting, was at least familiar. A window on this Dickensian world is offered in many categories of street licenses issued by Brooklyn mayor James Howell in 1878:

SECTION 1. Licenses shall be granted by the mayor from time to time to such persons as he may deem proper residents of the city of Brooklyn, of the age of 21 years, and of good moral character . . . and not otherwise, to carry on the business of coachman, porters, owners and drivers of hacks, trucks, cabs, omnibuses, stages, railroad cars, express wagons, peddlers'

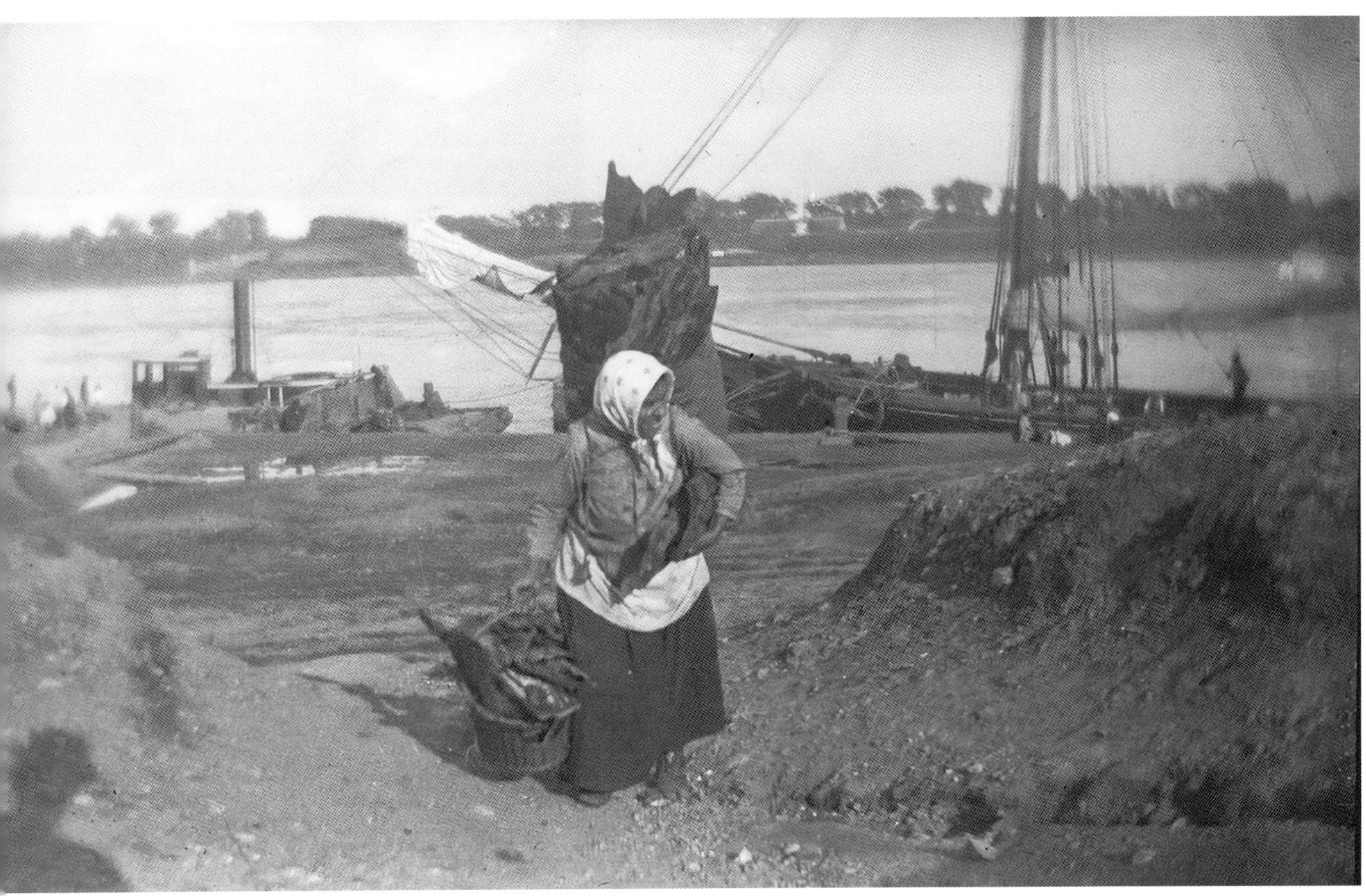

The Bark Woman, Brooklyn, 1870s. One of Brainerd's most poignant images, "The Bark Woman," is seen plodding up from the waterfront with her enormous burden. Like "The Soap Fat Man," the photograph is a record of a long-vanished industry, the gathering of tree bark for the tanning of animal hides. Brainerd used a concealed camera to get close to his subject, but he left his fingerprints here in the form of a shadow (in his bowler hat) appearing in the left corner. George Bradford Brainerd Photograph Collection, Brooklyn Public Library/Center for Brooklyn History.

wagons and junk wagons or carts, and of common criers, hawkers, peddlers, pawn brokers, keepers of intelligence offices, junk shopkeepers, sweeps, butchers, and meat sellers.

Brainerd's iconography also harkens back to the "street cries" tradition, the picturesque street peddlers whose short lyrical calls hawking their wares became a distinctive feature of 18th-century European urban life. Such colorful characters peppered the pages of Dickens and Thackeray. But nowhere would they be described with such feeling as in Henry Mayhew's *London Labour and the London Poor*, published in 1851, which includes the unforgettable portrait of "Jack Black, Her Majesty's Rat Catcher":

In the sporting world, and among his regular customers, the Queen's rat catcher is better known by the name of Jack Black. He enjoys the reputation of being, the most fearless handler of rats of any man living, playing with them—as one man

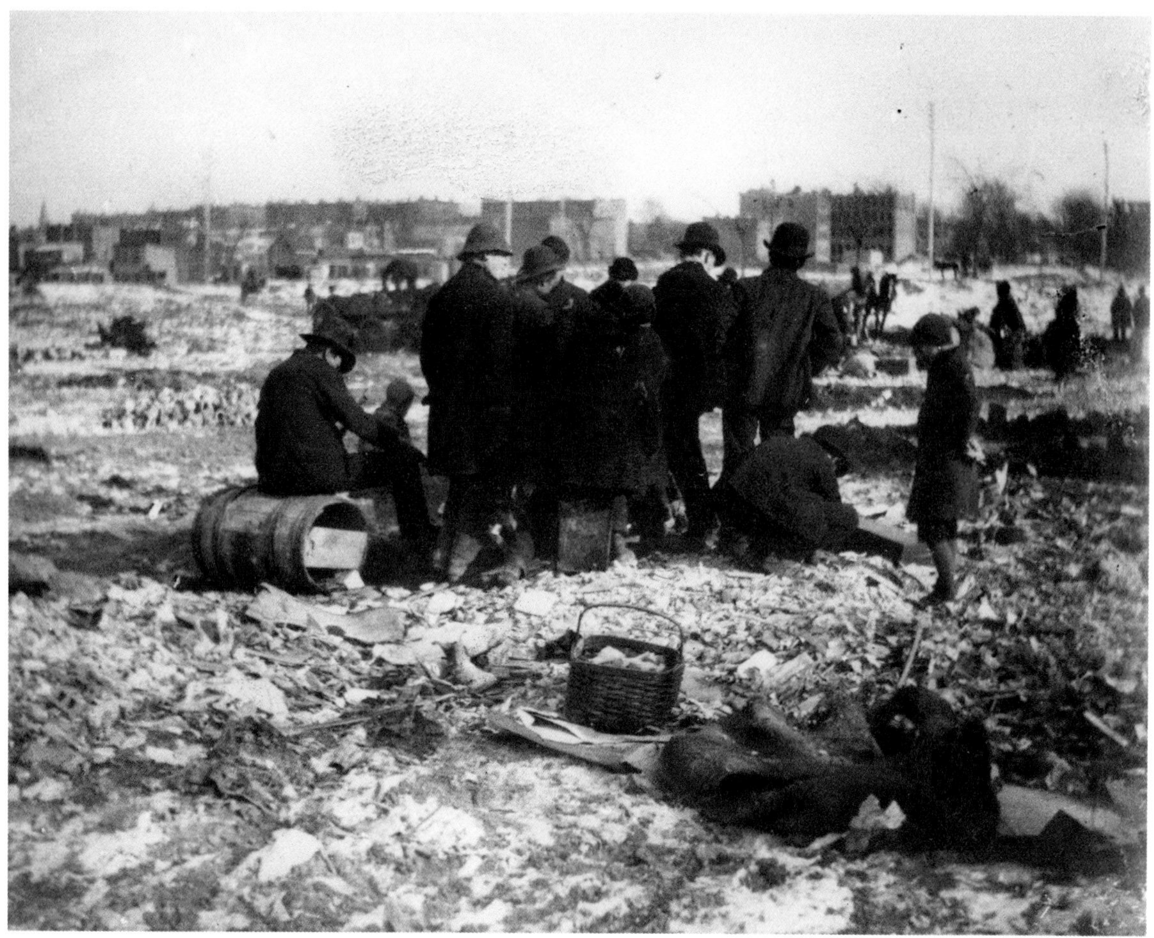

expressed it to me—"as if they were so many blind kittens." The first time I ever saw Mr. Black was in the streets of London, at the corner of Hartstreet, where he was exhibiting the rapid effects of his rat poison, by placing some of it in the mouth of a living animal. He had a cart then with rats painted on the panels, and at the tailboard, where he stood lecturing; he had a kind of stage rigged up, on which were cages filled with rats, and pills, and poison packages.

Echoes of *London Labour* reverberate in Brainerd's best street photography, in particular "The Soap Fat Man," and "The Rag Picker," as well as "Shanties on Fourth Avenue," in which Brainerd captures a group of women in shabby dress clustered about some shacks, possibly washing clothes, at the southern edge of what is now Brooklyn's Park Slope neighborhood. There is also the grim "Prospect Park Dump,"

Prospect Park Dump, 1870s. Salvaging, though filthy work, was a good source of income for the residents who sifted through the regularly arriving dumps of fill for salable material ranging from old rag paper and shoes to bricks and tin cans. More than eking out a living, some pickers were able to enjoy comfortable lives in homes they owned. This practice had been going on since the 1830s. George Bradford Brainerd Photograph Collection, Brooklyn Public Library/Center for Brooklyn History.

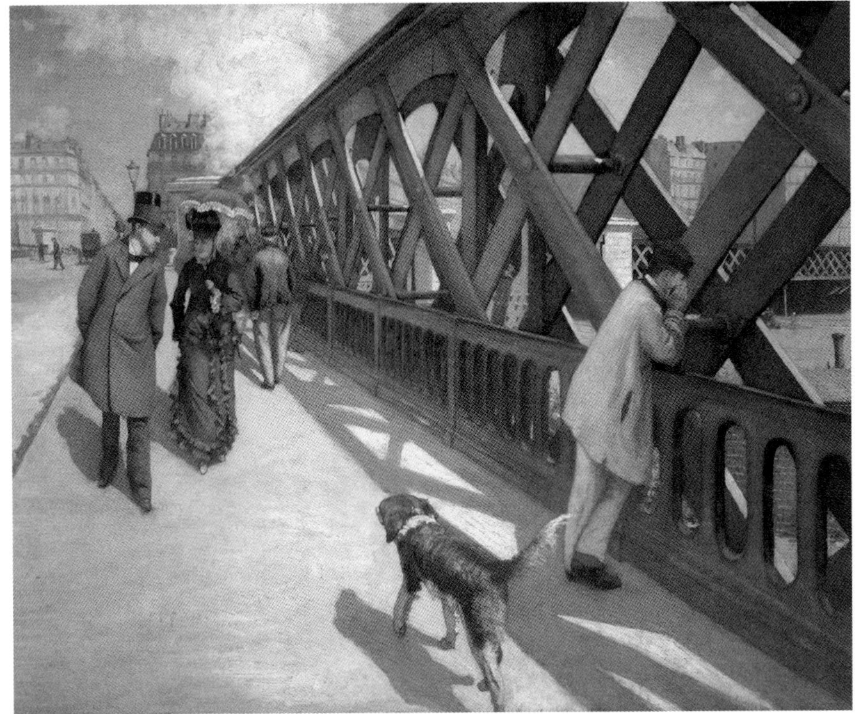

Le Pont de l'Europe, 1876 by French Impressionist Gustave Caillebotte. Like Degas, Caillebotte was heavily influenced by photography and his bold compositions and unusual cropping suggest he may have employed the new medium to help map out his pictures. It is not known whether Brainerd was familiar with Caillebotte's work, but both drew inspiration from the urban bustle, the busy streets and market squares thronged with pedestrians and horses and carriages in hundreds of variations.

showing groups of pickers hunting for valuables in the eponymous park, designed, like Central Park, by the renowned landscape architect Frederick Law Olmsted. Perhaps out of respect, Brainerd photographs the crowd from a distance with their backs to the camera. Like the protagonist in *I Am a Camera*, the play derived from Christopher Isherwood's touching memoir *Goodbye to Berlin*, Brainerd was there to record not to judge. It's this matter of fact, unsentimental approach that gives Brainerd's work its power.

A lovely portrait in the Mayhew tradition is "The Bark Woman." Similar to "The Soap Fat Man," it documents a vanished industry, the gathering of tree bark, usually hemlock, for the tanning of animal hides. Like a character in a German fairy tale, the bark lady is seen with her burden coming up from the waterfront in a headscarf and long dress. Her pose is so natural, one is apt to miss the enormous bundle of tree bark on her back, surely more than any one person could carry. If that's not enough there is more under one arm and overflowing a basket. Just as with Millet's *The Gleaners*, the circa 1878 image pays tribute to humble laborers and

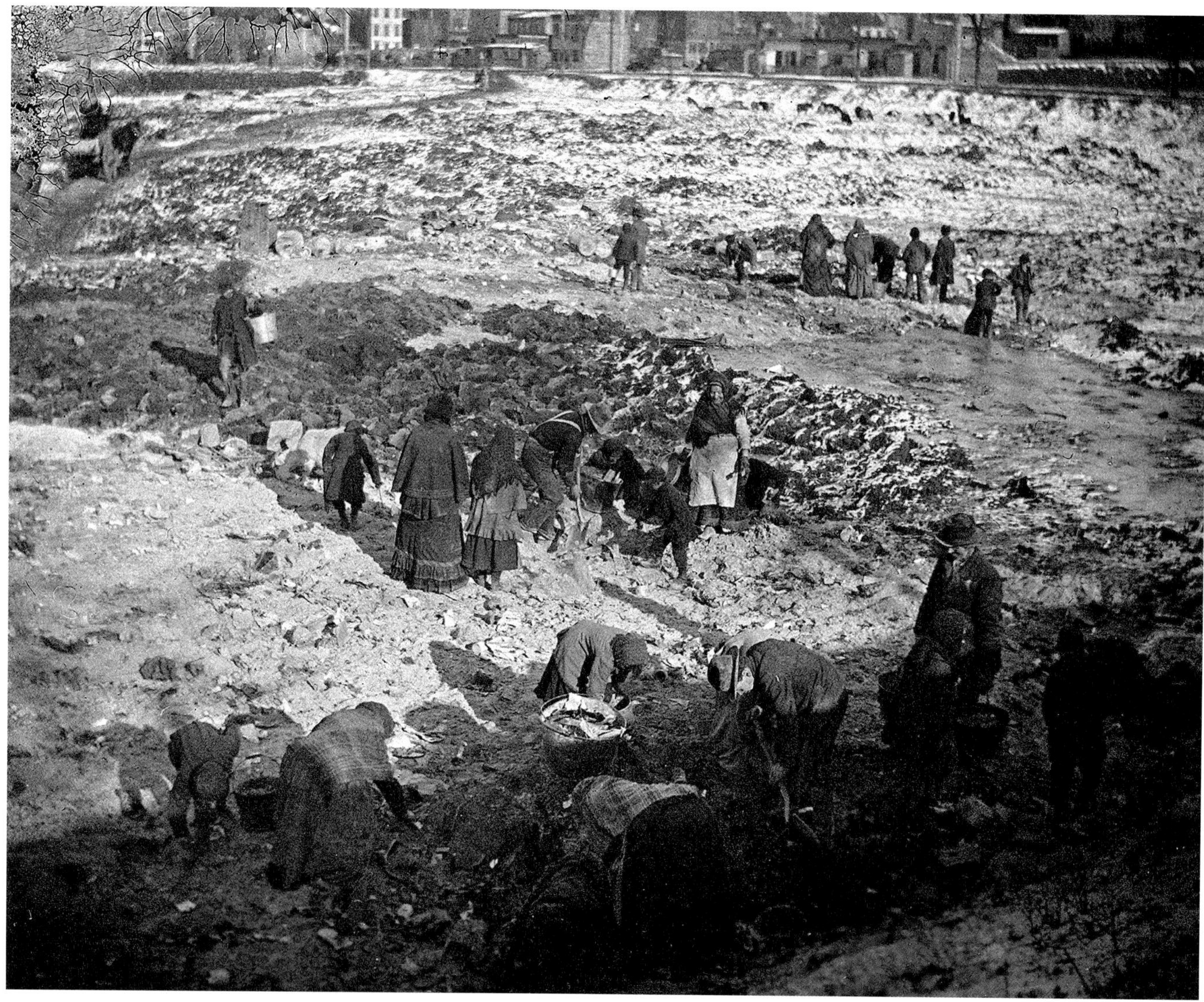

the dignity of those who toil at the fringes of society. Though a snapshot, the picture captures a moment of intense concentration and physical exertion, which underscores the resilience and determination of the working poor.

The dignity of work is a theme running through much of Brainerd's photography. He clearly had great respect for common laborers on whom he was utterly dependent as a public works director, managing so many key projects for the city of Brooklyn. The Water Department was always tearing up streets to lay new water pipe, and Brainerd, with his interest in movement and freezing action, used the opportunity to hone his craft. Brainerd's best street photography recalls

Prospect Park Dump, 1870s. Another view of pickers sifting through the trash at the Prospect Park Dump. George Bradford Brainerd Photograph Collection, Brooklyn Public Library/Center for Brooklyn History.

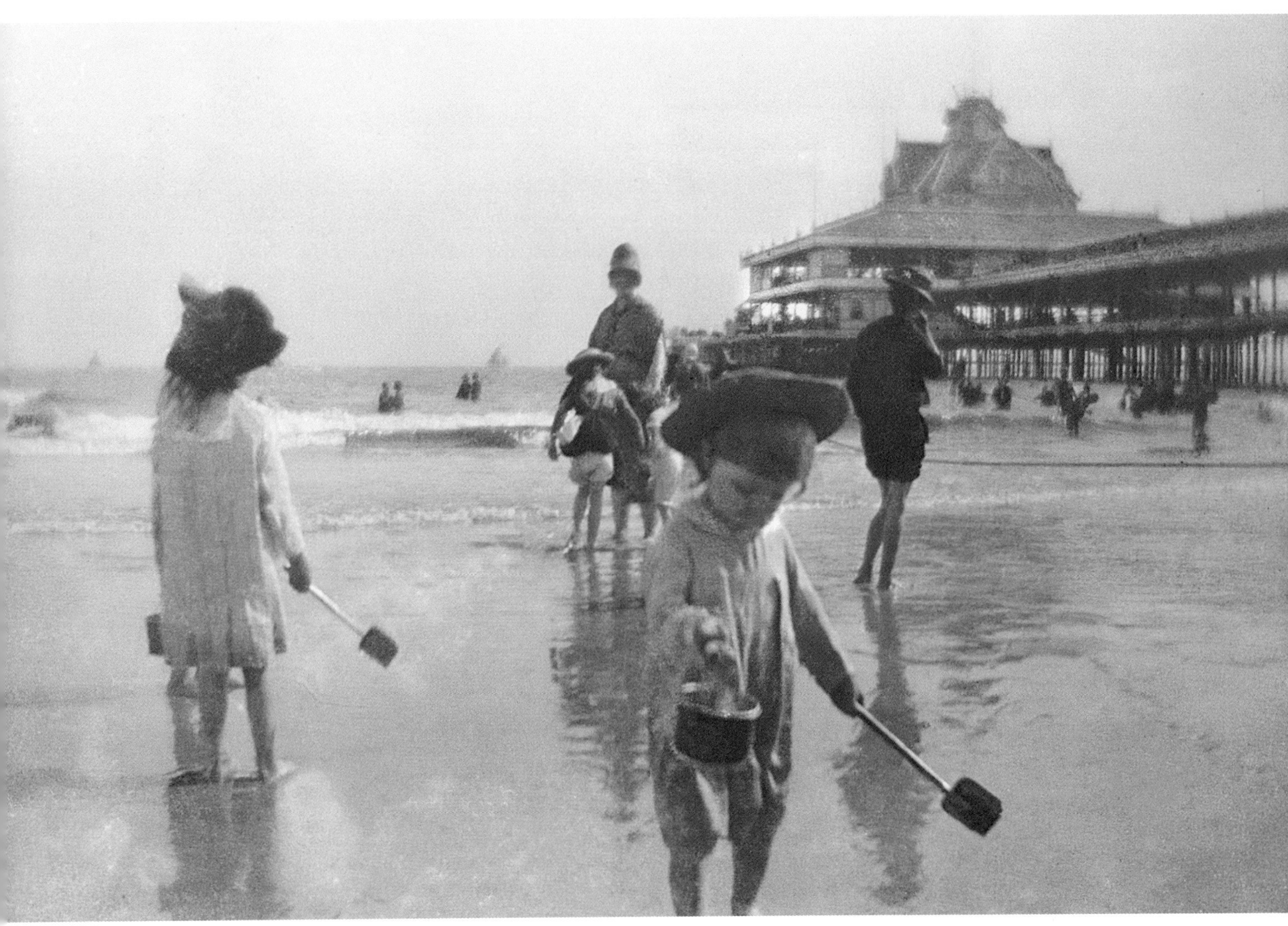

the fin de siècle images of the French photographer Eugène Atget, who also recorded workers known as "asphalt layers," repairing Paris streets. One is also reminded of Caillebotte's *The Floor Scrapers*, depicting men with muscled backs and arms stripping the varnish off the floors of an elegant Parisian apartment, probably Caillebotte's.

Just as with Caillebotte, Brainerd offers no clue as to interpretation. Is his street photography a paean to the common man and the mastery of work? Or is Brainerd's simply a comment on the efficiency of government in carrying important public works projects on behalf of the new monied classes? There is also the possibility Brainerd's is merely an aesthetic point of view—a perceptive vision

Brainerd's ebullient depictions of Victorians at play—splashing in the waves at Coney Island or gliding across the ice at Prospect Park and Central Park, are in stark contrast to his sometimes grim depictions of the poor and working class. Just as his camera had probed the darker side of urban life, so too would Brainerd seek out the myriad amusements city dwellers looked forward to after the Civil War. With his hand camera, Brainerd probably waded in himself to get this tight shot of a little girl with shovel and pail at Coney Island's Iron Pier.

emphasizing not so much the toil, as the beauty of form and movement and the rhythms of work. This ballet of the street, as it were, is most evident in an image entitled "Repairing Clinton Street," showing a road crew in a graceful curving line, with shovels and picks in the air, attacking the pavement near a sumptuous brownstone with an iron lacework railing. Framing the picture at the right is a man in a bowler hat, probably the foreman, leaning heavily on one leg; but our attention is drawn to the figure at the left, a smartly dressed gentleman in a straw boater bounding over the cobblestones with his gaze firmly down, determined, it seems, to shut out the picks and shovels and the road crew tearing up the ground just a feet away. It's the modern city distilled in a moment.

In contrast to Brainerd's grim views of the poor are his ebullient depictions of Victorians at play—splashing in the waves at Coney Island, gliding across the ice at Prospect Park and Central Park, or just showing off at the zoo. Just as his camera probed the darker side of urban life, so too would it seek out the many amusements city dwellers looked forward to after the Civil War, when an emerging middle class with more time on their hands and dollars in their pockets sought diversions as never before. It was the Gilded Age, when the business tycoon "Diamond" Jim Brady, sporting a 10-carat stone on his shirtfront cried, "Hell! I'm rich. Now it's time to have some fun!" This was also the era of luxurious steamboats churning up the East River on their way to palatial summer resorts on Long Island Sound. "Their paddle boxes were painted lavender and their smokestacks deep yellow, and their outside decks were replaced with alternating strips of black walnut and yellow pine," one commentator wrote of the "floating palaces." "Grand staircases of mahogany swept up to their 300-foot saloons from which rosewood doors opened into state rooms, brilliantly lighted from gas chandeliers illuminating the white and gold trimmings and the acres of velvet pile

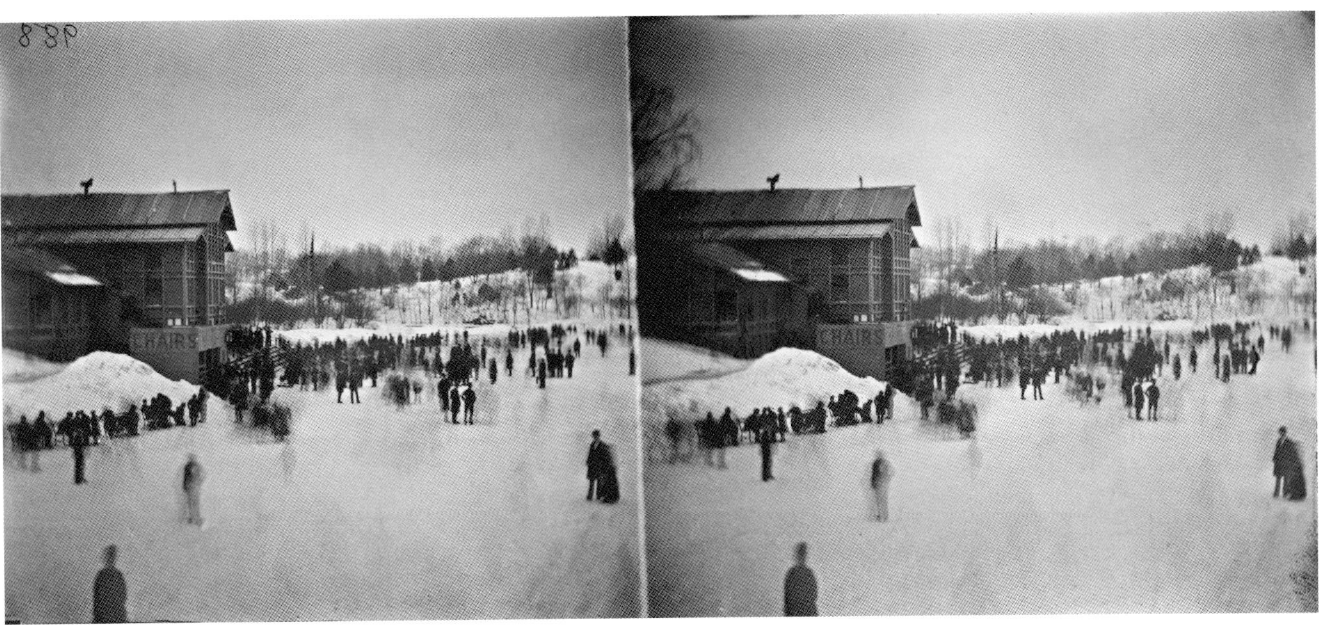

carpeting. A concert orchestra played on each vessel, joined by the trilling of 200 canaries in gilded cages. . . ."

As a member of Brooklyn's financial and cultural elite, one might have expected Brainerd to dwell more on Gilded Age glamor in the same way the aristocratic French photographer, Jacques Henri Lartigue, recorded Parisian high society of which he was a member. Such images are the exception. Brainerd only hints at the great wealth being generated by the money kings in the form of palatial mansions and glimpses of their exclusive pastimes, such as yachting and lawn tennis, and parading ultra-expensive carriages each afternoon in Central Park. Perhaps because his roots were on the Connecticut River, where the old ways persisted long after disappearing elsewhere, Brainerd leaned more toward the timeless and eternal—ice skating, "surf bathing," and strolling in the city's lush parks.

In the late 1870s, Brainerd began experimenting with improved handheld cameras and faster dry-plate technology, which drew him more and more to scenes of movement and action. He had developed his own emulsions, carefully working out the right combination of

An enchanting winter panorama of skaters in Central Park, stereoscopic print dating to 1877. George Bradford Brainerd Photograph Collection, Brooklyn Public Library/Center for Brooklyn History.

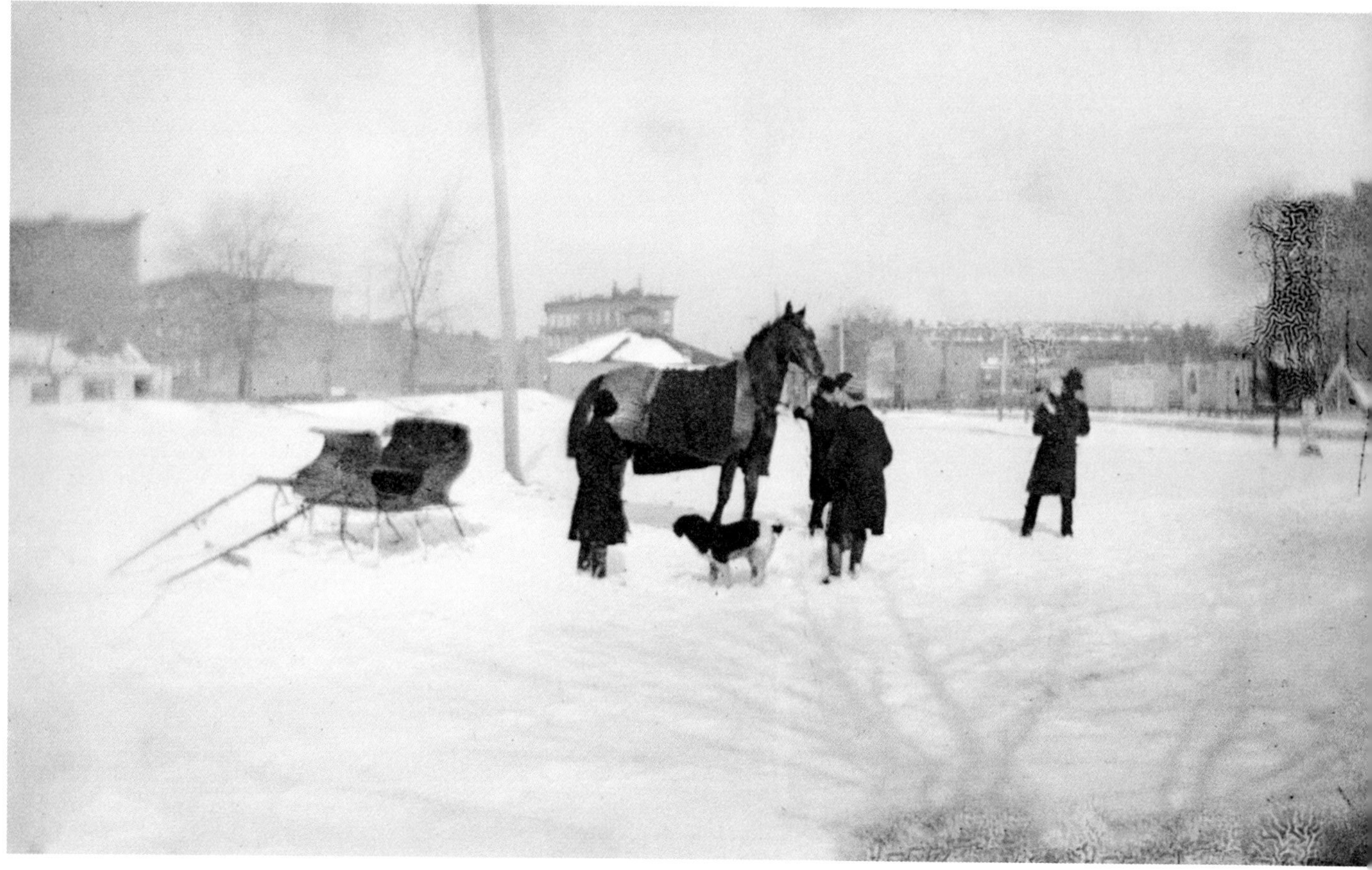

Another evocative winter scene from the late 1870s, probably Brainerd's own family, getting ready for sleighing. George Bradford Brainerd Photograph Collection, Brooklyn Public Library/Center for Brooklyn History.

light-sensitive silver halides suspended in the gelatin binder, the sticky mixture spread onto thin glass plates. However, as Brainerd's emulsions got faster, there developed a need for an improved shutter device. The first photographic shutter was simply a cap removed from in front of the lens and replaced at the appropriate time. As plate sensitivity increased, mechanical shutters were needed. The earliest mechanical shutter, developed in the 1840s, was known as a "drop" or "guillotine" shutter, and was basically a board or plate with a hole in it sliding past the lens opening. Mathew Brady probably used such a guillotine shutter for his famous photograph of Lincoln, depicting the unusually beardless candidate moments before he delivered his address at Cooper Union.

Brainerd adopted a modified version of the guillotine shutter, in which a vertical sliding plate, fitted behind the

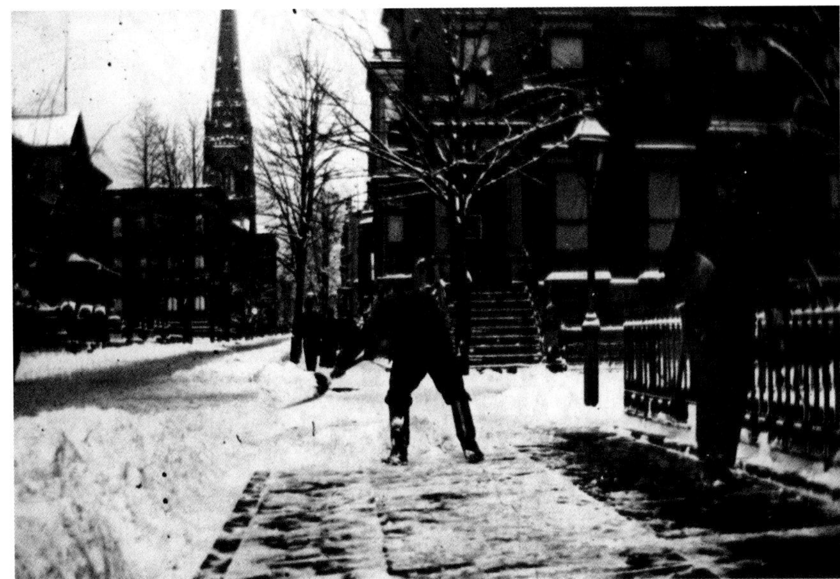

Shoveling snow, Brooklyn late 1870s. Such quotidian scenes of city life were not considered worthy subject matter before Brainerd began to document them with his "hand" cameras.

lens, was drawn by a string with rubber bands pulling it down again when the exposure had been made. A series of pins allowed tension on the rubber bands to be increased, thereby increasing the shutter speed. With his rubber-band shutter, Brainerd was able to achieve the speeds he needed to stop action. The engineer was even able to freeze the motion of sprinters on a track, which usually requires exposures of 1/250th of a second or more. The problem now was to devise a method for quick focusing. As Brainerd confided to a fellow amateur, he was making "too many errors in aiming," thus ruining precious photographic plates, which had to be cleaned and recoated. Brainerd's solution was nothing less than a twin-reflex lens, with a viewing lens focused by the same mechanism as the taking lens. This novel focusing method was described in a patent Brainerd received for his hand camera, No. 331, 677, which, while issued in December of 1885, was in use many years before:

> When, therefore, the lens is moved by the carrier until an image of any object opposite is seen sharply defined on the Finder screen, the lens is simultaneously adjusted to project a nearly similar, equally sharp image of the same object upon

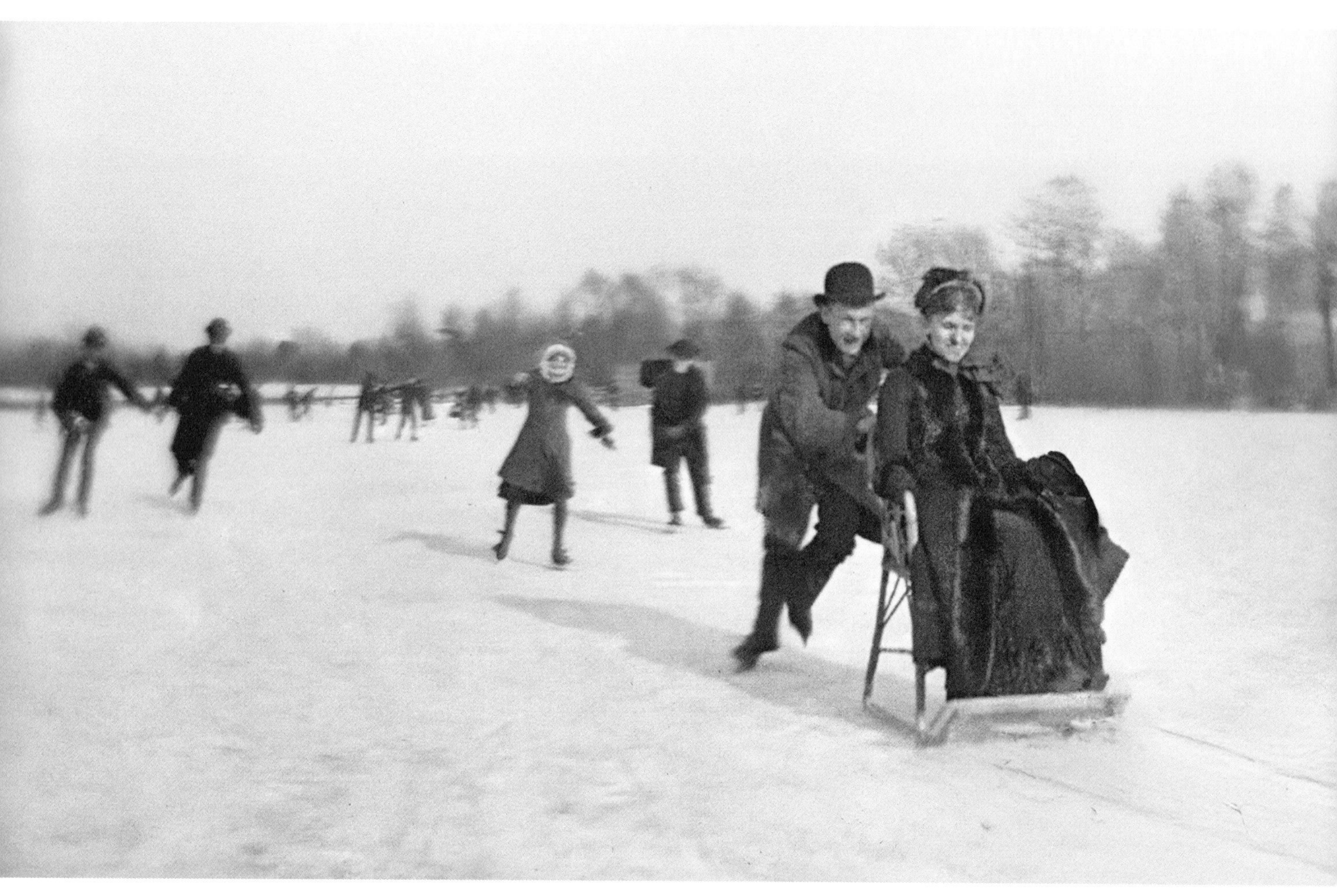

the sensitive plate. In case it be desired to fix the focus for any special distance, the carrier may be clamped to the partition by the thumbscrew. The focusing of the picture may be equally affected by the modification or method shown in Figure 3 in which the partition terminates at the frame.

With his new instant technology, Brainerd was able to capture the speed and excitement of winter sports like sleighing, sledding, and especially ice skating, producing some of the first candid "snapshots" of skaters in New York. Whether he knew it or not, the Brooklyn engineer was capturing a craze. Indeed, before bicycle mania there was ice-skating mania, which in winter saw virtually every frozen lake or pond covered with skaters, twirling, spinning, or just gliding happily along. Part of this was climate

Skating chair, 1870s. The craze for skating in the Victorian era spawned a few rather odd inventions. One of these was a skating chair—more or less a dining chair armed with runners. Brainerd was almost certainly using one of his surreptitious cameras to capture this image of a woman smiling—a display of emotion unheard of in stiff, formal portrait photography of the time. The lack of smiles was not the result of poor dental hygiene, as has sometimes been suggested; rather, such gushing was not considered proper for a lady. George Bradford Brainerd Photograph Collection, Brooklyn Public Library/Center for Brooklyn History.

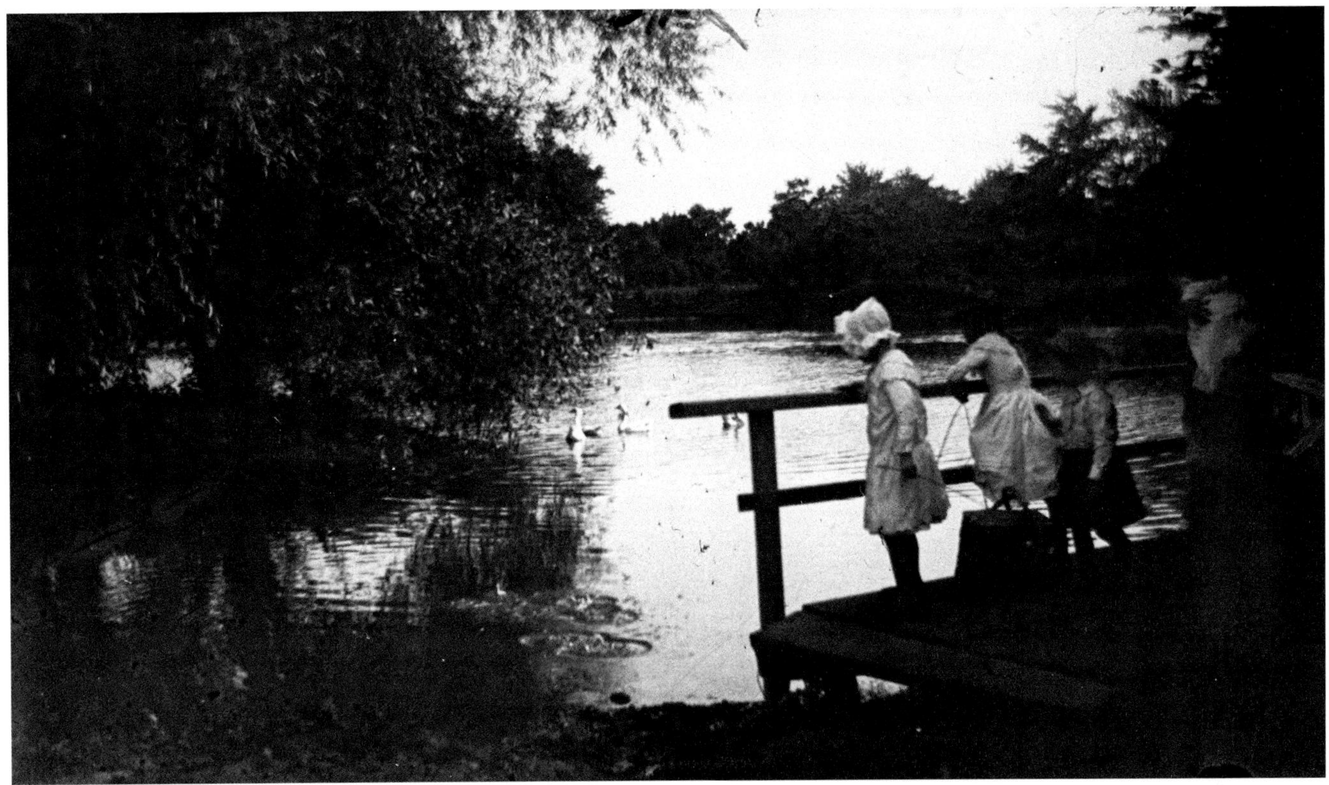

Prospect Park, Brooklyn, 1875. An impressionistic view of children on a bridge in Brooklyn's Prospect Park. Once again, Brainerd's feel for composition and balancing of light and shadow is first rate, evidence of the great care he took with his photographs. George Bradford Brainerd Photograph Collection, Brooklyn Public Library/Center for Brooklyn History.

driven, something called the Little Ice Age, which saw more frozen natural waters than today. Fueling the trend was also advances in the skates themselves, making them more comfortable, safer, and more accessible to the masses. Perhaps more significant were changing societal norms that permitted men and women to interact in a freer manner under certain prescribed circumstances—ice skating being one of the morally acceptable ways for men and women to flirt and have fun. The new relaxed spirit was noted by the *Brooklyn Daily Eagle*, which went so far as to suggest the winter pastime was doing more good for "the heart of humanity" than "half the sermons preached in the various sectarian temples of the Metropolis":

> The ice boats did not occupy the large lakes yesterday . . . so the sixty acres of clear glistening ice were thrown open for the use of the skaters, and the scene from Lookout Hill at 4 PM was one to be remembered. Hundreds came from their uptown residences in New York to enjoy the skating facilities

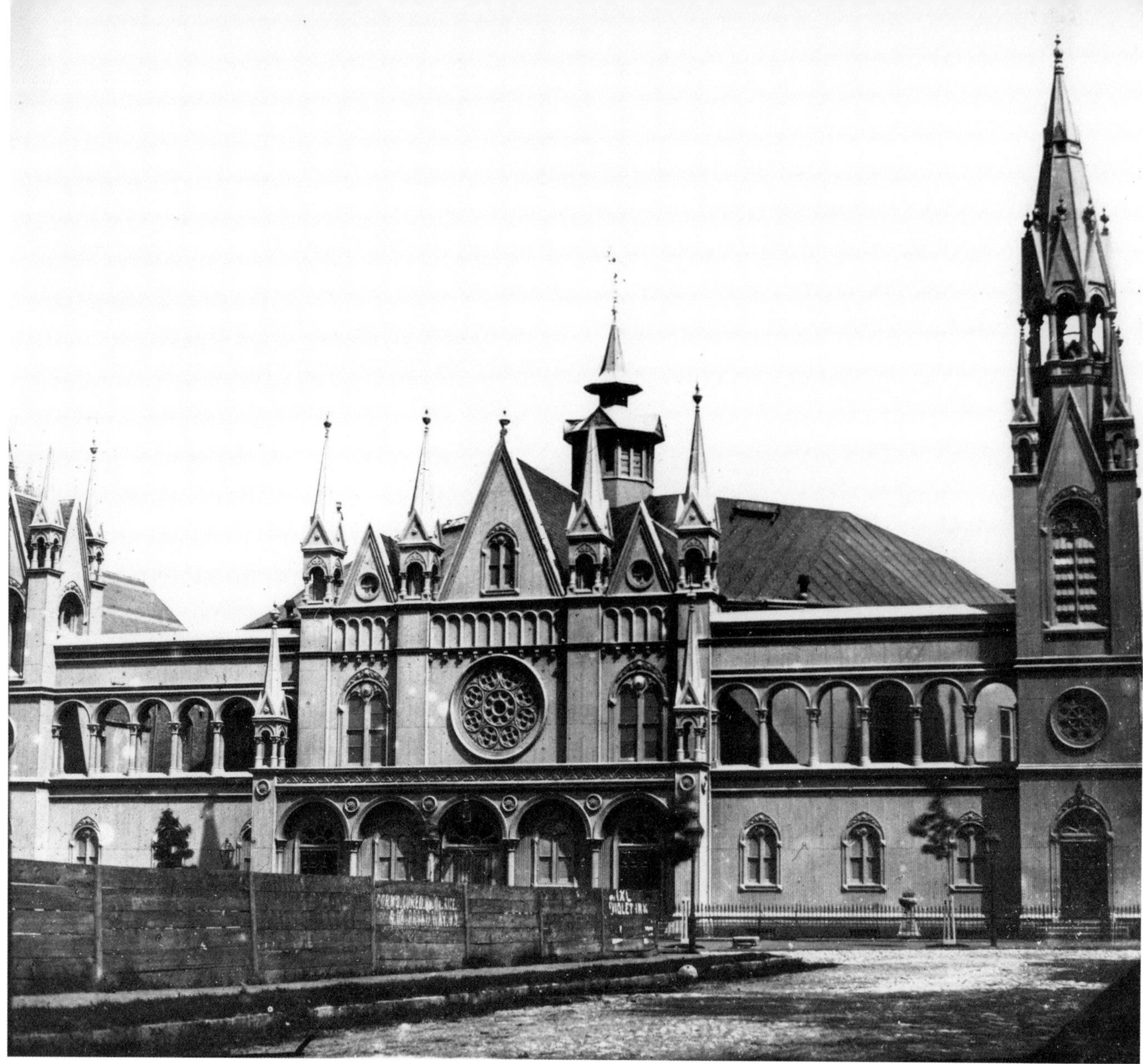

at Prospect Park which they could not have at Central Park. It was a gala Sunday . . . and one of the best skating days, both as regards the condition of the ice and the immense crowd present, among the largest known in the history of skating at Prospect Park.

Along with new forms of entertainment, Brainerd continued to document the growing metropolis—like Berenice Abbott in later years—with new buildings going up all around him.

Dr. Reverend Scudder's immense cast iron cathedral in Brooklyn, New York. Known as "The Iron Church," the cast-iron-fronted Gothic-style Scudder's Church was a landmark in Brooklyn when it was erected in the 1870s. Long since demolished, the glorious structure was photographed in the late 1870s by Brainerd, who had an eye for eclectic architecture. The church was named in honor of Rev. Henry Martyn Scudder (1822–1895), a Presbyterian minister and missionary in India. George Bradford Brainerd Photographic Collection, Brooklyn Public Library/Center for Brooklyn History.

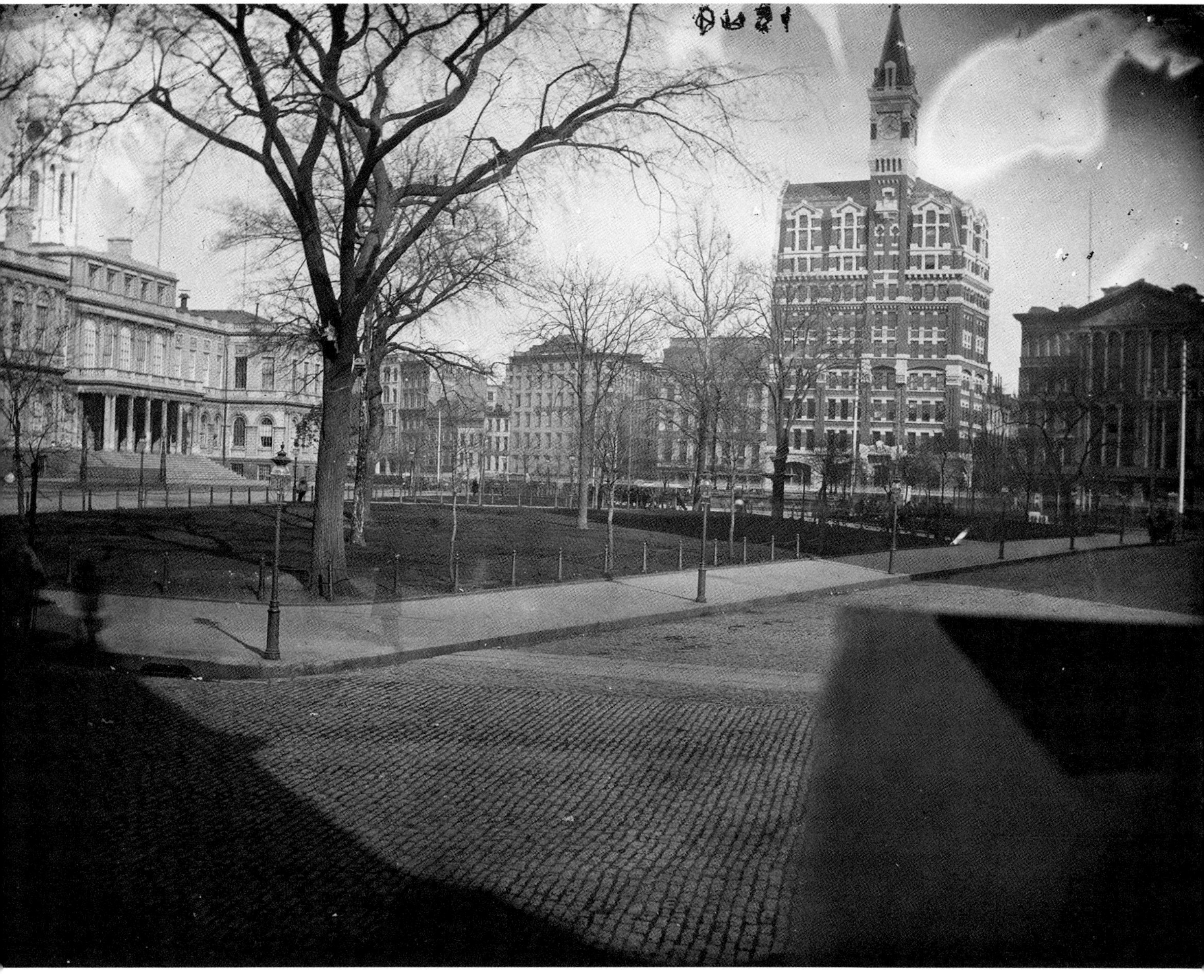

"I walk, I look, I see, I stop, I photograph."

—Leon Levinstein

Tribune Building, 1878. The 10-story Tribune Building, designed by Richard Morris Hunt, for a site on Park Row, stood 260 feet high, making it New York's tallest building in 1875. George Bradford Brainerd Photograph Collection, Brooklyn Public Library/Center for Brooklyn History.

L eopold Eidlitz, the Prague-born New York architect, once described American architecture as "the art of covering one thing with another thing to imitate a third thing, which, if genuine, would not be desirable." His words apply uncannily well to the many eclectic revival

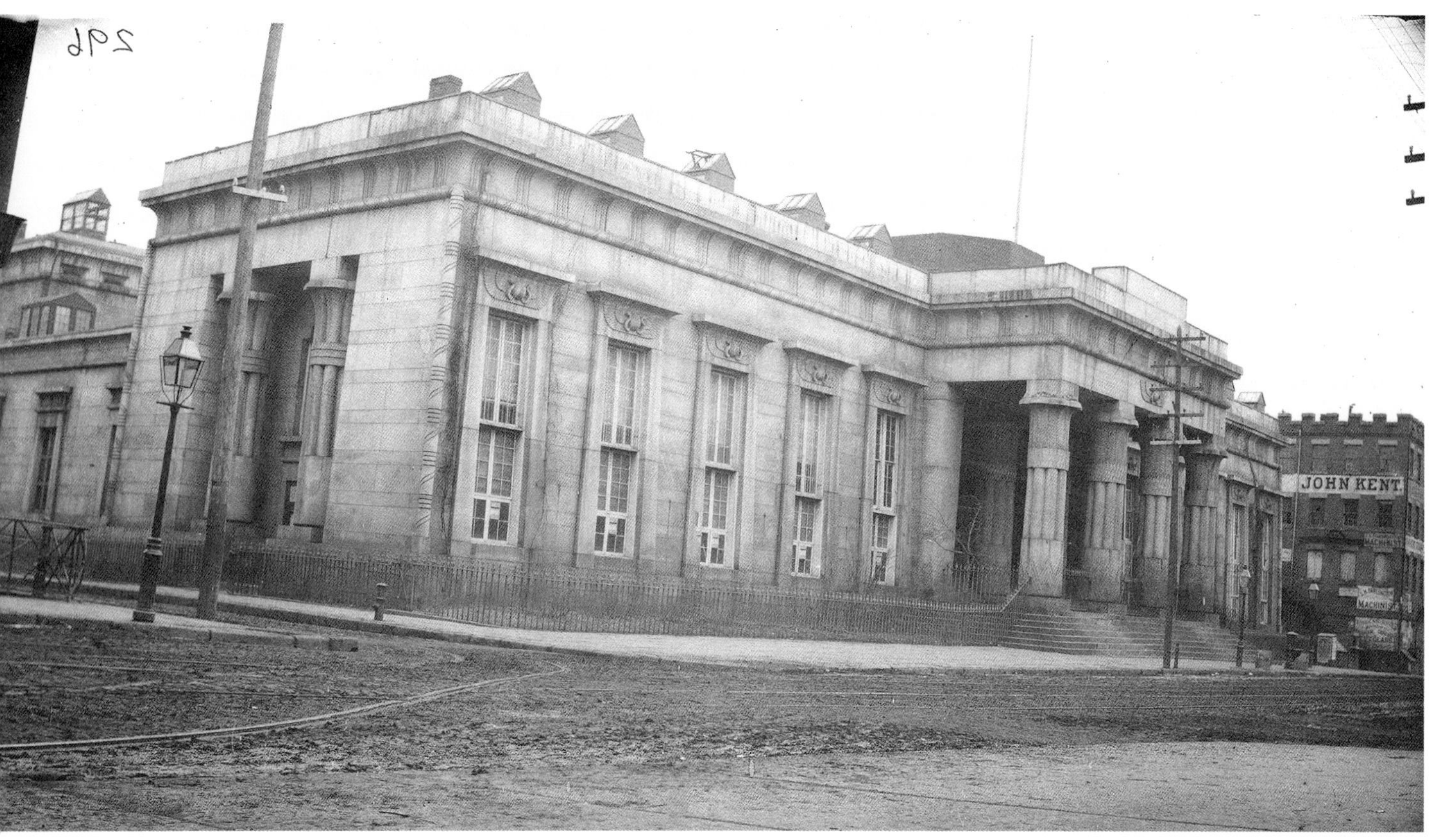

styles that sprung up during the Victorian era, often in bizarre combinations, leading the spectator to gaze in awe at the preposterousness of such an outlandish imagination. Whether it was his eye for the odd and unusual or just pride in his city, Brainerd would record dozens of the wondrous buildings that gave 19th-century New York and Brooklyn their beauty and charm. Among these were the monumental City Hall Post Office and Court House, designed by the architect Alfred B. Mullett, and New York's House of Detention, dubbed the "Tombs," which James Gordon Bennett called for to be torn down soon after it was erected. A beloved building, instead, was the ten-story Tribune Building designed by Richard Morris Hunt, which stood on Park Row.

There is also an early image of the Metropolitan Museum of Art, and one of the Brooklyn Bridge, which Brainerd photographed just as the first strands of cable

The Tombs, 1878. "The Halls of Justice," the excitable editor of the *New York Herald*, James Gordon Bennett, wrote in 1838, "will never deserve the name unless the architect who designed it and the jackasses that fixed on the location shall have been sentenced for life in one of the dreary cells of their own contriving." Bennett was talking about New York's old "House of Detention," better known as "The Tombs," which as many plainly saw, was an all too convincing copy of the Egyptian mausoleum its architect, one John Stevens of Hoboken, sought to emulate. The public immediately took to speaking of it as "the Tombs," and the name stuck. George Bradford Brainerd Photograph Collection, Brooklyn Public Library/Center for Brooklyn History.

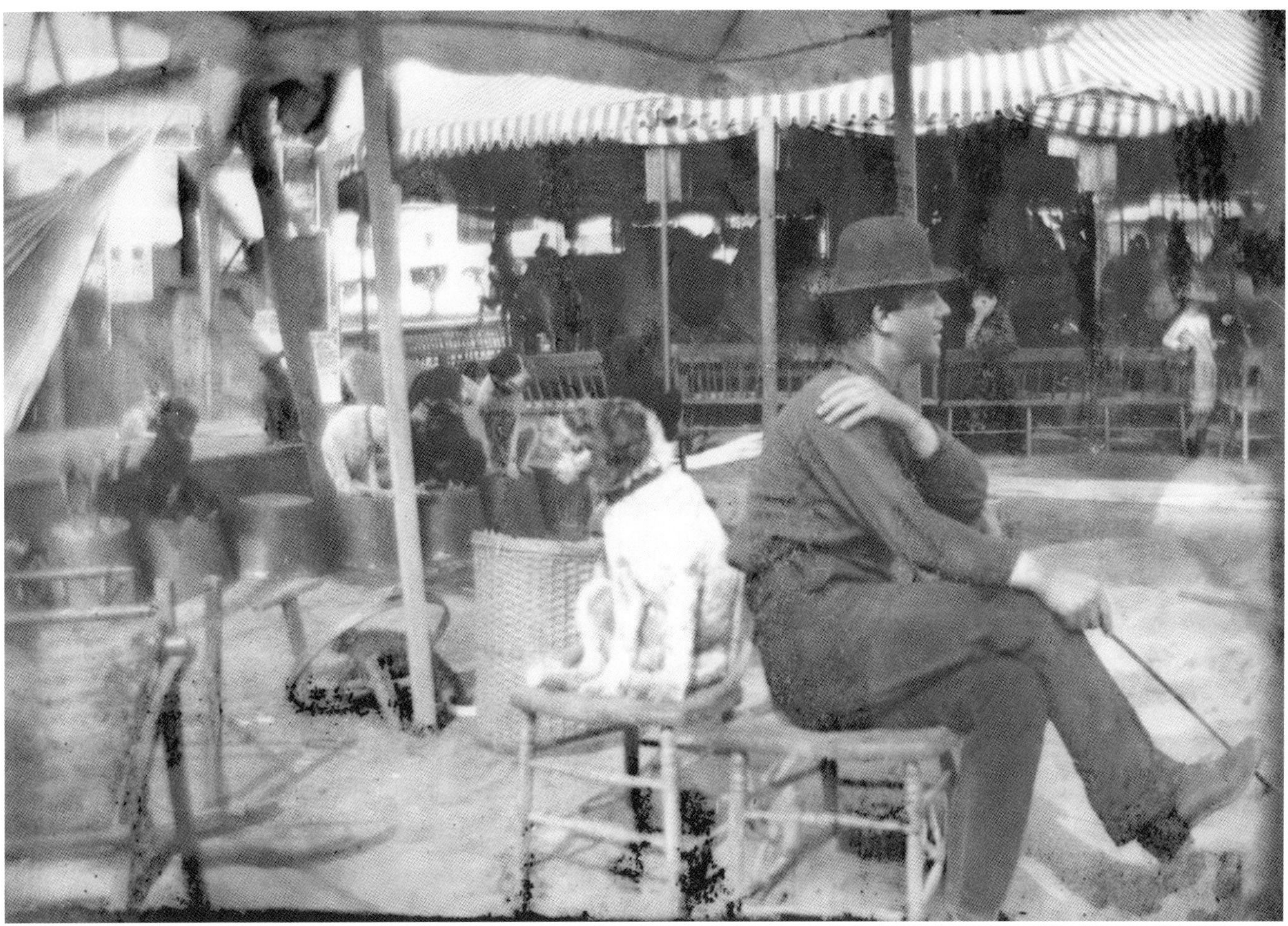

were being strung between the towers rising in the East River. It was August 14, 1876, a milestone the *Brooklyn Eagle* celebrated with the headline, "Wedded!"

George Brainerd had been entranced with Coney Island ever since he was a little boy when the barrier island on Gravesend Bay was just dunes and a few bathing shacks huddled together on the beach. Things started to change after the Civil War when, first, horse-drawn trolleys and, after, a railroad was built out to Coney Island and the ocean areas of Brighton Beach and Manhattan Beach, transforming all three into major summer destinations. In Brainerd's remarkable photographic record of Coney Island, we see the resort's transformation from a collection of rude bathing shacks to a bustling beach resort, poised to become America's largest amusement park.

Performing Dog Act, Coney Island, 1870s. Brainerd took some of the earliest, if not the earliest, pictures of Coney Island side shows. Here, we see a trainer with his pups taking a break between shows. Most histories date Coney Island sideshows to around 1880, but thanks to Brainerd's keen eye we know the tradition is even older. George Bradford Brainerd Photograph Collection, Brooklyn Public Library/Center for Brooklyn History.

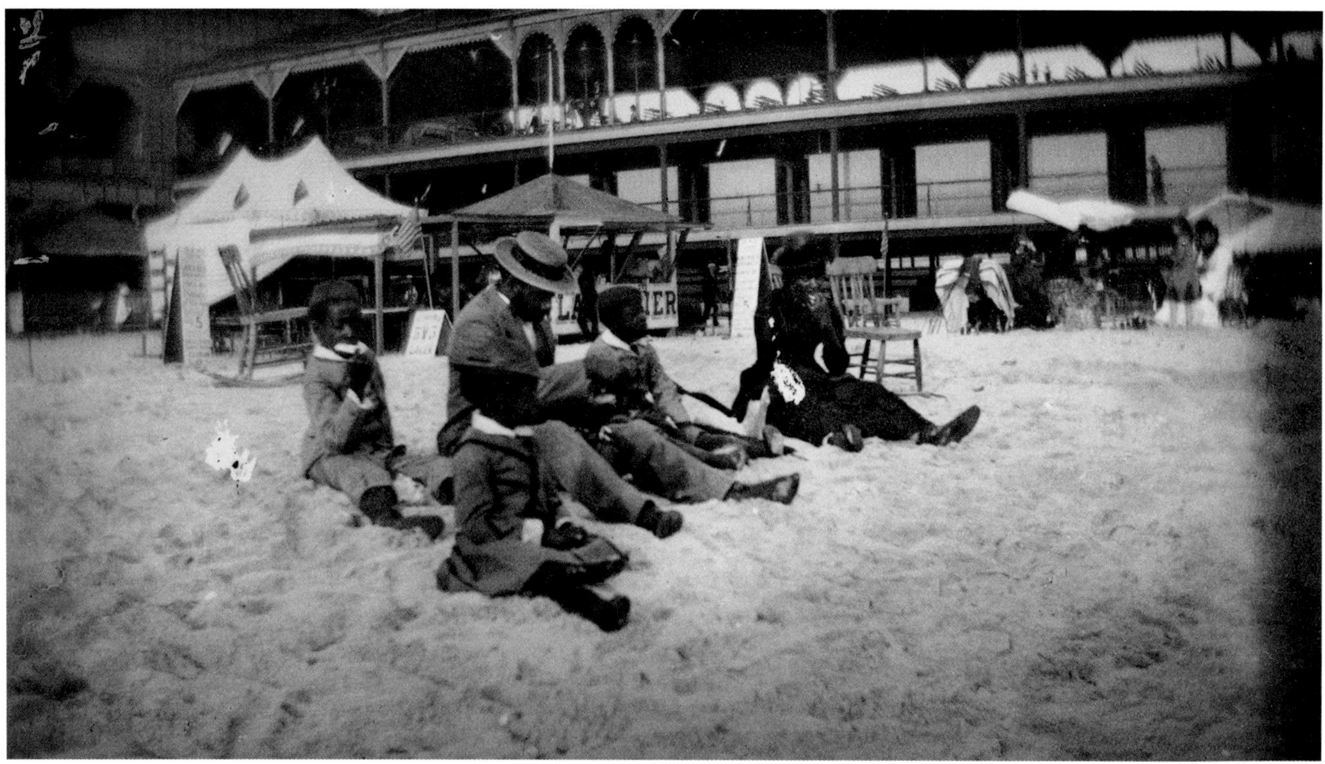

Several rare images also suggest Coney Island's side shows and "freak" displays had begun earlier than the 1880 date usually ascribed to this phenomenon. The photographer's camouflaged camera allowed him to move about unnoticed in the circuslike atmosphere of tents and stands with their brash lettering advertising the latest bizarre attraction. Among the curiosities were a dancing dog act and a legless acrobat.

The photographer's clandestine camera also captured a middle-class African-American family in their Sunday best enjoying a picnic on the beach, evidence of the democratic spirit for which Coney Island was known.

Brainerd's early record of Coney Island shows the uncertainty with which Victorians first approached the seashore. Indeed, a steamboat captain who brought the first crowds to the island before there was even a dock, recalled excursionists being rather hesitant in their attitudes toward saltwater and sand. While some spent the day "aimlessly gathering unnecessary clam shells," others clung to the safety of

African-American family, Coney Island, 1870s. As Coney Island became more physically and economically accessible, a growing number of tourists from a variety of classes visited the seaside locale. Here, an African-American family sits in the sand and enjoys a day off. The family's presence is indicative of the democratic spirit of Coney Island, which allowed for a mixing of different races and ethnicities. George Bradford Brainerd Photograph Collection, Brooklyn Public Library/Center for Brooklyn History.

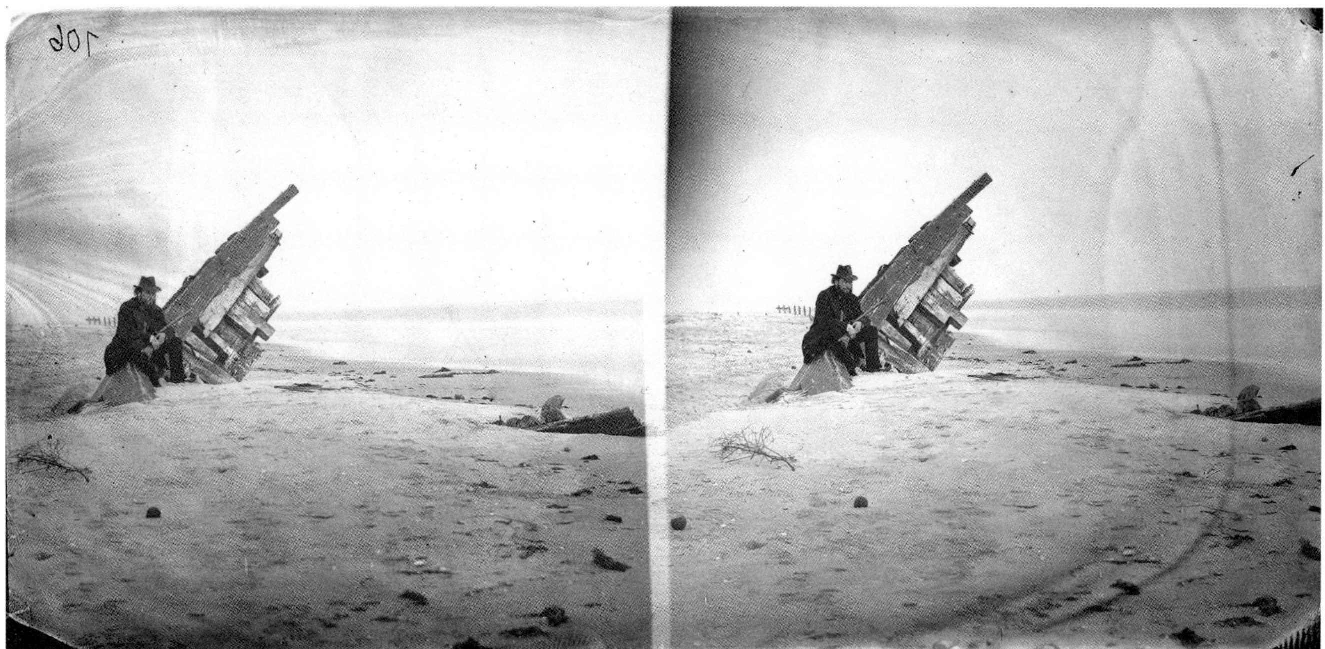

vessel, fearing "the island would be swept away when they were standing on it."

Especially fascinating is the evolution in swimwear. Many beachgoers in Brainerd's early photographs from the 1870s donned city clothes: boys in knickers and girls in the frilly white frocks with ribbons as if they were heading to Sunday service. Everyone, even the littlest tot, has some form of headgear to shield them from the blistering sun. And there are the ubiquitous parasols, making Brainerd's pictures appear rather like a painting by Georges Seurat. Why is no one swimming? Of course, visiting the seashore in the early days was really a pretext for sociability, a chance to put one's fashion on display and partake in a variety of entertainments.

Gradually, however, we see beachgoers start to wade in—the kids first, followed by Mommy and Daddy. The evolution seems complete around 1880, when Brainerd recorded a couple, probably husband and wife, emerging from the surf at the Iron Pier. He sports a manly Victorian full-length swimming suit; she, a long bathing gown.

Brainerd took dozens of photographs of Coney Island, more than any other place, even the Brooklyn waterfront,

The beaches of Coney Island were rather remote in the early days, as evidenced by this solitary figure beside the wreck of an old sailing ship on Brighton Beach in the mid-1870s. Visitors to the seaside resort in those days often donned street clothes, as bathing attire hadn't really caught on. George Bradford Brainerd Photographic Collection, Brooklyn Public Library/Center for Brooklyn History.

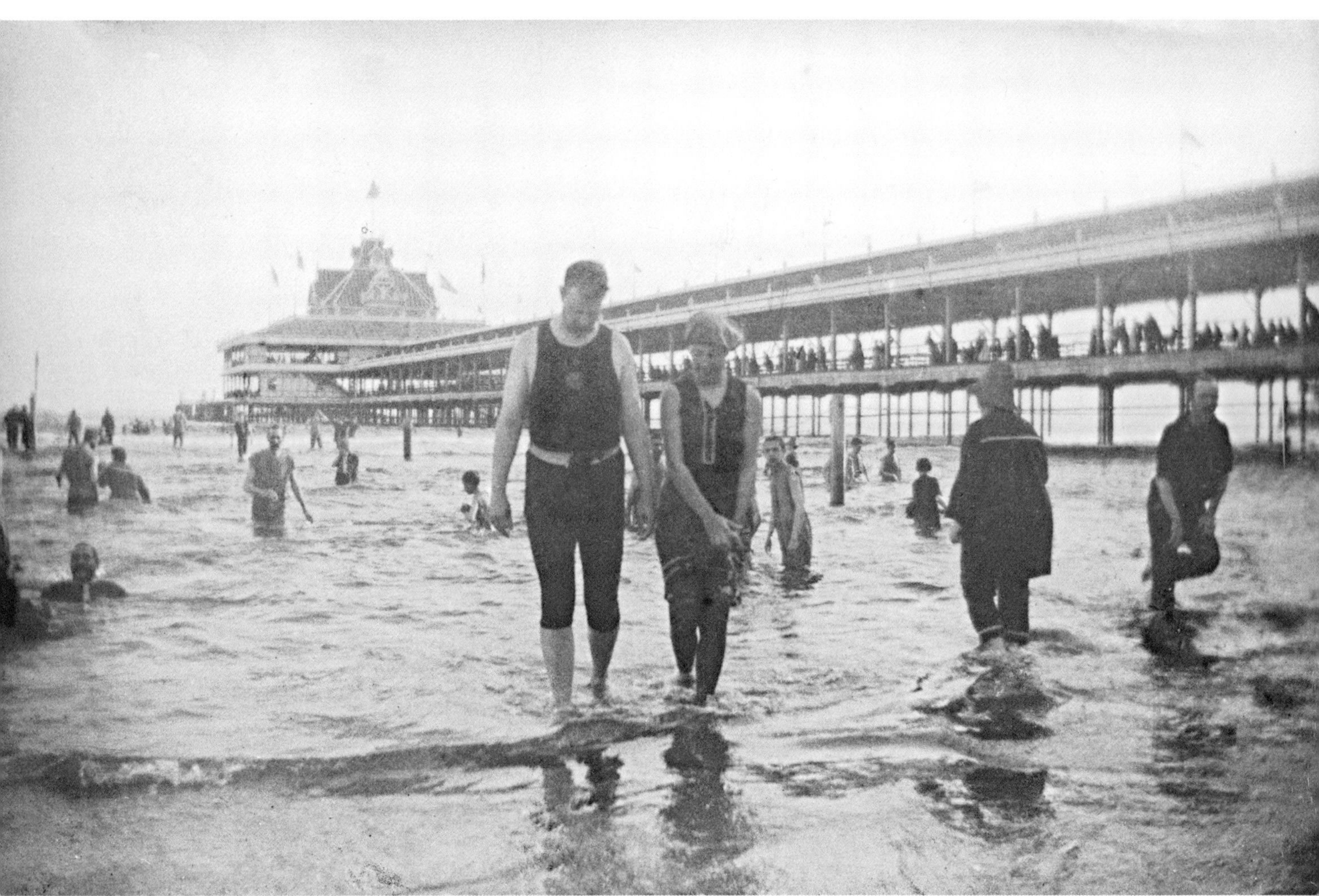

which he adored. It might have been that the Brooklyn engineer was spending more time at the beach for his own health reasons. The seashore then was advertised as a cure for almost every disease. Might it not restore the health of an ailing photographer? By 1884, Brainerd was already showing signs of the illness that would later claim his life, probably a form of cancer, which manifested itself first in the form of an acute throat infection. In all likelihood, Brainerd's illness was a result of his years of exposure to toxic photographic fumes. Instead of despairing, his illness became a springboard for study, with Brainerd devising the first photographic camera in existence capable of taking pictures of the human larynx. It was here that an abscess had developed that hampered Brainerd's breathing.

Coney Island bathers, 1880. Just as with ice skating, the new fad for "surf bathing" in the Victorian era offered a morally acceptable way for men and women to interact—provided one was covered from head to toe in some garment that insured modesty and decency in the water were not threatened. In this lovely picture, a couple, perhaps husband and wife, stand quite close in their dripping suits, hands almost touching—as if their immersion together has given them a new bond. George Bradford Brainerd Photograph Collection, Brooklyn Public Library/Center for Brooklyn History.

Brainerd worked with Dr. Thomas R. French, a noted laryngoscopic surgeon at Brooklyn's St. Mary's Hospital and professor of laryngology and diseases of the throat at the Long Island College Hospital Medical School. It took a year and over 2,500 unsuccessful attempts before Brainerd and French successfully photographed a larynx, a milestone in medical imaging. "Dr. French and George Brainerd made sure that their process could be easily reproduced by any doctor, even one unfamiliar with cameras," wrote Rebekah Abramovich, in an article on the medical breakthrough:

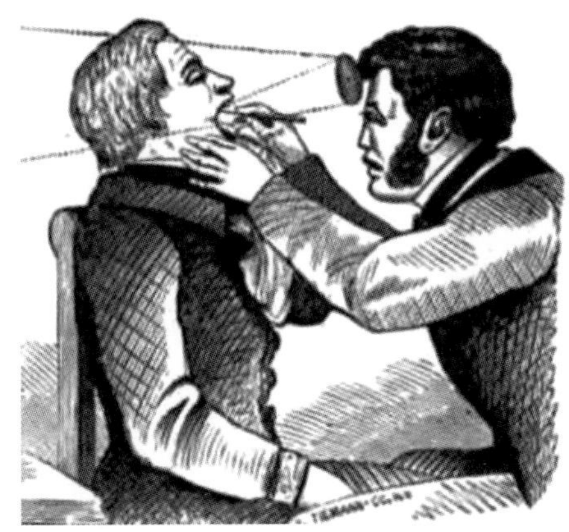

> Their technique was refined so that it would only take a doctor five minutes to set up the camera and accessories and not more than ten minutes to photograph the patient, making the process appealing to a wide range of practitioners. The resulting documents of the larynx could take a number of forms adaptable for a variety of situations. For instance, the plates could be developed and then processed into enlarged photographic prints for close-up examination. The plate could also be placed on a projector and used as in a classroom situation at a medical school or conference. Finally, the plate could be transferred to a black background for a wood engraving that could then be reproduced or published, not to mention it is then easier to store.

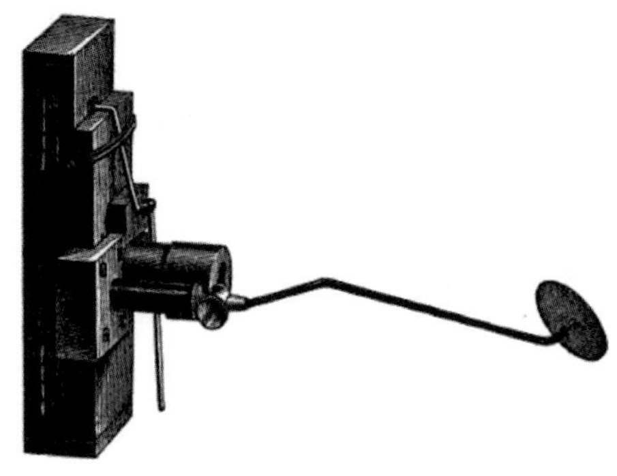

George Brainerd was also a pioneer in medical imaging, designing the first photographic camera capable of taking a picture of the human larynx. It was Brainerd's own illness, an acute throat infection, that prompted the Brooklyn engineer to design the novel apparatus, a small camera equipped with a special mirror. However, it would take a year and over 2,500 unsuccessful attempts before Brainerd and his collaborator, Dr. Thomas R. French, successfully photographed the larynx, a milestone in medical photography.

However, like nearly all of his other innovations, Brainerd did not patent this latest device, just as he had not sought to spread or reproduce his early photographic innovations to the public. One of the few mentions of Brainerd's remarkable achievements would appear in the *Brooklyn Eagle* shortly after Brainerd's death on April 15, 1887. The cause of death was a stroke resulting from a brain tumor. Brainerd died at home in his rooms at Lafayette Avenue in Brooklyn. He was just 42.

> In George B Brainerd now deceased the [Brooklyn] Academy had a man of unusually broad experience, he having been an amateur photographer in the days when wet plates were used and half hour exposures were the rule. He was also an

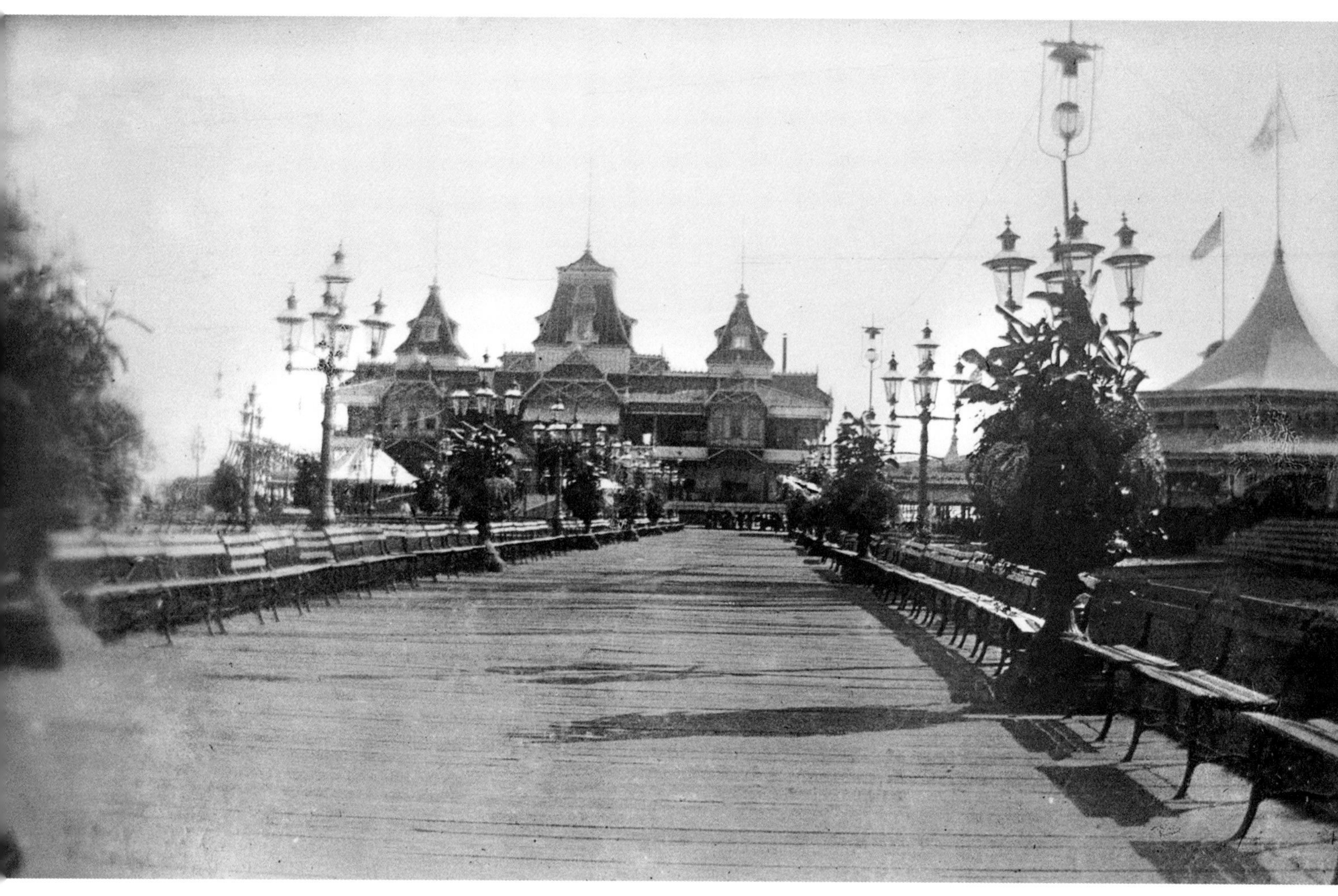

inventor and it is through his experiments that instantaneous picture taking was evolved his time was spent principally in investigating and studying how to improve the art, and the various apparatuses which he made were by no means few and helped materially to bring the science to its present state of perfection.

George Bradford Brainerd was buried in the family plot in Rock Landing Cemetery in Haddam Neck, high on a bluff overlooking the Connecticut River. His body had been carried up the river to Haddam on the steamboat *Capitol City*, one of the largest and most elegant of the Hartford line vessels, after a quiet service the day before at his house in Brooklyn on Lafayette Avenue. Brainerd had paid tribute to his hometown of Haddam some years earlier in an article

Coney Island Boardwalk, 1870s. George Bradford Brainerd Photograph Collection, Brooklyn Public Library/Center for Brooklyn History.

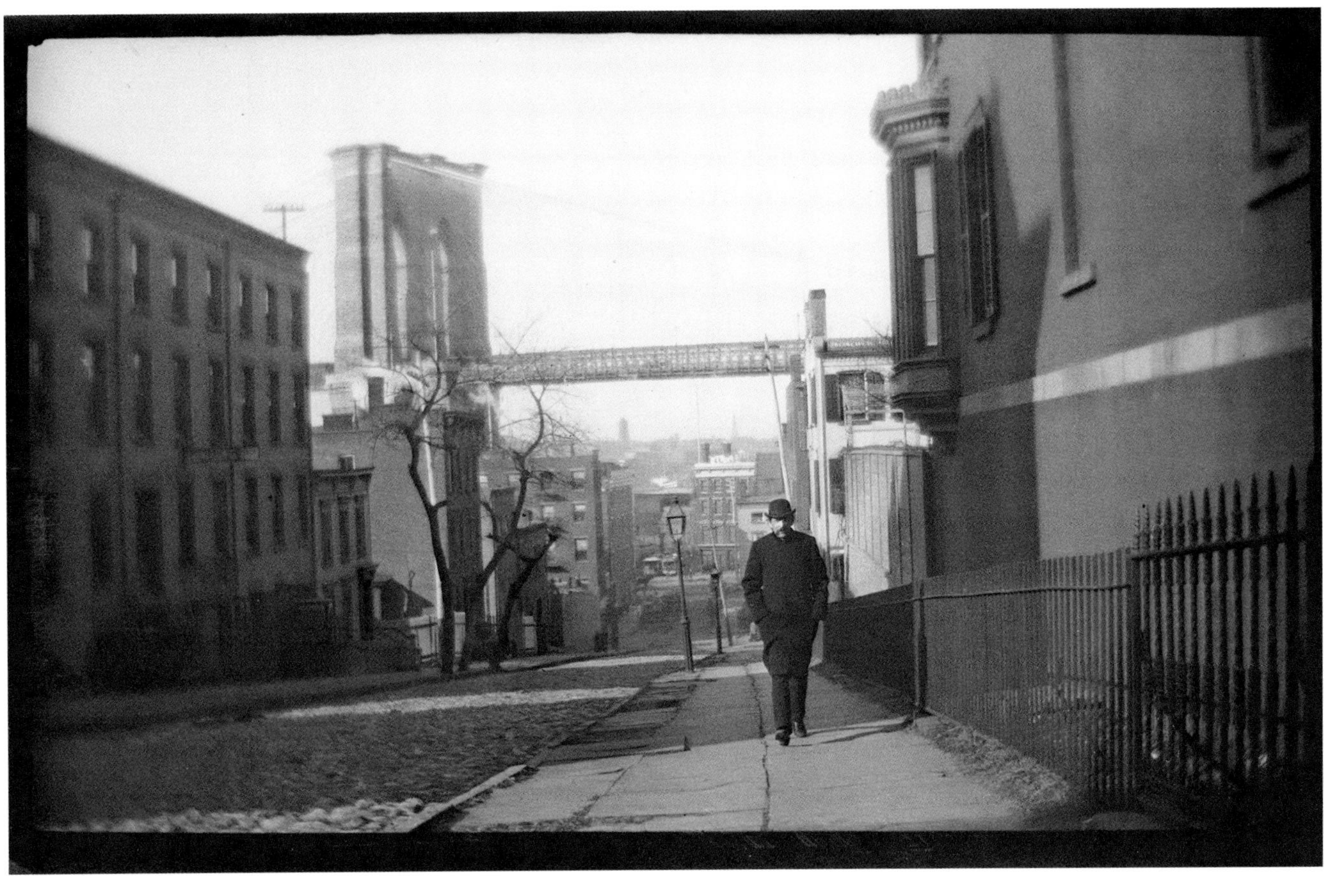

published in the *Brooklyn Eagle*, although somewhat reluctantly, he said, as he feared word would get out, spoiling his tranquility. "The address which I have written above is one that has seldom appeared in your columns," he wrote of the tiny hamlet on the river's left bank, "not, I am sure, because it is unworthy of a place there, nor that none of your legion of readers have ever wandered thither, but rather, having found in it a quiet, attractive and secluded spot, they have chosen to preserve it so by silence." The Man of the Crowd had come home.

Another image where the photographer has worked himself into the composition, Here, Brainerd is seen walking up a street in Brooklyn with the recently completed Brooklyn Bridge in the background. George Bradford Brainerd Photograph Collection, Brooklyn Public Library/Center for Brooklyn History.

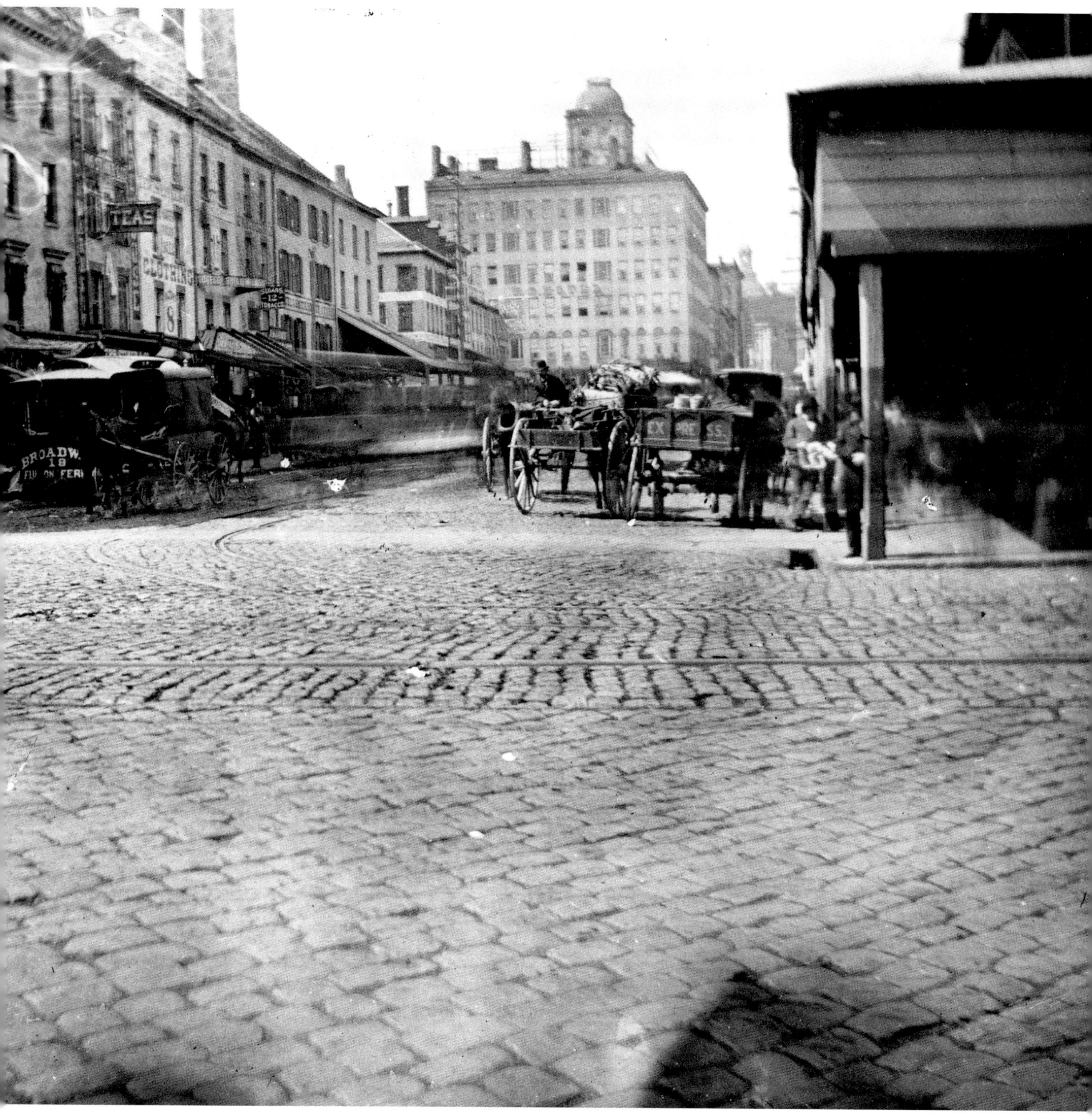

A lovely view of old New York with a broad expanse of cobblestone streets crowded with horse-drawn carts and drays drawn up near the Fulton Street docks in Lower Manhattan. The busy waterfront was a favorite theme of Brainerd's from his job with the Brooklyn Water Department provisioning ships with fresh supplies of drinking water for their sea journeys. George Bradford Brainerd Photographic Collection, Brooklyn Public Library/Center for Brooklyn History.

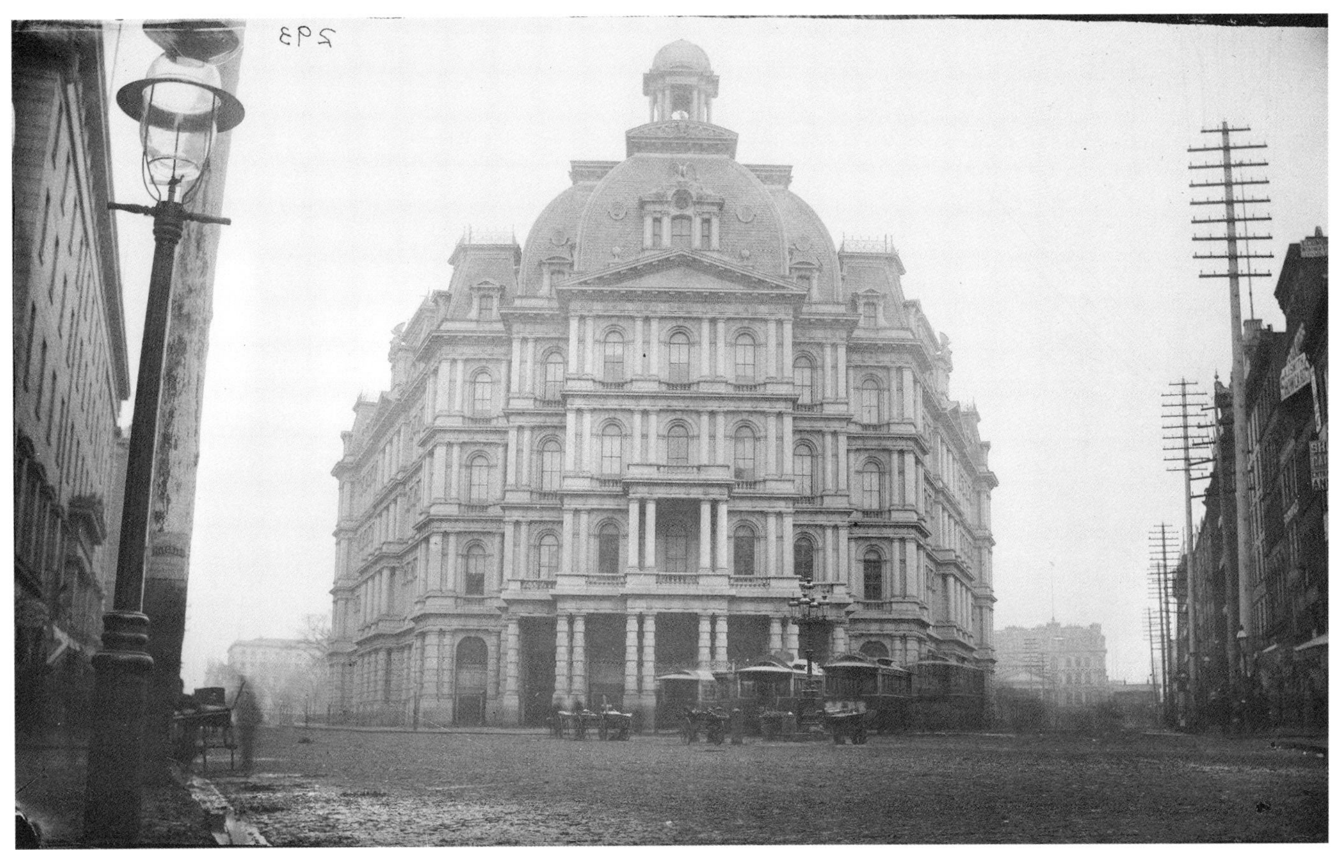

A City's Ghosts

"**M**emories are the specific invisible remains in our lives of what belongs in the past tense," Janet Flanner once wrote. Then, there is photography to come along and spoil our lovely imaginings with a claim of "objective reality," and "truth." In many ways, George Brainerd's pictures of old New York and Brooklyn are shocking to our modern eyes—as the images he serves up through the miracle of photography are nothing like what we envision life to be during that glorious era Mark Twain famously named the "Gilded Age." This was the time of opulent mansions on Fifth Avenue and 70-room "cottages" in Newport, where monied elites

Beauty truly is in the eye of the beholder. This is the long-vanished City Hall Post Office and Courthouse, which rose over a triangular site in Lower Manhattan along Broadway. Designed by the British American architect Alfred B. Mullet in the 1870s, its soaring domes and tiers and tiers of columns were considered a masterpiece of the Second Empire style by some, while other decried its grandiosity, dubbing the great pile "Mullett's Monstrosity." The latter won out, for the glorious old municipal building was torn down a little over 50 years after it was built, reminding one of the quip by *Harper's Magazine* in the 1860s, that "New York is a series of experiments, and [that] everything which has lived its life and played its part is held to be dead, and is buried, and over it grows a new world." George Bradford Brainerd Photograph Collection, Brooklyn Public Library/Center for Brooklyn History.

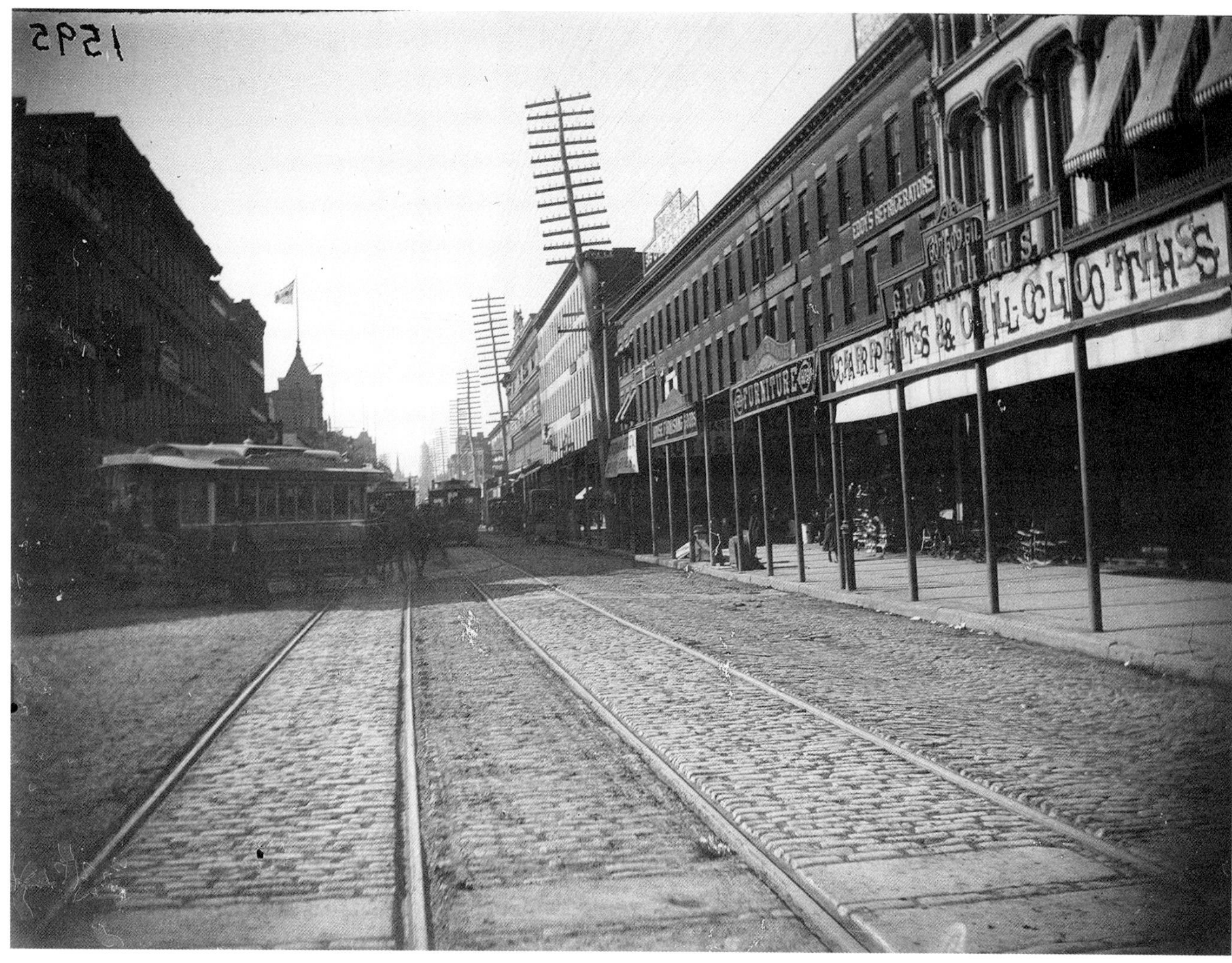

threw lavish parties lasting for days. Among the excesses were ultra-expensive carriages drawn by glossy-black teams of horses and private zoos filled with all manner of exotic creatures plucked from the four corners of the globe. Amid this speculative frenzy, the social arbiter, Ward McAllister, coined the phrase "the Four Hundred," declaring that there were "only 400 people in fashionable New York Society." "If you go outside that number," he warned, "you strike people who are either not at ease in a ballroom or else make other people not at ease."

In contrast to this Gilded Age glamor are street scenes like "Prospect Park Dump," "The Rag Picker," and "The Mugio," showing a legless beggar, perhaps a maimed Civil

Fulton Street in Brooklyn, the main thoroughfare down to the wharves and the ferry across the East River to Manhattan.

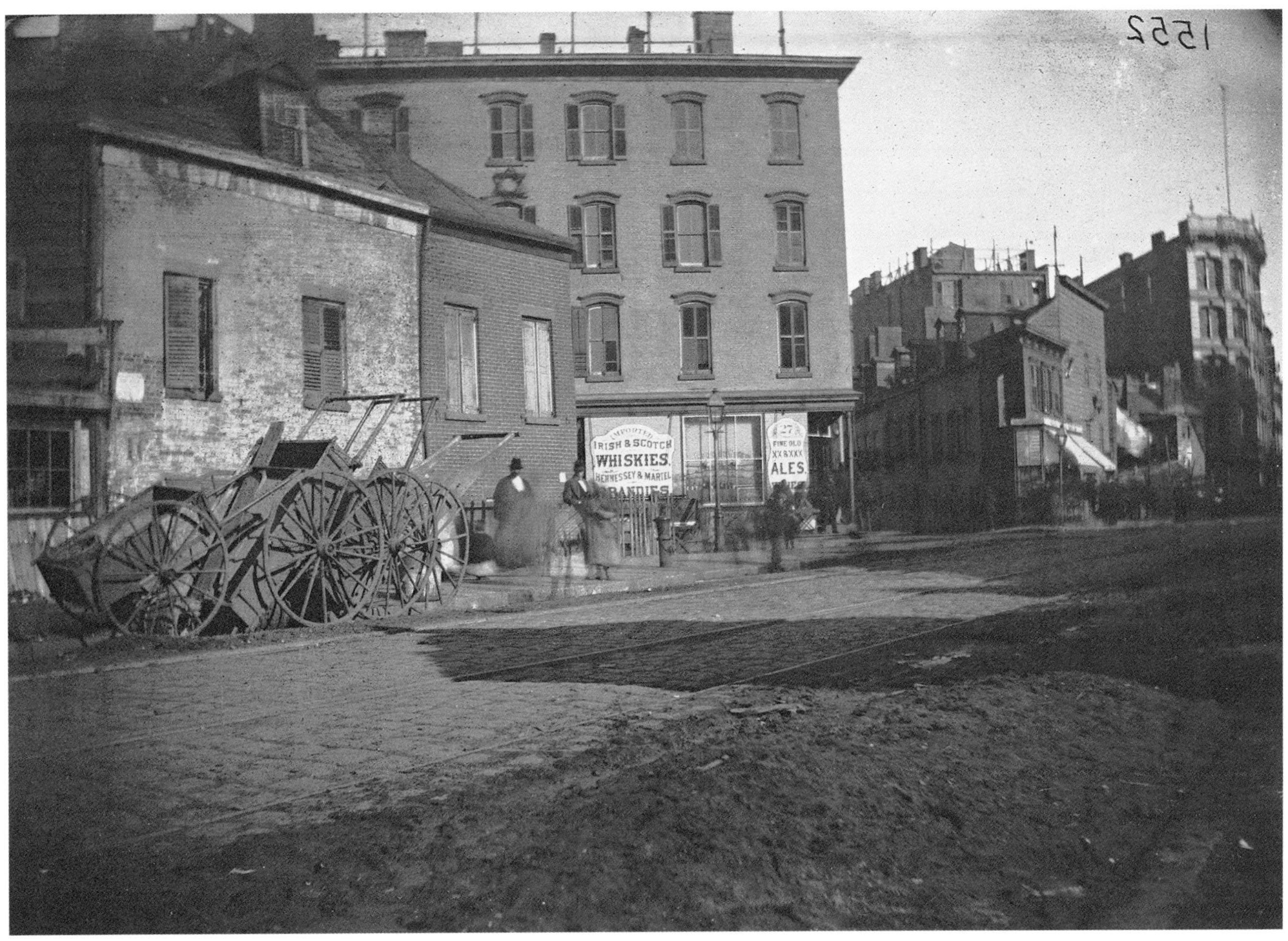

War veteran, panhandling on a New York sidewalk. Such grim depictions are perhaps the exception rather than the rule. Nonetheless, they hint at a harsher reality below the surface gaiety. In fact, one can't help but feel an undercurrent of melancholy in some of Brainerd's pictures. A dreary haze seems to hang over everything, even on the brightest days. This gray grimness was perhaps a result of the burning of anthracite coal, which muted even Old Glory's brilliant red, white, and blue, in just a few days in the smutty air. "By the time the Civil War was over," Lewis Mumford wrote, in the *Brown Decades*, a portrait of the postbellum years, "Browns had spread everywhere: mediocre drabs, dingy chocolate browns, sooty browns that merged into black. Autumn had come. The whole country looked darker, sadder, soberer."

The Five Points, 1877. "Debauchery has made the very houses prematurely old," Charles Dickens wrote of New York's Five Points District, in his *American Notes,* published in 1842. "See how the rotten beams are tumbling down, and how the patched and broken windows seem to scowl dimly, like eyes that have been hurt in drunken frays." Brainerd's wet-plate image of the Five Points, with shadows slanting across the cobblestones and a few figures in the distance—is perhaps less menacing than Dickens's description, yet we still feel a hint of danger. George Bradford Brainerd Photograph Collection, Brooklyn Public Library/Center for Brooklyn History.

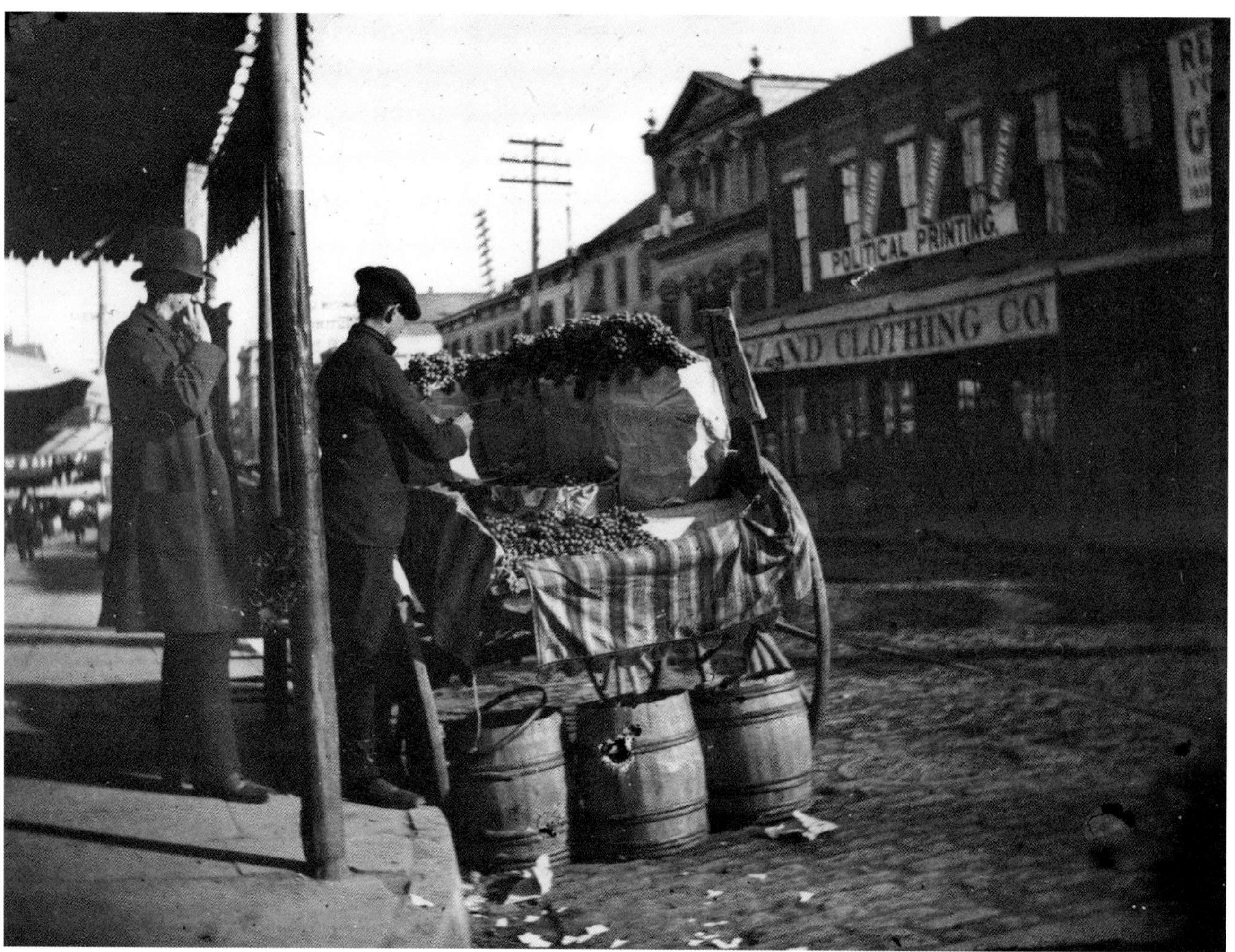

Yet beneath the crass surface, a new life was stirring. People were starting to have fun again. And George Brainerd was there to capture it as faithfully as he knew how: "I am a camera with its shutter open, quite passive, recording, not thinking," wrote Christopher Isherwood, in his novel *Goodbye to Berlin*, which could have been penned for Brainerd. "Recording the man shaving at the window opposite and the woman in the kimono washing her hair. Some day, all this will have to be developed, carefully printed, fixed."

Grape vendor, Lower Manhattan, late 1870s. The bowler hat, the moustache, and the tall lanky frame betray the figure of the photographer himself, who often worked himself into his compositions. Right, a boy dashes across muddy cobblestones in the rough and tumble Canal Street area in New York. Canal Street formed the northern boundary of the infamous Five Points District, home to homicidal gangs like the Plug Uglies, the Bowery Boys, and the Dead Rabbits, featured in Martin Scorsese's *Gangs of New York*. Worth noting is the fact Brainerd appears to have employed a handheld camera with faster dry plates, which would have given him some anonymity in dangerous neighborhoods such as these. George Bradford Brainerd Photograph Collection, Brooklyn Public Library/Center for Brooklyn History.

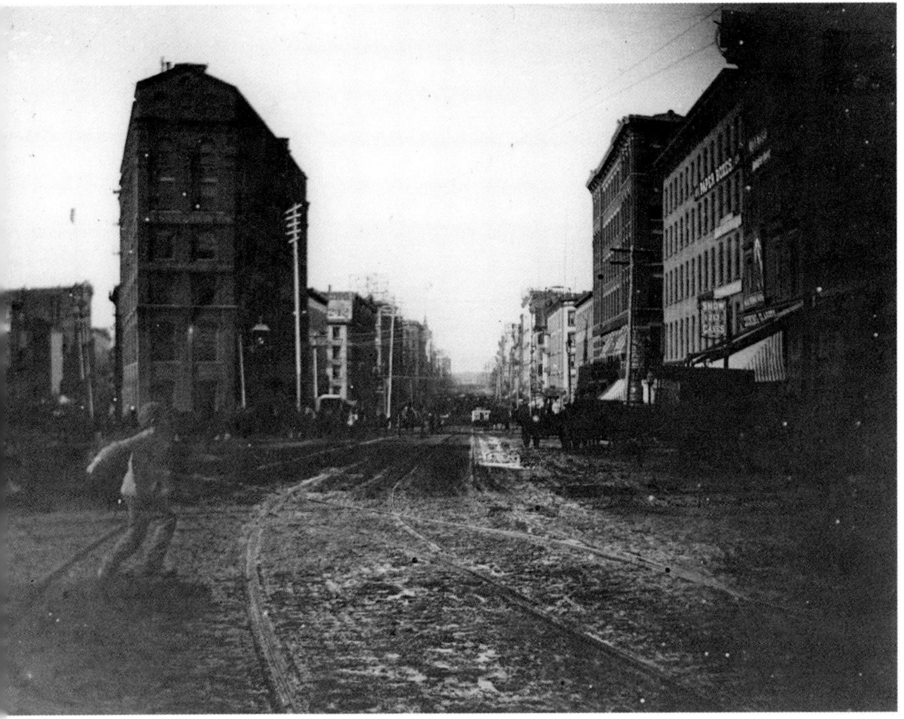

Below, New York City Hall, 1878. Nestled in the heart of Lower Manhattan is a national landmark, New York's City Hall, oldest city hall in the United States still in continuous use. Built between 1803 and 1812, few buildings in the country have witnessed so much history. It was outside the stately classical-style building that the bloody New York City Police Riot of 1857 broke out between the recently dissolved New York Municipal Police and the newly formed Metropolitan Police in June of that year. The violence was sparked by rumors that the newly appointed Street Commissioner, Charles Devlin, had paid then Mayor Ferdinando Wood $50,000 for the job, ousting his rival, Daniel Conover. Armed with bricks, bats, and their own bare fists, the two sides went at it, and though the scuffle lasted only 30 minutes, fifty-three men were injured, some seriously. George Bradford Brainerd Photograph Collection, Brooklyn Public Library/Center for Brooklyn History.

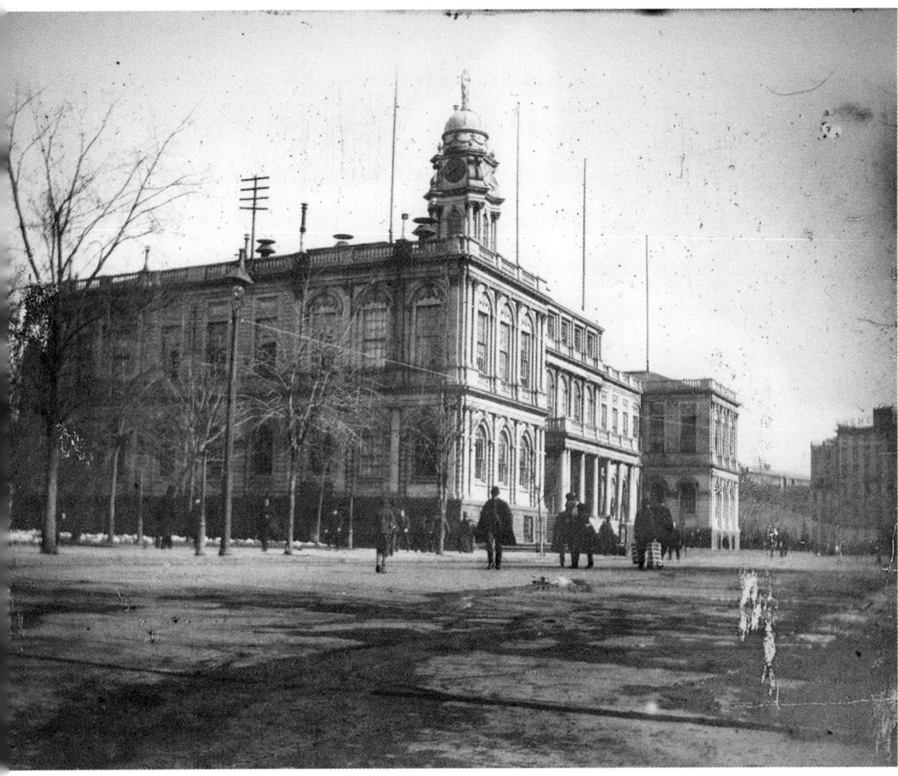

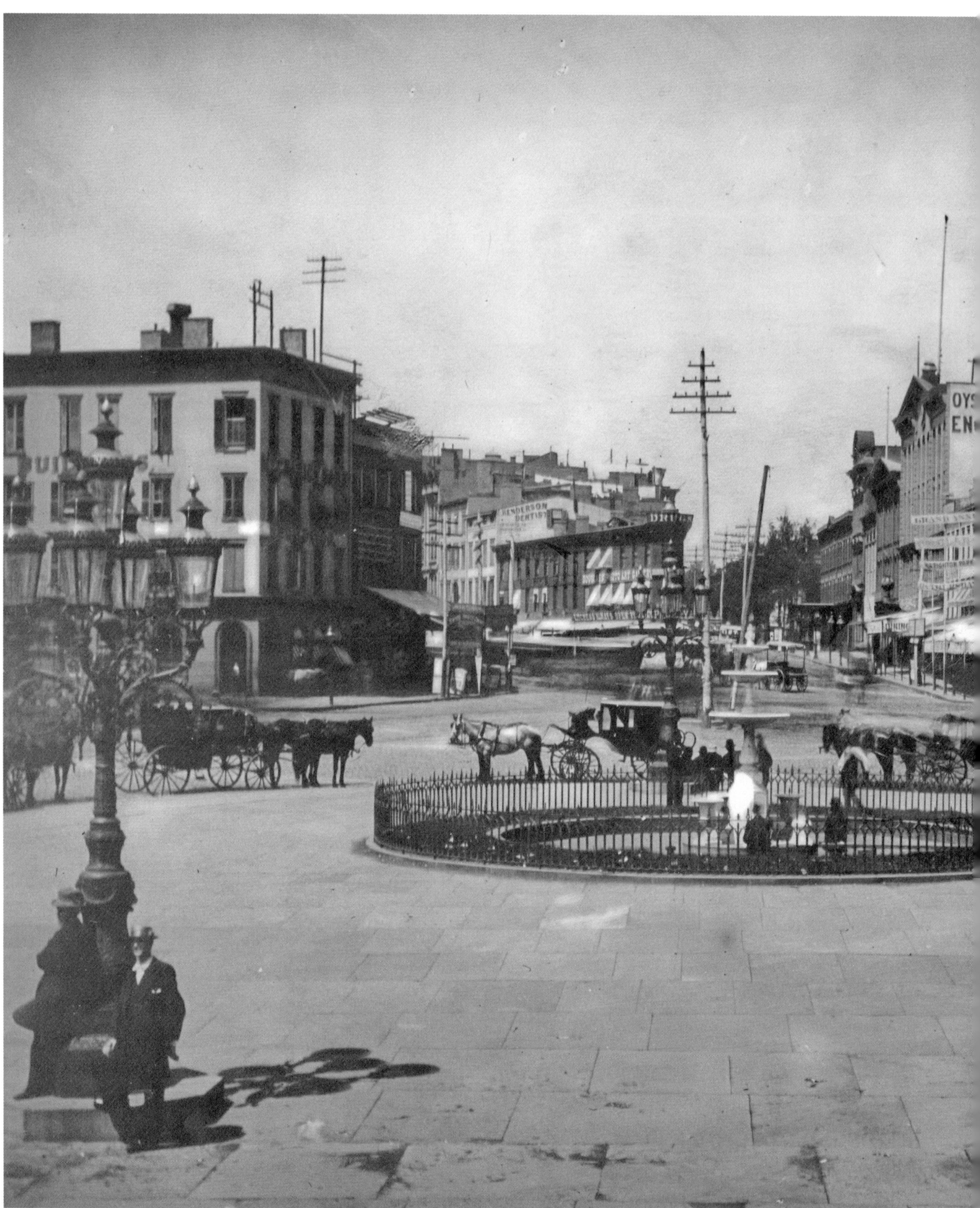

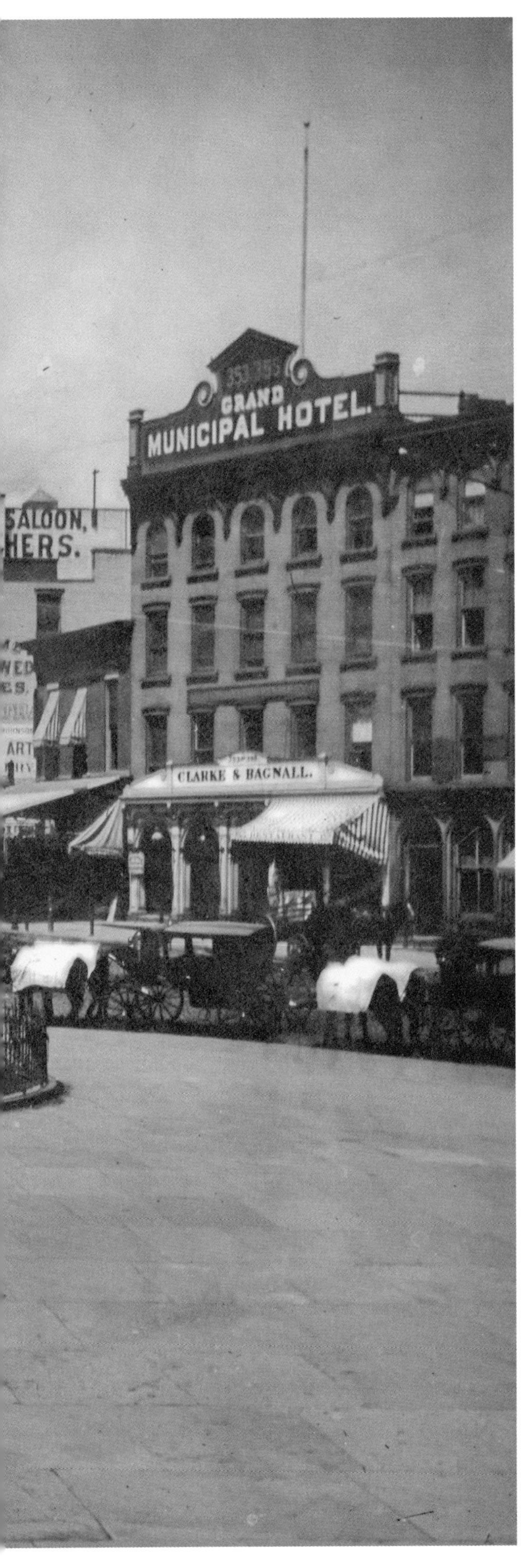

City Hall Park, Brooklyn 1880. Horse-drawn carriages line up at the edge of City Hall Park in the business district of downtown Brooklyn. George Bradford Brainerd Photograph Collection, Brooklyn Public Library/ Center for Brooklyn History.

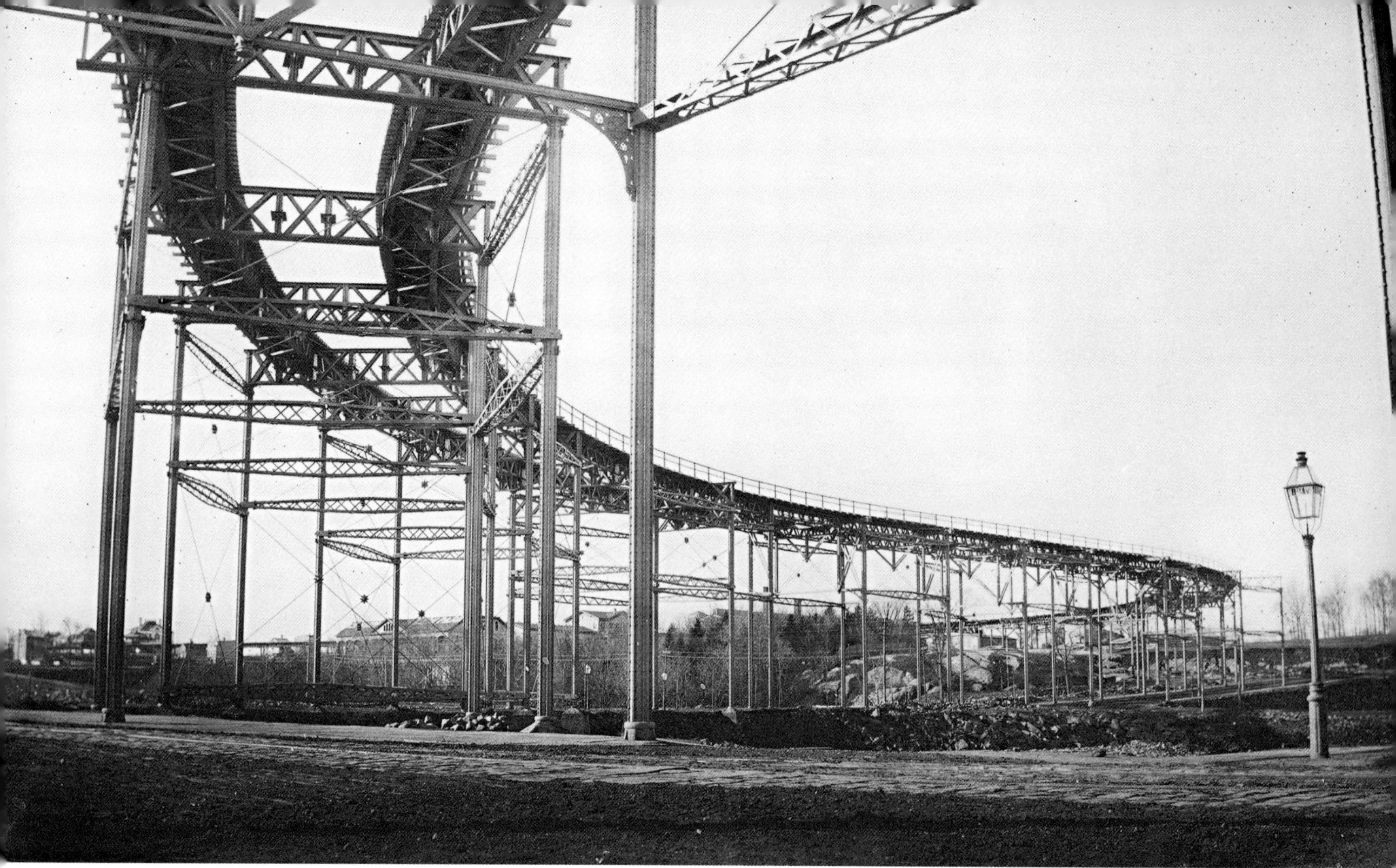

Poetry of Structure

A Changing City —*Brooklyn Daily Eagle*, 1870

"The changes of a decade impelled by the rapid growth of a progressive city have been many and marvelous. . . . The amount of labor here already accomplished and still in progress seems almost incredible. Hills have been levelled, trees uprooted, hollows and ponds filled, soft, yielding meadows and muddy marshes made firm and solid, and the whole covered converted into building lots, intersected by broad avenues and streets well graded, and paved and lined with thousands of buildings, comprising dwellings of every description, from the small frame cottage to the imposing brownstone mansion and business structures, from the one story frame office to the mammoth factory and mills. Dashing equipages and horses have superseded lumbering farm wagons and wearisome stagecoaches, while the plodding farmer . . . has been succeeded by hundreds of artisans in factories and workshops and hundreds of laborers by whom the tide of improvement is daily continued. . . ."

Brooklyn Bridge, 1880s. The 1880s saw the rapid expansion of New York City's transit system, with the introduction of elevated railroads, which revolutionized urban transportation. To carry pedestrians across the new Brooklyn Bridge, the New York and Brooklyn Railway operated a cable car system. Like the French Impressionist Caillebotte, Brainerd was fascinated with the forms of these engineering marvels and sought to convey their bold pattens through the new medium of photography. Brainerd's plates come a full two decades before the work of Charles Sheeler, the painter and photographer whose work would also celebrate the beauty of industrial forms. George Bradford Brainerd Photograph Collection, Brooklyn Public Library/Center for Brooklyn History.

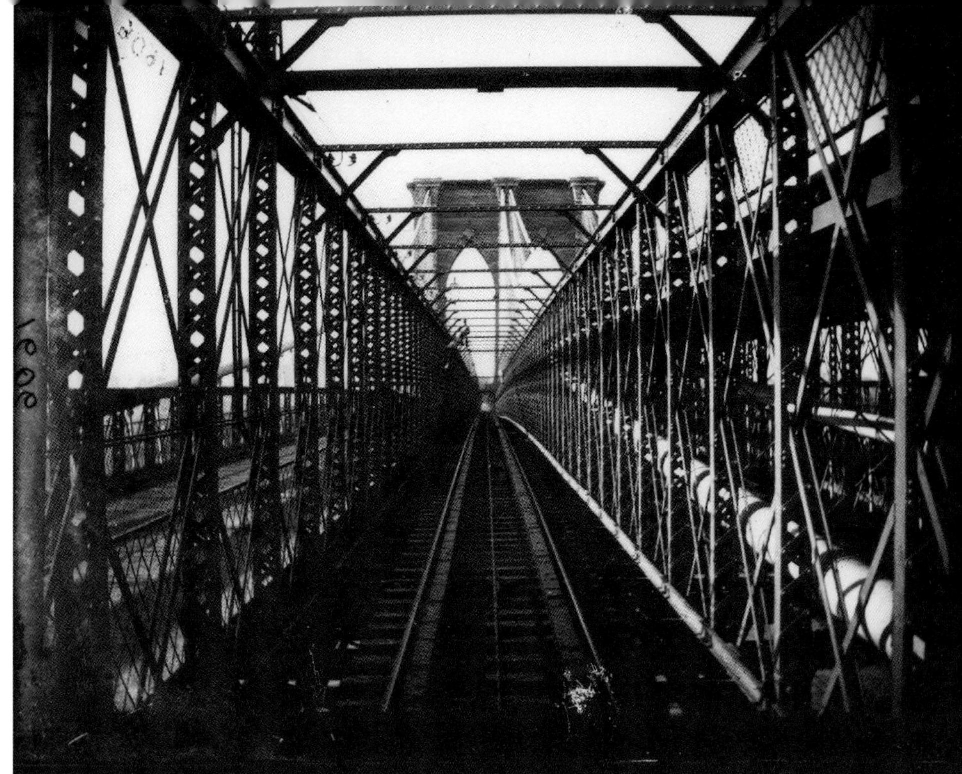

Worker, Brooklyn Bridge, 1880s. A striking composition of a bridge worker high in the air, seemingly caught in a web of suspension cables. George Bradford Brainerd Photograph Collection, Brooklyn Public Library/Center for Brooklyn History.

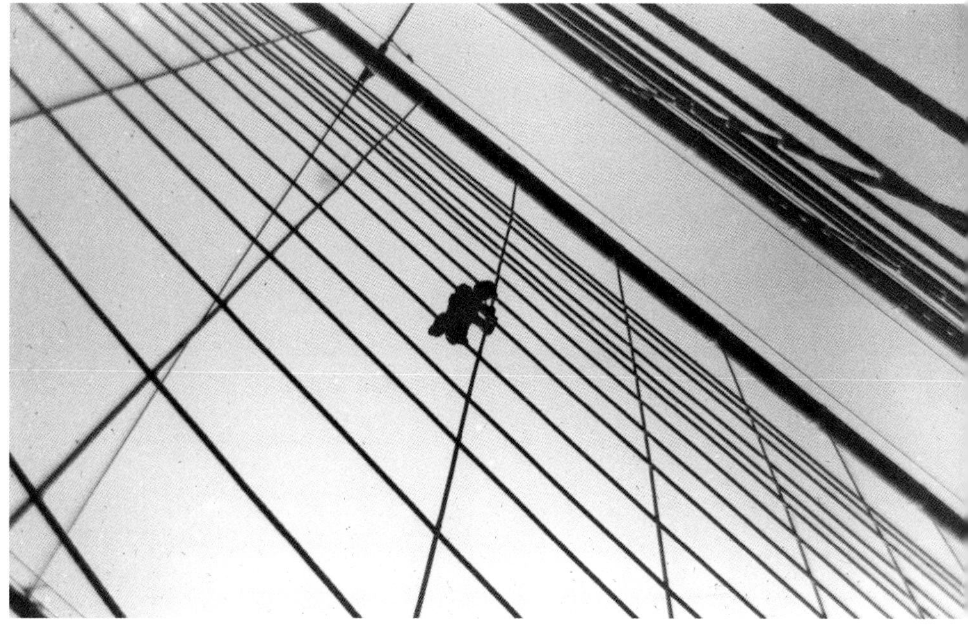

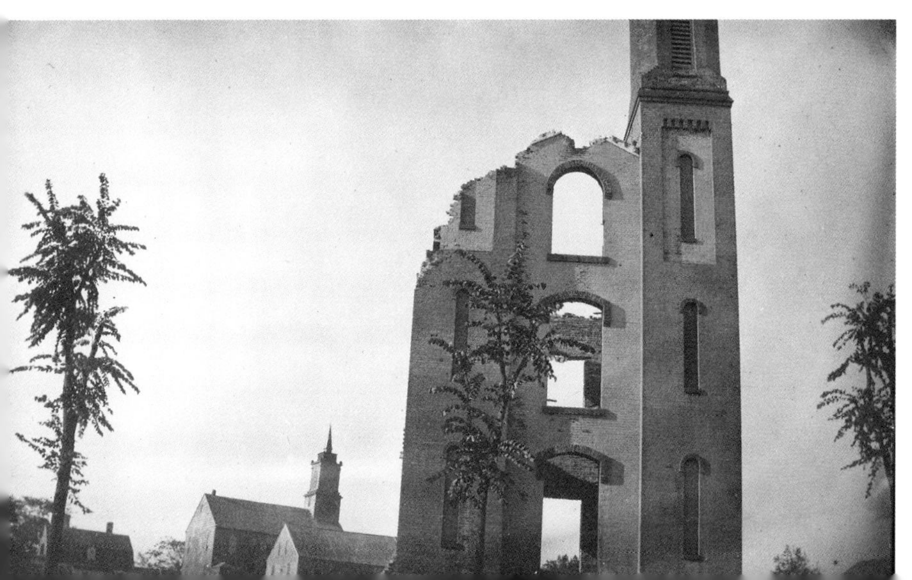

Fragment of a wall, unknown location, 1870s. Another unusual composition by Brainerd, emphasizing the abstract patterns of what appears to be a partially demolished church, probably in Brooklyn. George Bradford Brainerd Photograph Collection, Brooklyn Collection, Brooklyn Public Library/Center for Brooklyn History.

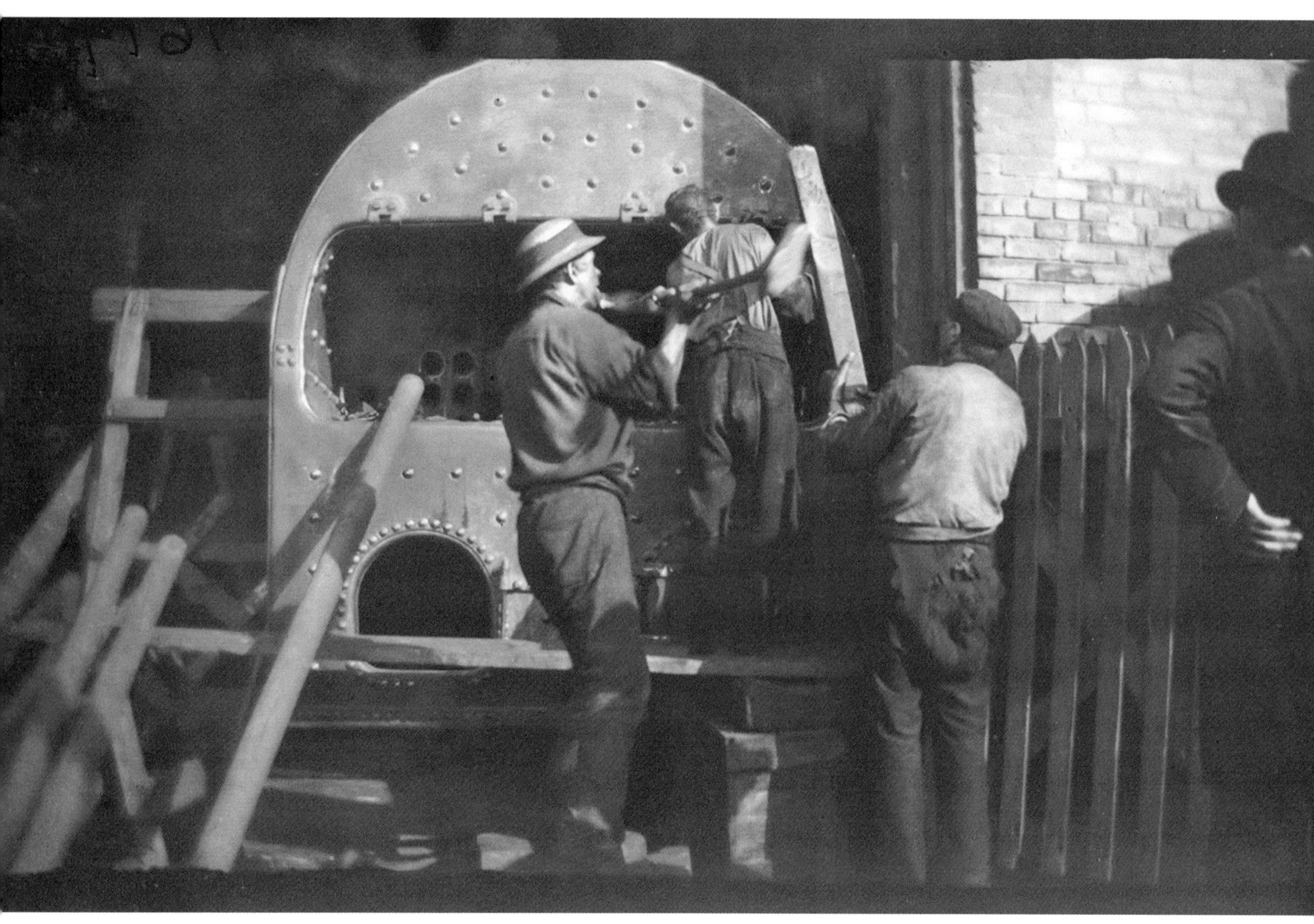

Making a Boiler, 1876. The Industrial Age rendered to abstraction. George Bradford Brainerd Photograph Collection, Brooklyn Public Library/ Center for Brooklyn History.

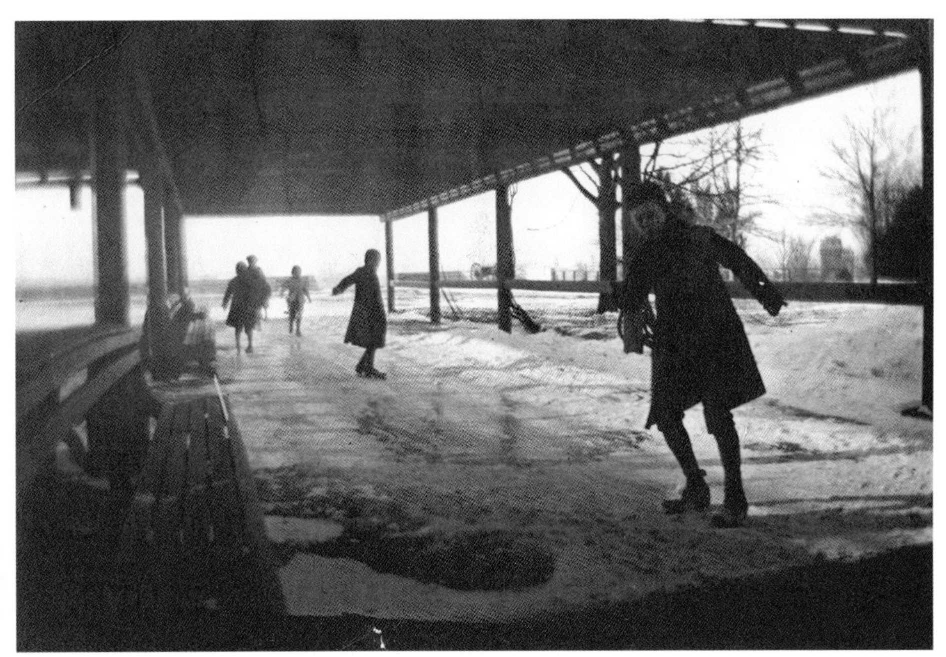

Boys sliding under an elevated railroad probably in Brooklyn, 1874. Another remarkable early dry plate, showing the photographer had perfected the technology for freezing motion far earlier than anyone had suspected. Below, Brooklyn Bridge, early 1880s. The first cars to operate on the Brooklyn Bridge, which opened on May 24, 1883, were horse-drawn trolleys, as it was feared the bridge could not support the weight of steam locomotives. The chuffing locomotives, like the one pictured below, did run at either end of the great span, although they did not cross. Brainerd produces a masterful composition in the tradition of the art photographer Alfred Stieglitz, who began making pictures in the late 1880s. George Bradford Brainerd Photographic Collection, Brooklyn Public Library/Center for Brooklyn History.

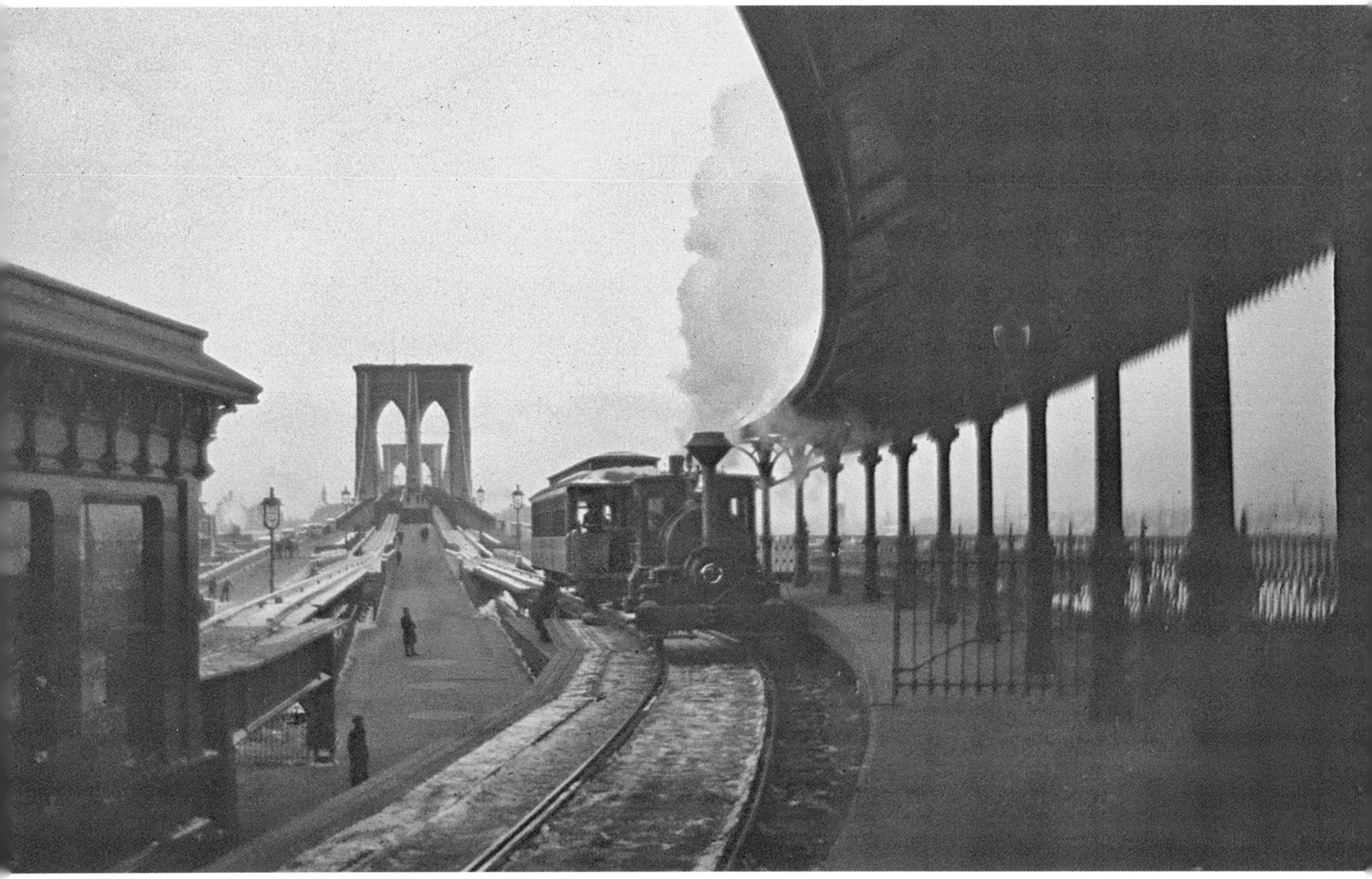

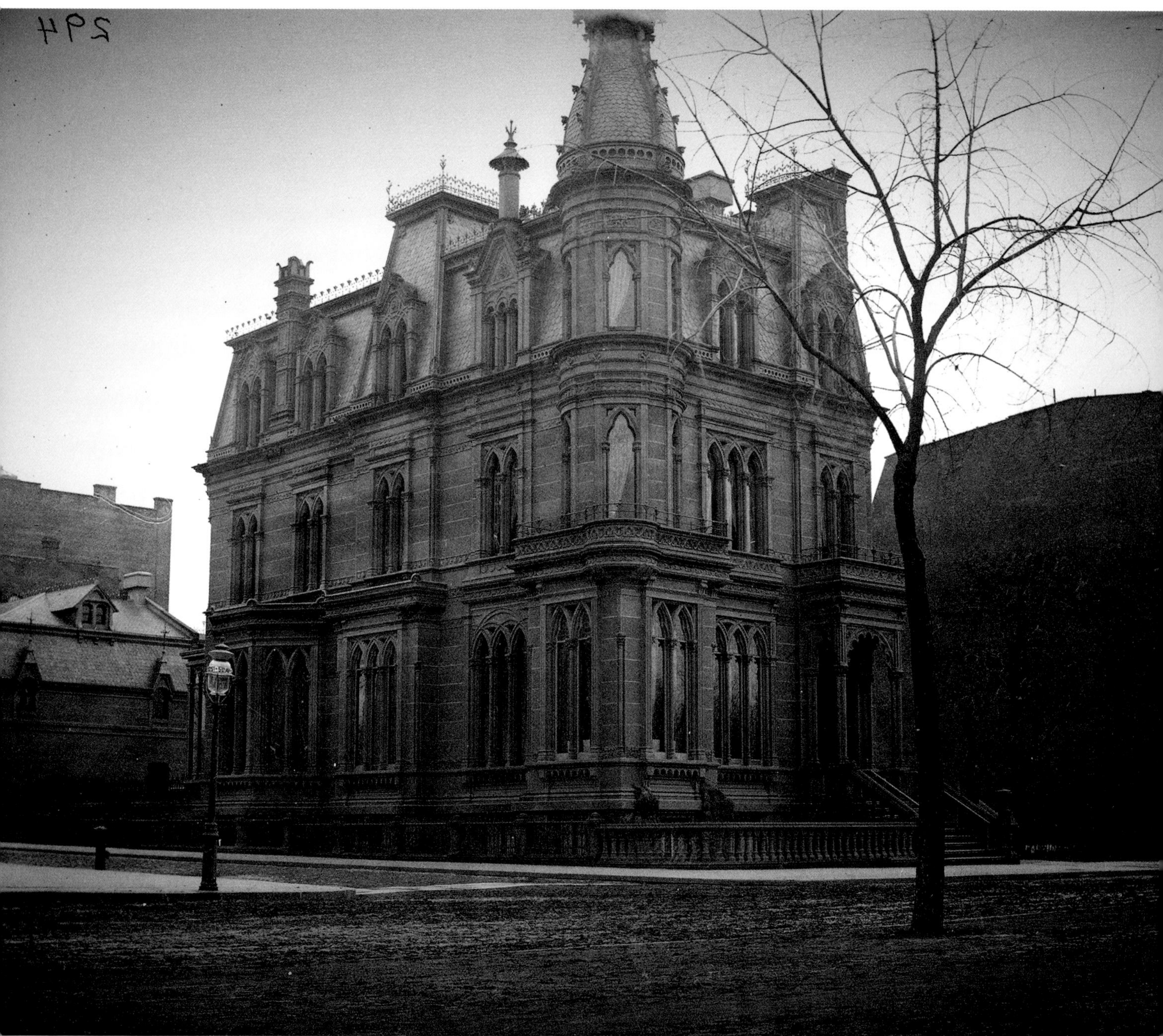

A glorious brownstone mansion at an unidentified location along 5th Avenue in New York City in the late 1870s. Following the Civil War, 5th Avenue became an upscale residential address with palatial homes going up in an area known as "Marble Row." With the succession of fabulous Gilded Age mansions erected between 59th to 78th Street, the street would dubbed the "Gold Coast," and "Millionaires' Row." George Bradford Brainerd Photographic Collection, Brooklyn Public Library/Center for Brooklyn History.

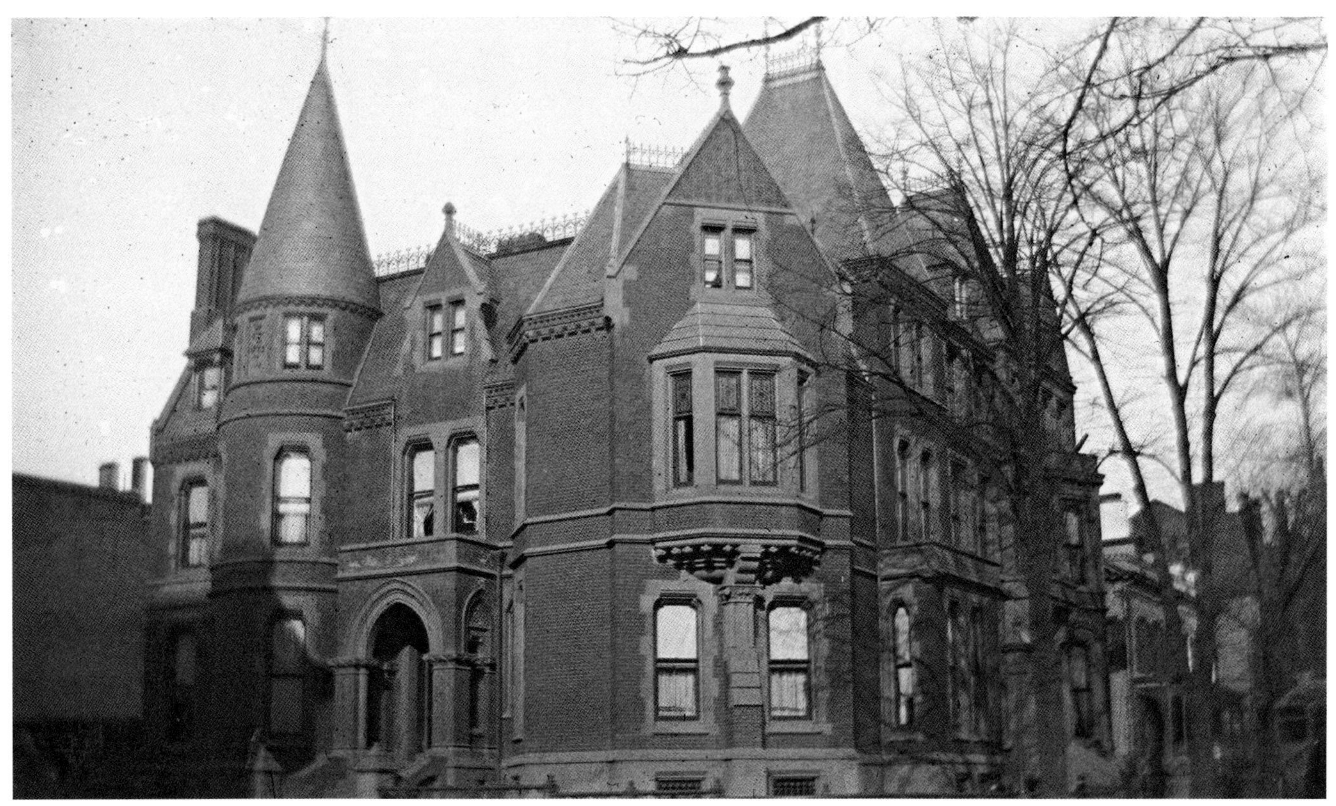

Turret and Tower

During the late 19th century, New York's most esteemed families built extravagant mansions along Fifth Avenue, turning it into one of the most desired residential streets in the United States. The catalyst for Fifth Avenue's transformation came in the form of the Astor family. Patriarch John Jacob Astor had purchased large swaths of Manhattan land in the area, allowing William Backhouse Astor Sr. to present his son and the new Caroline Astor (née Webster Schermerhorn) with a parcel of land on 34th Street and 5th Avenue as a wedding gift in 1854. Old money didn't need to flaunt, however, so the first Astor home, like this stately Fifth Avenue brownstone

Packard Mansion, Brooklyn, 1885. Well-heeled Brooklynites also built handsome mansions, though, perhaps, less ostentatious than their New York counterparts. In Brooklyn, few dwellings matched the turreted splendor of the Packard mansion in Brooklyn Heights (it stood on the corner of Henry and Joralemon Streets) built in the 1870s for the department store magnate Edwin Packard. The Packards were listed in the social register, the Brooklyn Blue Book, and the family's three daughters Mildred, Elizabeth, and Clara, made their well noted debuts. Edwin Packard, a direct descendant of John Alden of the *Mayflower* and Captain Samuel Packard, was a linen buyer for the hugely successful A. T. Stewart and Co., a groundbreaking department

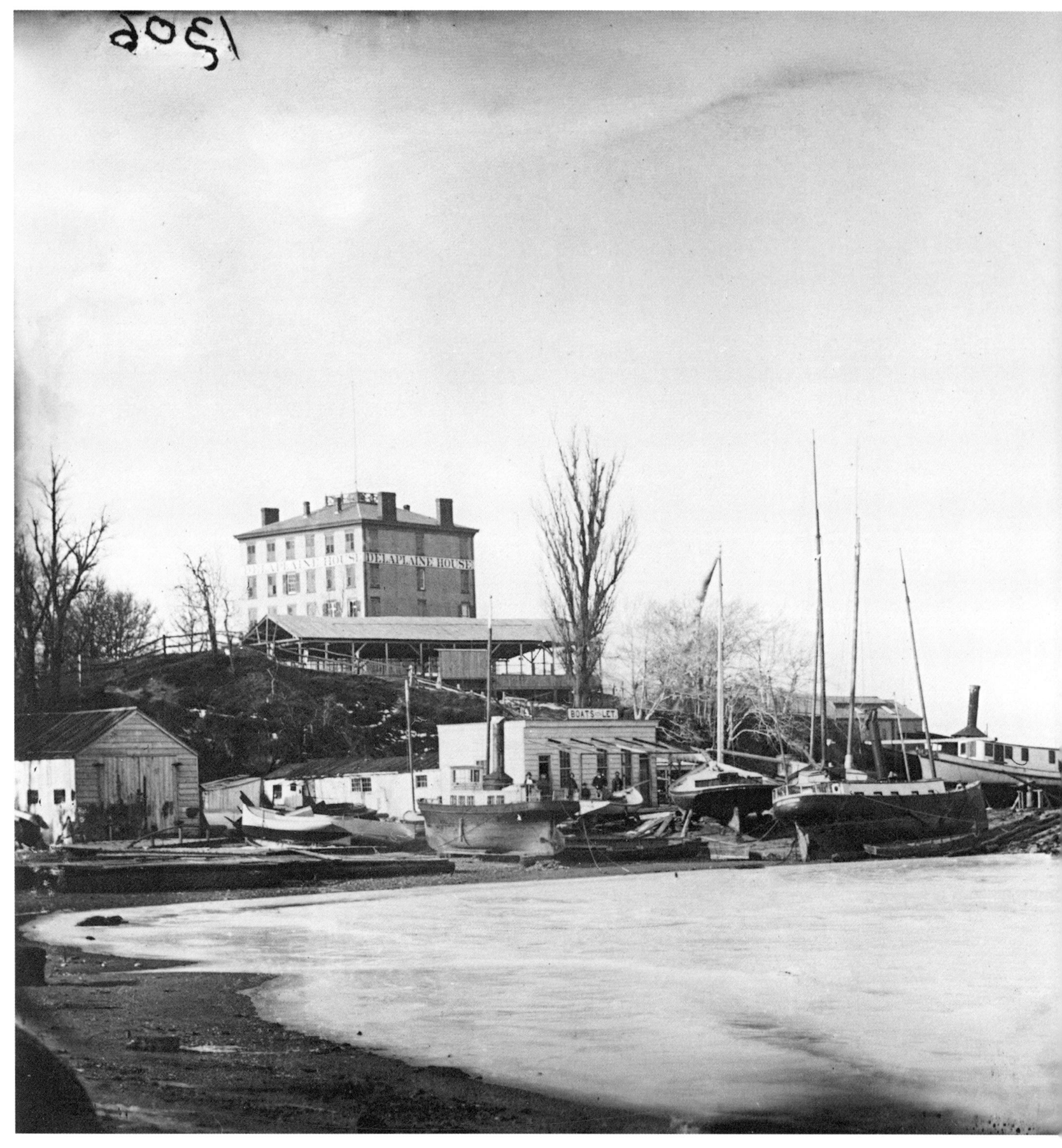

store located on Broadway near Grace Church in New York City. The marble-fronted emporium was owned by Alexander Tur-ney Stewart, one of the richest men of the day, who sent Packard on buying trips to Europe. Edwin married Julia Hutchinson, son of Samuel Hutchinson, himself a wealthy owner of the dry goods company, Wickhams & Hutchinson, located on Pearl Street in New York. George Bradford Brainerd Photograph Collection, Brooklyn Public Library/Center for Brooklyn History.

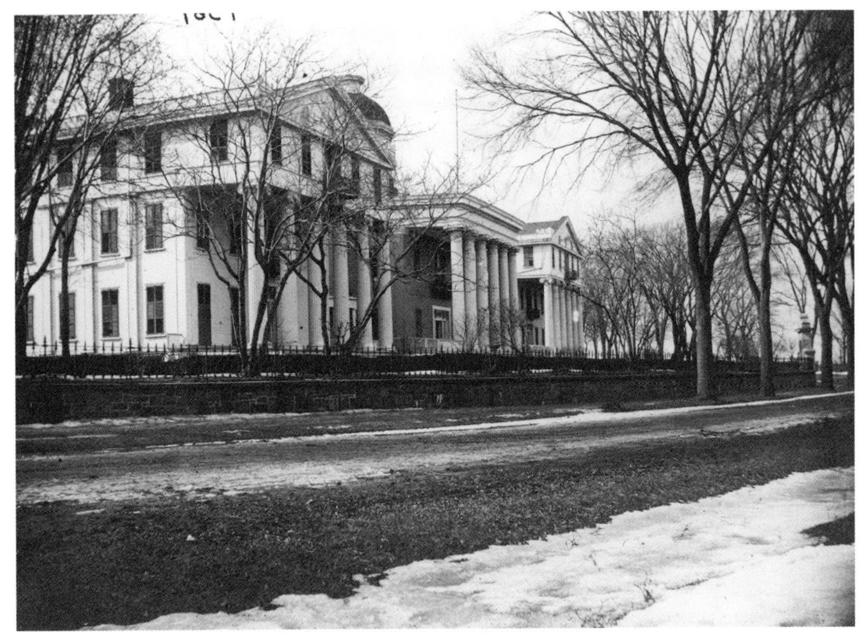

photographed in the mid-1870s by George Brainerd, was
a rather modest affair. However, with new fortunes being
made overnight in the hub of commerce that was New
York, the new millionaires began to vie with one another in
the home-building department, each new dwelling rising
on Fifth Avenue more palatial than its predecessor. Among
the most glorious of these now vanished residences was
the French chateau–style abode Caroline Astor had built
for herself on 65th Street and Fifth Avenue. It was actually
two separate buildings connected on the inside by a great
ballroom that could host 1,200 guests, the same number
her rival, Alva Vanderbilt, the new Gilded Age queen, had
invited to her fancy dress ball.

New Brighton, Staten Island, 1871.
One of Brainerd's earliest images when
he picked up photography again after
graduating from Rensselaer Polytechnic
Institute in Troy, New York, the image
shows elegant villas along the tree-
lined streets of New Brighton on Staten
Island, a once fashionable retreat where
moneyed New Yorkers and Brooklynites
enjoyed elegance on par with Newport,
Rhode Island, and Cape May, New Jersey.
The posh residential community, named
after the 18th-century English seaside
resort, was the brainchild of Thomas E.
Davis, who envisioned a tony enclave
of detached villas in their own sylvan
settings, in the fashion made popular
by landscape architect, Andrew Jackson
Downing. By the 1840s, elegant hotels
had sprung up and New Brighton became
a destination, with fashionable crowds
enjoying amusements like "sea bathing,"
yachting, and fishing. Although many of
the villas are gone, scattered remains of
this once grand resort remain and can be
viewed today. George Bradford Brainerd
Photograph Collection, Brooklyn Public
Library/Center for Brooklyn History.
Left, Gowanus Bay, Brooklyn, 1874. A
bit of faded grandeur is seen in this
plate from the early 1870s of Brooklyn's
Gowanus Bay, showing the old docks
with a great square house crowning
the summit of the hill. The dwelling is
the old Delaplaine house, a pink stucco
villa erected on Gowanus Heights in the
early 1800s by the Delaplaine family,
New York shipping merchants. Brainerd must have known something of
its past glory and wanted to make a
record of an area that was being rapidly
transformed. George Bradford Brainerd
Photograph Collection, Brooklyn Public
Library/Center for Brooklyn History.

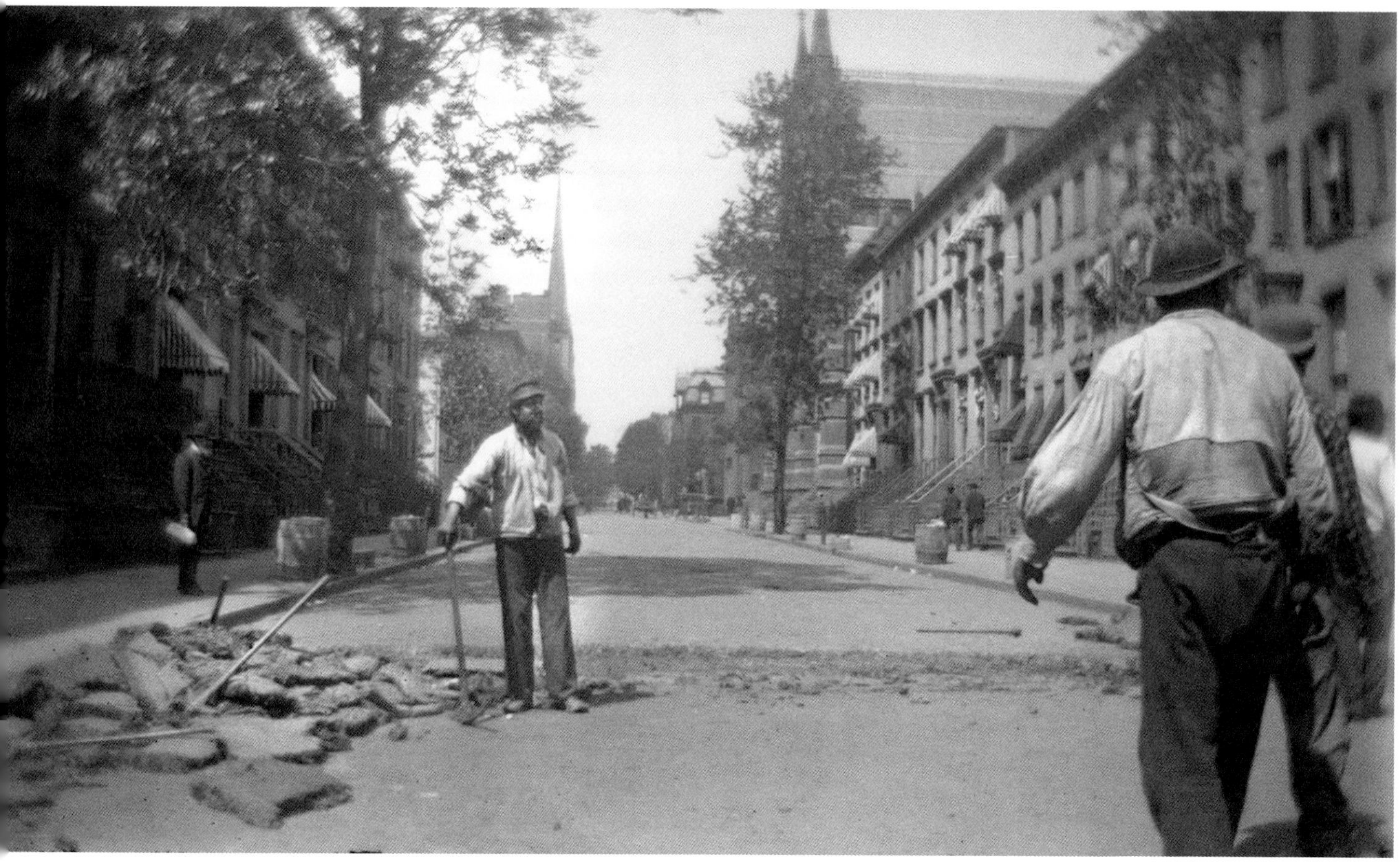

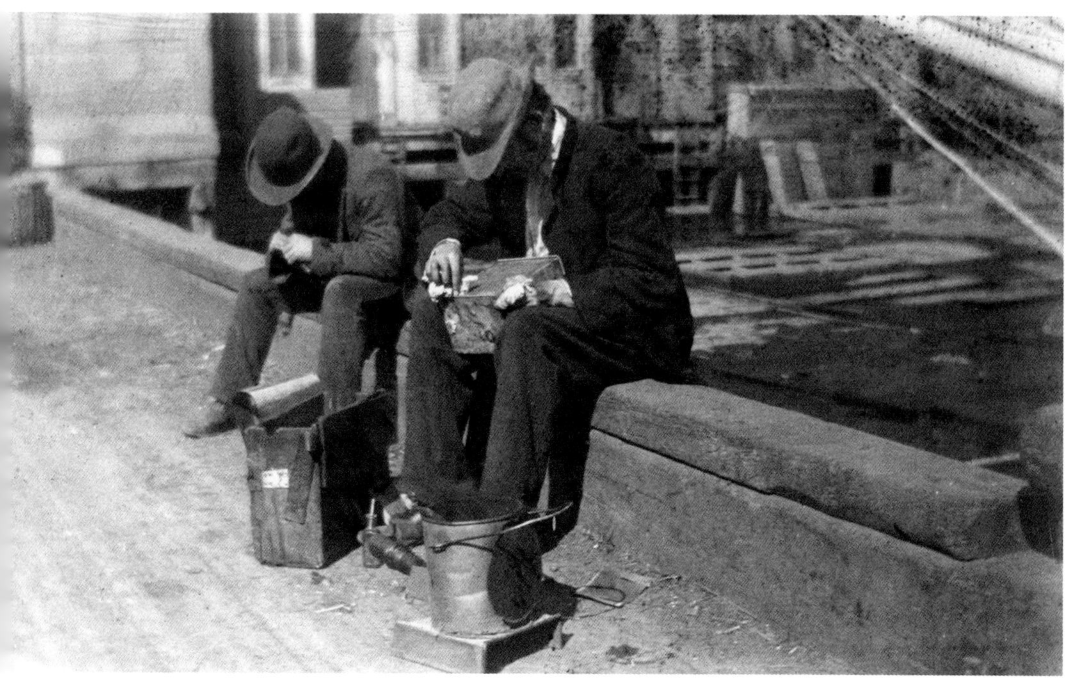

Tin workers, Brooklyn. Late 1870s. George Bradford Brainerd Photographic Collection, Brooklyn Public Library/Center for Brooklyn History.

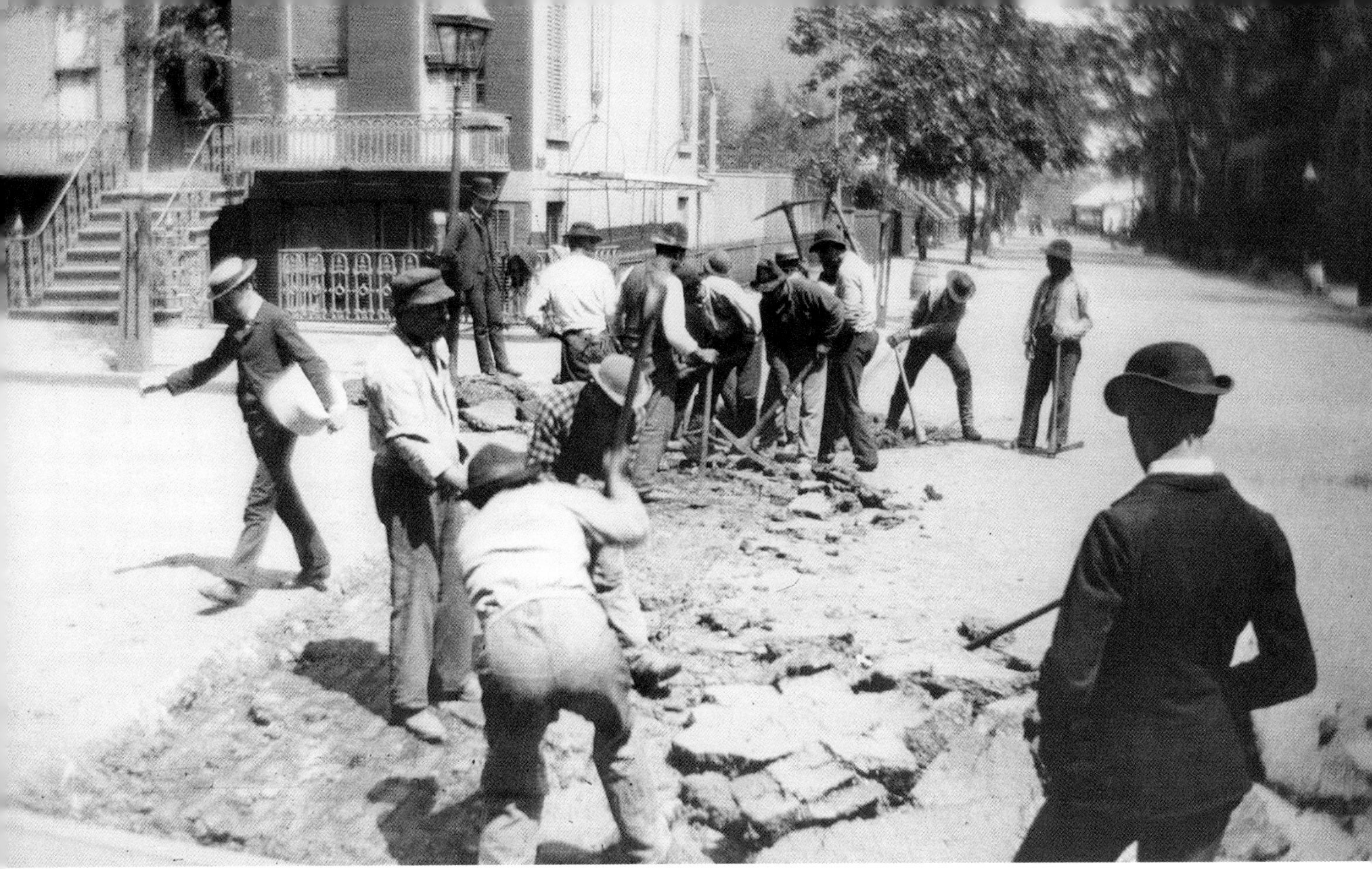

Sidewalk Ballet

" **T**hose who obtain their living in the streets of the Metropolis are a very large and varied class; indeed, the means resorted to in order to "pick up a crust," as the people call it, in the public thoroughfares (and such in many instances it literally is,) are so multifarious that the mind is long baffled in its attempts to reduce them to scientific order or classification. It would appear, however, that the street-people may all be arranged under six distinct genera or kinds. These are severally: street-sellers, street-buyers, street-finders, street performers, artists, and showmen, street artisans, or working peddlers, and street laborers." —**Henry Mayhew,** *London Labour and the London Poor,* **1851**

Left and above: Repairs to Clinton Street, 1875. The dignity of work is a theme running through much of Brainerd's photography. He clearly had great respect for common laborers on whom he relied as a manager of city public works projects. More than just a job site record, these two photographs rank with the very best 19th-century street photography, such as the work of Eugène Atget. Using a handheld camera, Brainerd has pulled off masterful compositions in both instances, drawing our eye across the picture plane through a hierarchy of figures (in the same way Degas arranged his ballerinas), beginning with a strong foreground element. George Bradford Brainerd Photograph Collection, Brooklyn Public Library/Center for Brooklyn History.

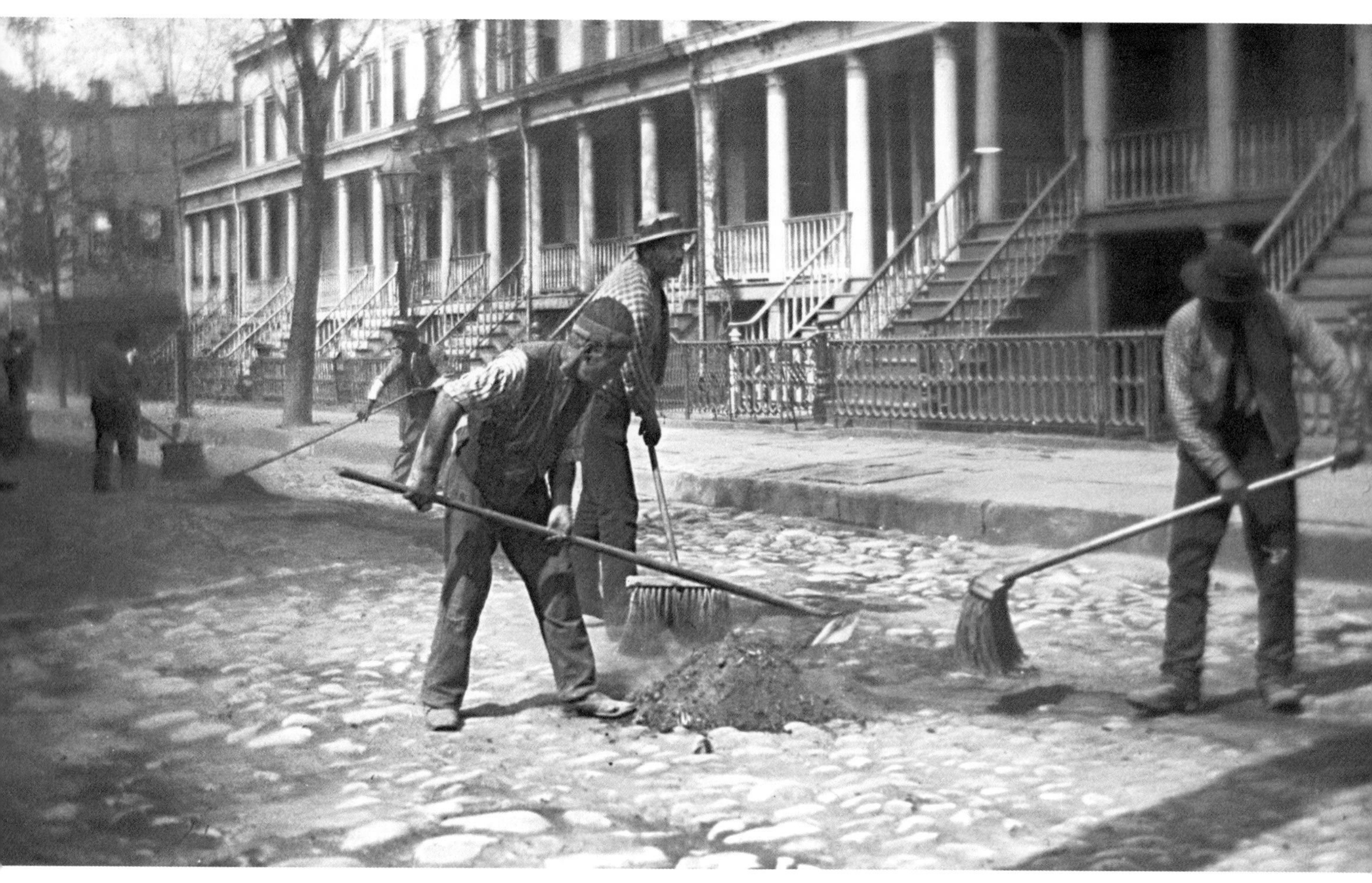

Street sweepers, 1875. Another powerful image in which the photographer elevates the drudgery of street sweeping to almost an art. George Bradford Brainerd Photograph Collection, Brooklyn Public Library/Center for Brooklyn History.

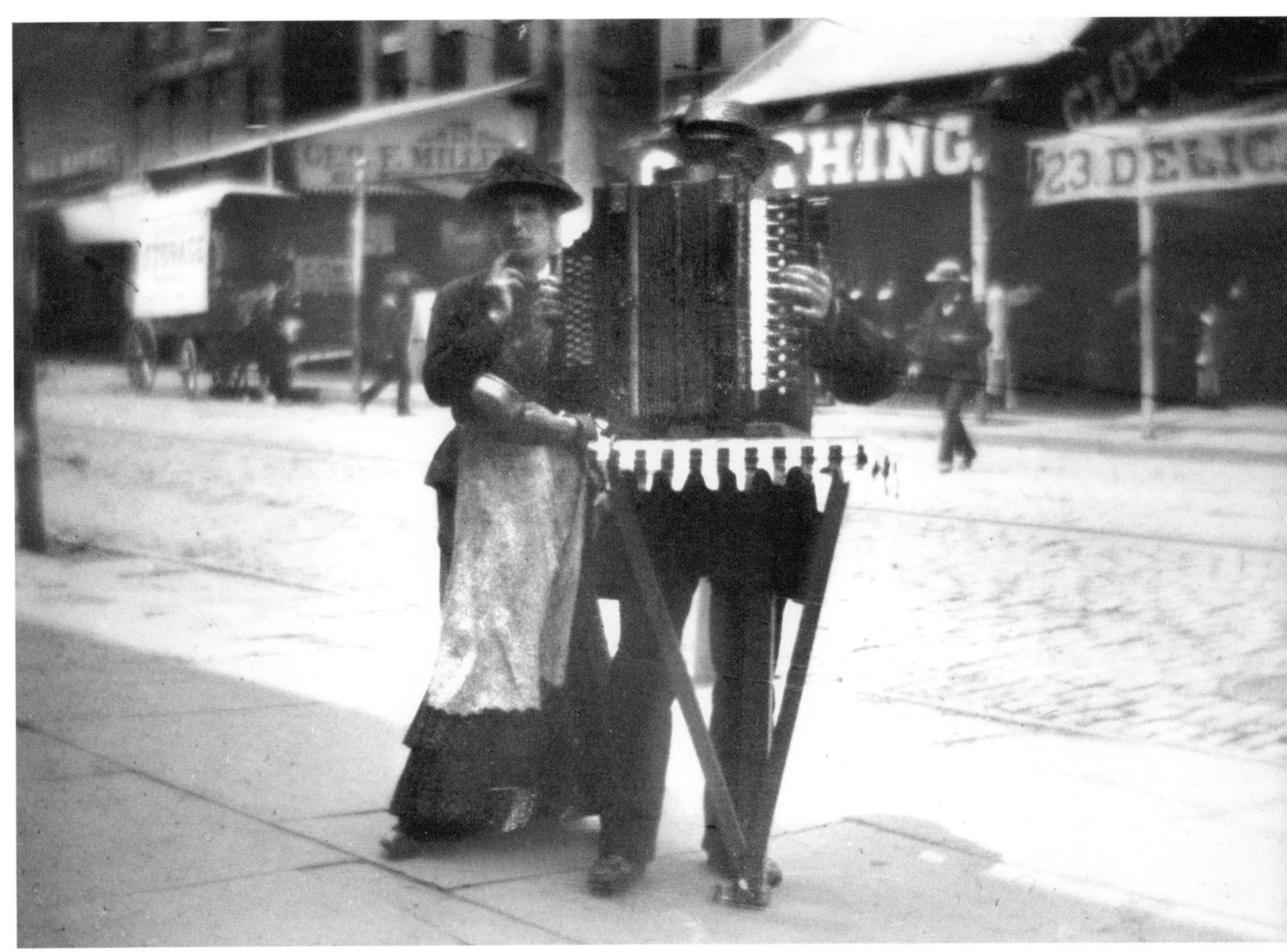

Accordion player, Brooklyn, 1870s. The face of this musician is hidden behind his instrument, but we can almost hear his rich, resonant melody filling the streets and mingling with the hum of a bustling city. There are two, probably a husband and wife, or a father and a daughter, working in tandem. On good days, they might draw a crowd. This day, however, it appears only the photographer was there to appreciate their artistry. George Bradford Brainerd Photograph Collection, Brooklyn Public Library/Center for Brooklyn History.

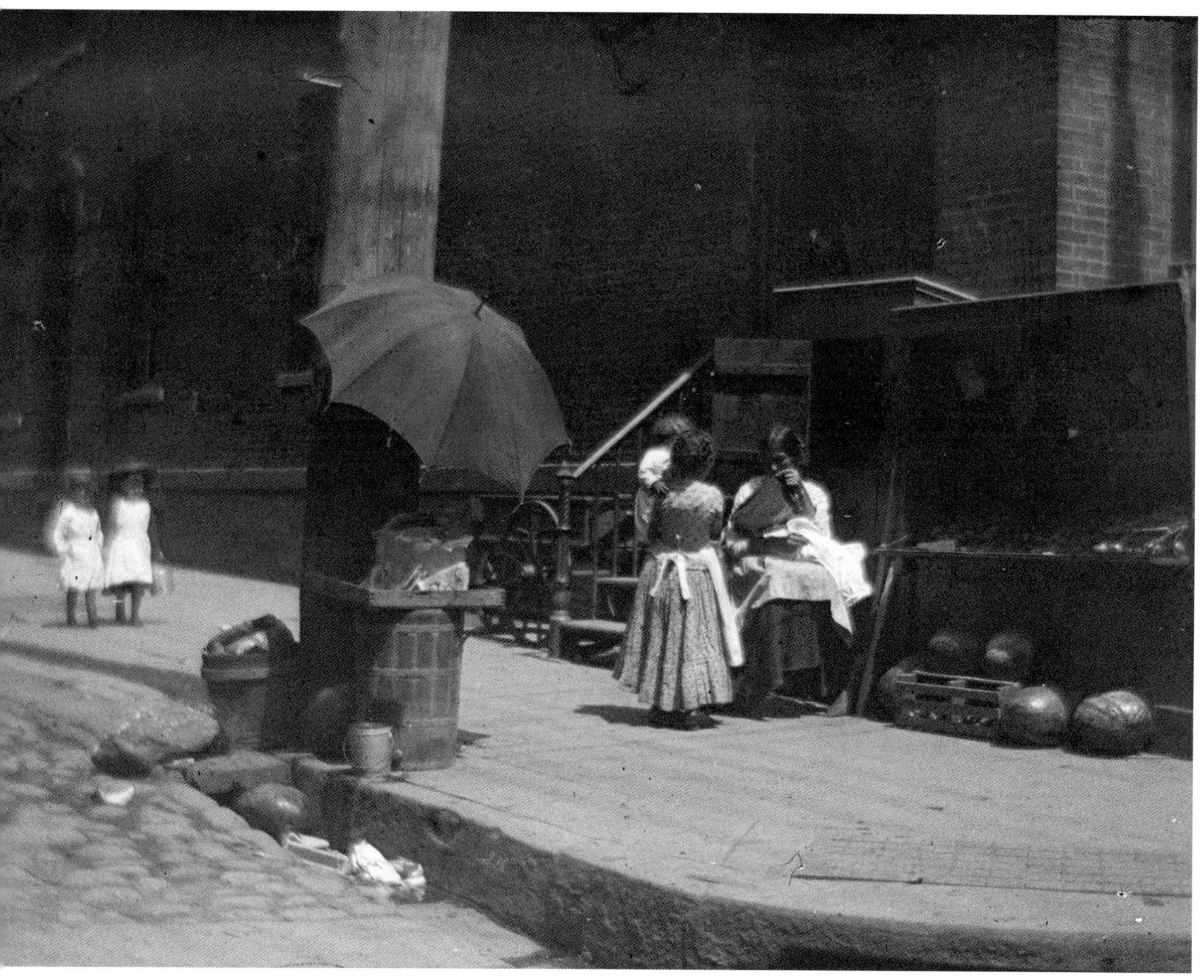

This pair of images—a fruit stand with an umbrella, and Brooklyn newsboys—once again show Brainerd's masterful use of chiaroscuro and feeling for composition. Brainerd's formal training is unclear, beyond the mechanical drawing classes he had in college. But it's likely he had some instruction in painting and composition, for many of his pictures, though often snapped with a handheld camera, show a deep knowledge of composition and balancing of positive and negative spaces. George Bradford Brainerd Photograph Collection, Brooklyn Public Library/Center for Brooklyn History.

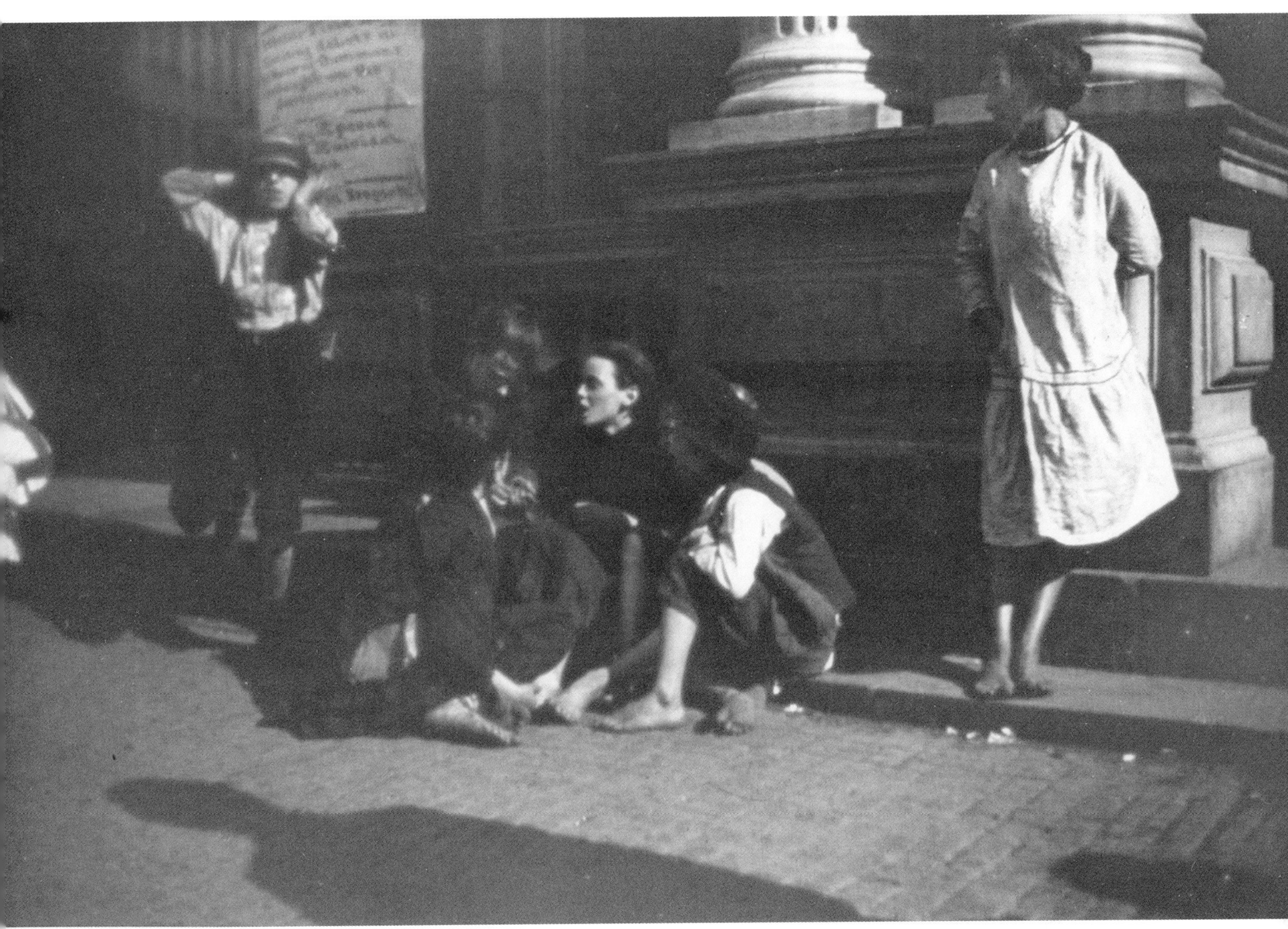

Brainerd's image of Brooklyn newsboys anticipates the work of the celebrated social documentary photographer, Lewis Hine, the New York City schoolteacher who traveled around the country photographing the working conditions of children in all types of industries. Hine worked in the early 1900s, whereas Brainerd's picture of bedraggled paperboys was produced in the late 1870s.

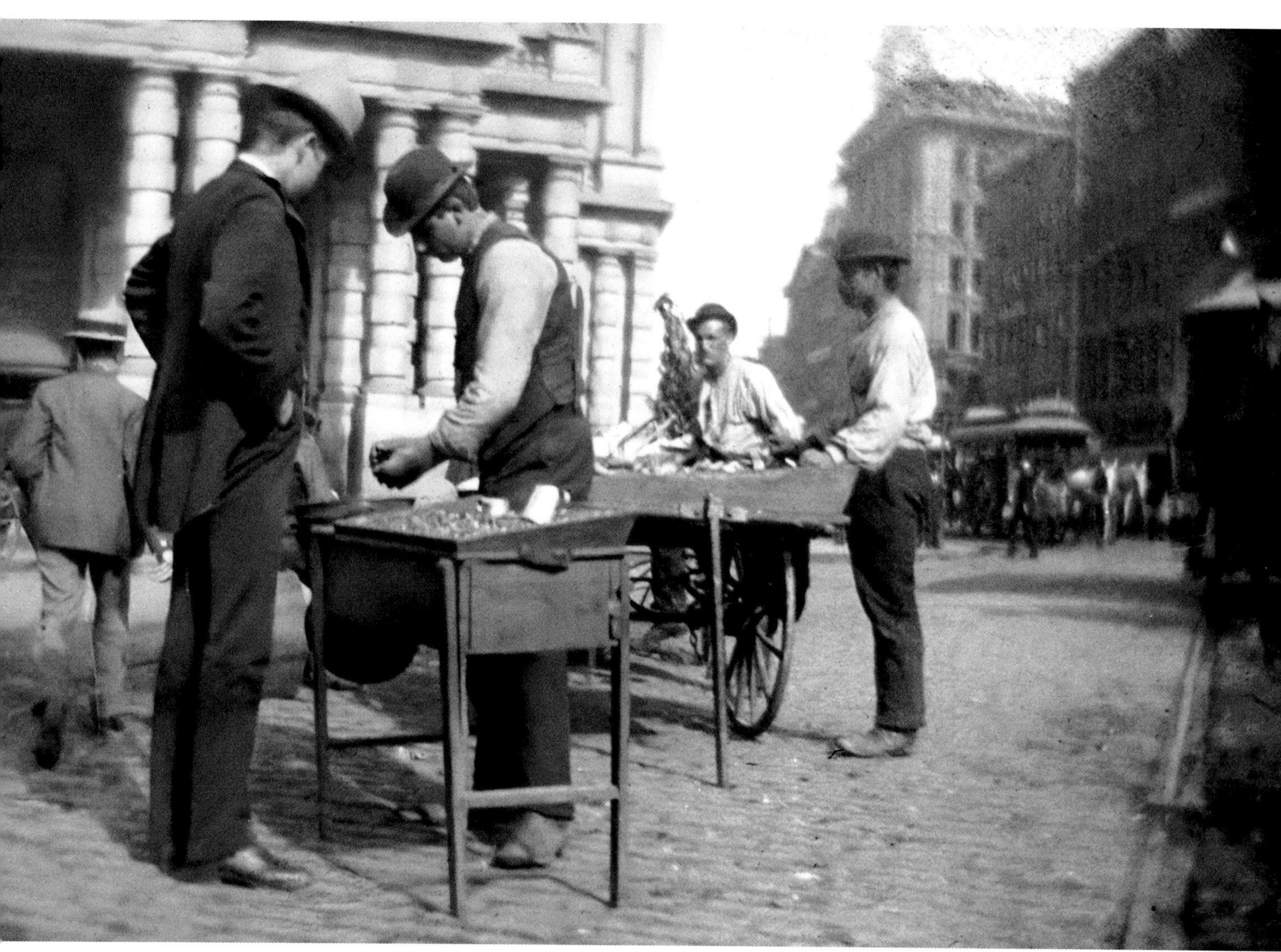

Chestnut stand, Lower Manhattan, 1870s. The toasty treat that Nat King Cole immortalized in "The Christmas Song" was a year-round staple of street vendors in New York City. Brainerd's image records a chestnut stand on Broadway in Lower Manhattan. Again, we see the photographer's ability to convey narrative in this brief transaction between a Victorian gentleman and a humble peddler, the latter having trundled his cart into the city at dawn and remained well after the lamps were lighted. George Bradford Brainerd Photograph Collection, Brooklyn Public Library/Center for Brooklyn History.

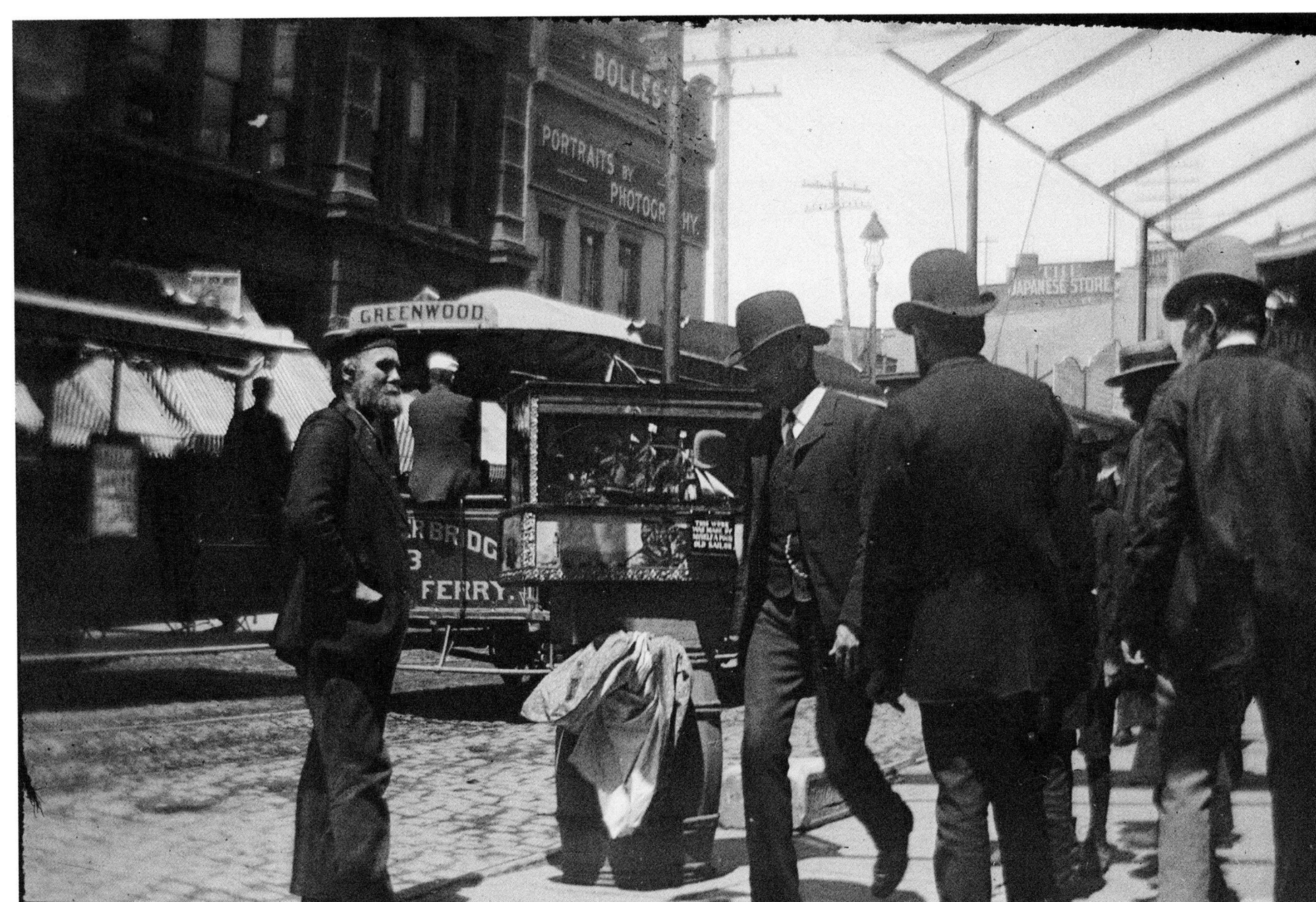

Old sailor with ship model, Brooklyn, 1885. "It is an
ancient Mariner/And he stoppeth one of three/'By thy
long grey beard and glittering eye/Now wherefore stopp'st
thou me?" We can almost hear the words of Coleridge's
Ancient Mariner ring out in this photograph taken in the
vicinity of the waterfront. Undoubtably a well-known
personality in Brooklyn, the old sailor would have possessed a sea chest of salty stories, ready to trundle
out whenever the situation called for a little entertainment. George Bradford Brainerd Photograph Collection,
Brooklyn Public Library/e Center for Brooklyn History.

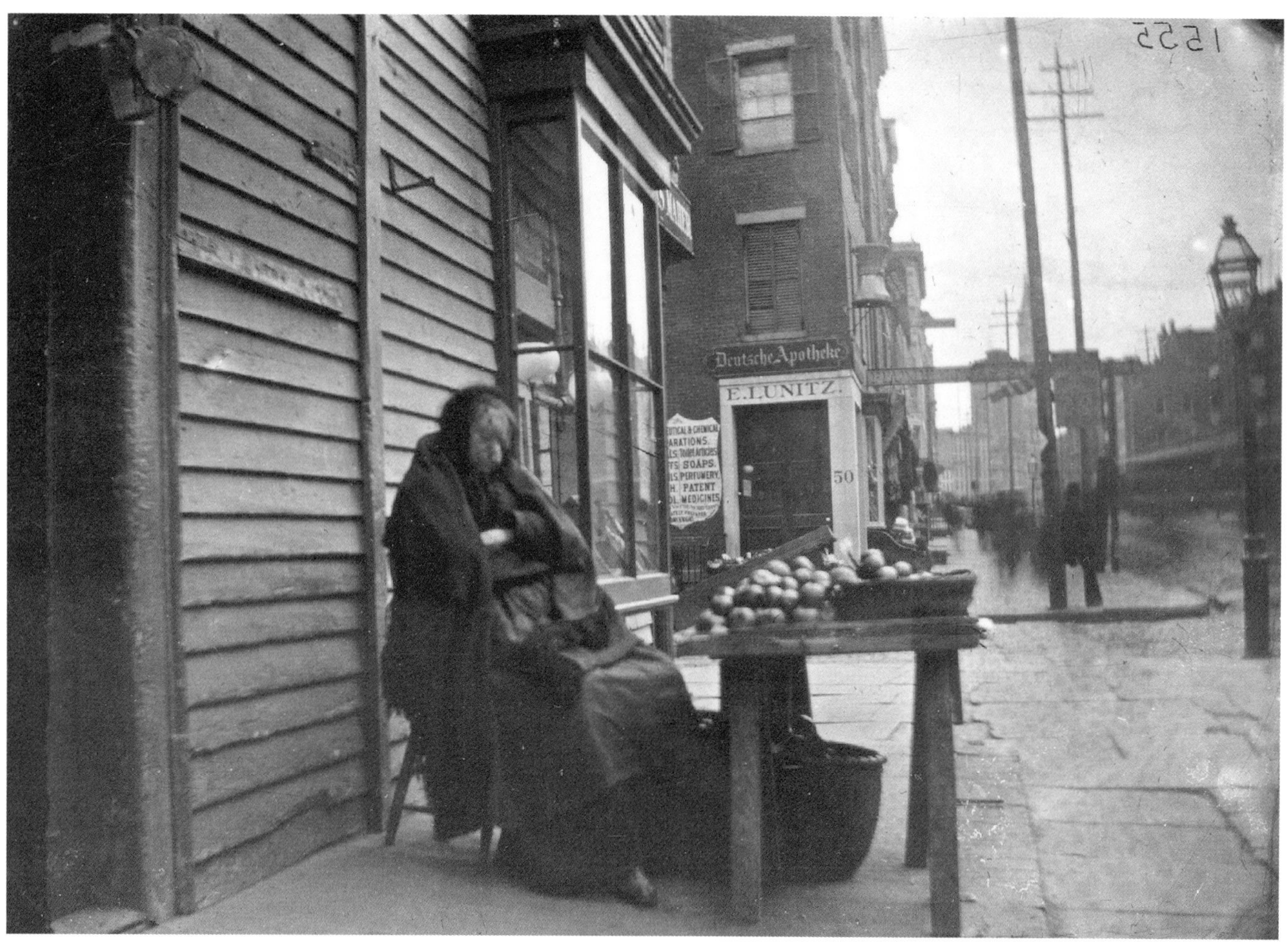

Old Apple Woman, New York, 1870s. Brainerd's feeling for the textures of the city is on display in this image entitled "Old Apple Woman," capturing an elderly lady peddler plying her trade on the streets of New York. George Bradford Brainerd Photograph Collection, Brooklyn Public Library/Center for Brooklyn History.

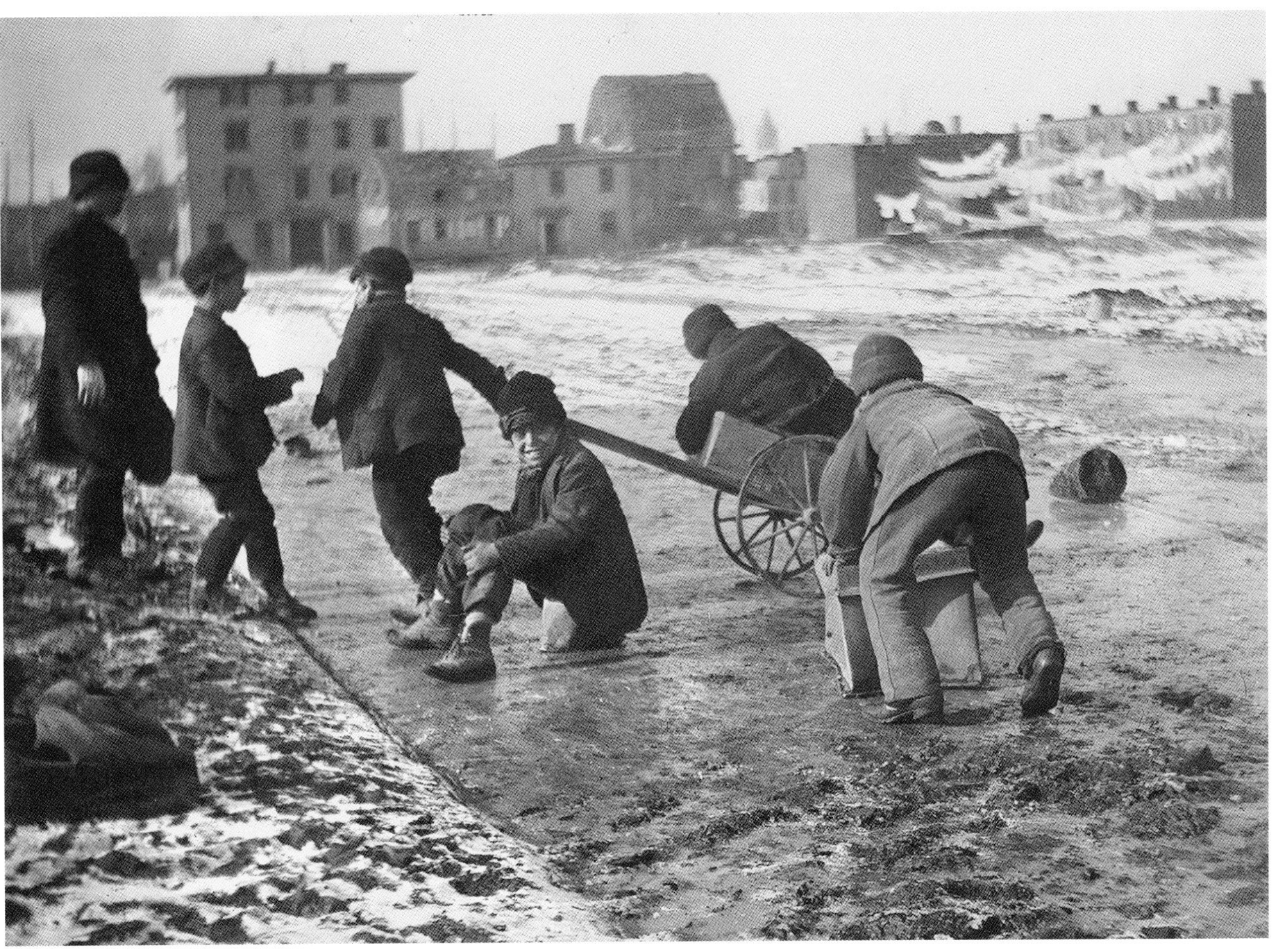

Boys sliding on tin cans, 1870s. A gang of boys has some improvised fun on the ice in one of the poorer districts of Brooklyn. Brainerd's job with the Water Department would have brought him into the neighborhoods of both rich and poor, but it was the latter where the photographer seemed to find the most compelling subjects. George Bradford Brainerd Photograph Collection, Brooklyn Public Library/Center for Brooklyn History.

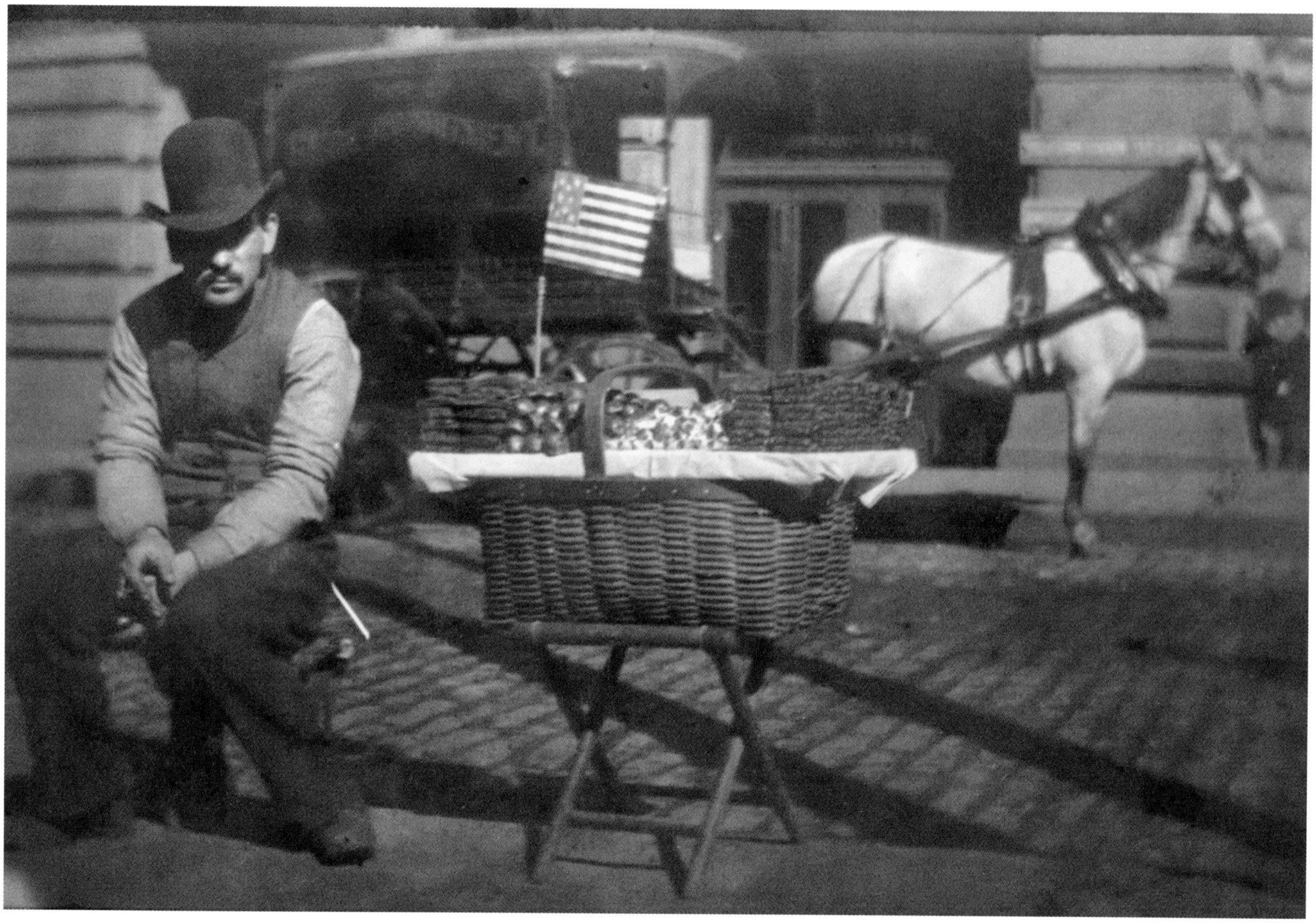

Candy Man, New York, 1870s. There's something a tad menacing about George Brainerd's "Candy Man," who regards the picture-taker suspiciously from under his bowler hat. Maybe it's his broad flat nose, which looks as if it might have been broken on more than one occasion, evidence perhaps of his former life as a brawler. But the little flag and pile of sweets add a cheerful note, and there's the old mare waiting patiently in the background for her driver. George Bradford Brainerd Photograph Collection, Brooklyn Public Library/Center for Brooklyn History.

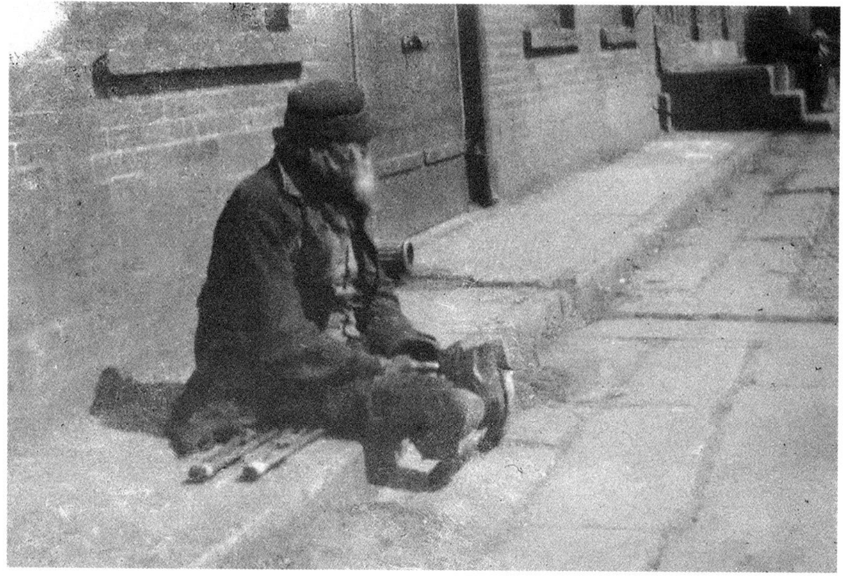

The Mugio, New York, 1870s. This grim image of a legless beggar is described simply as "The Mugio." Who was this pitiful medicant? Was he one of the tens of thousands of frightfully maimed Civil War soldiers? Or was he a victim of an industrial accident? Indeed, the job of railroad worker was once so hazardous companies employed their own surgeons to perform hasty amputations. Alas, we may never know his story. George Bradford Brainerd Photograph Collection, Brooklyn Public Library/Center for Brooklyn History.

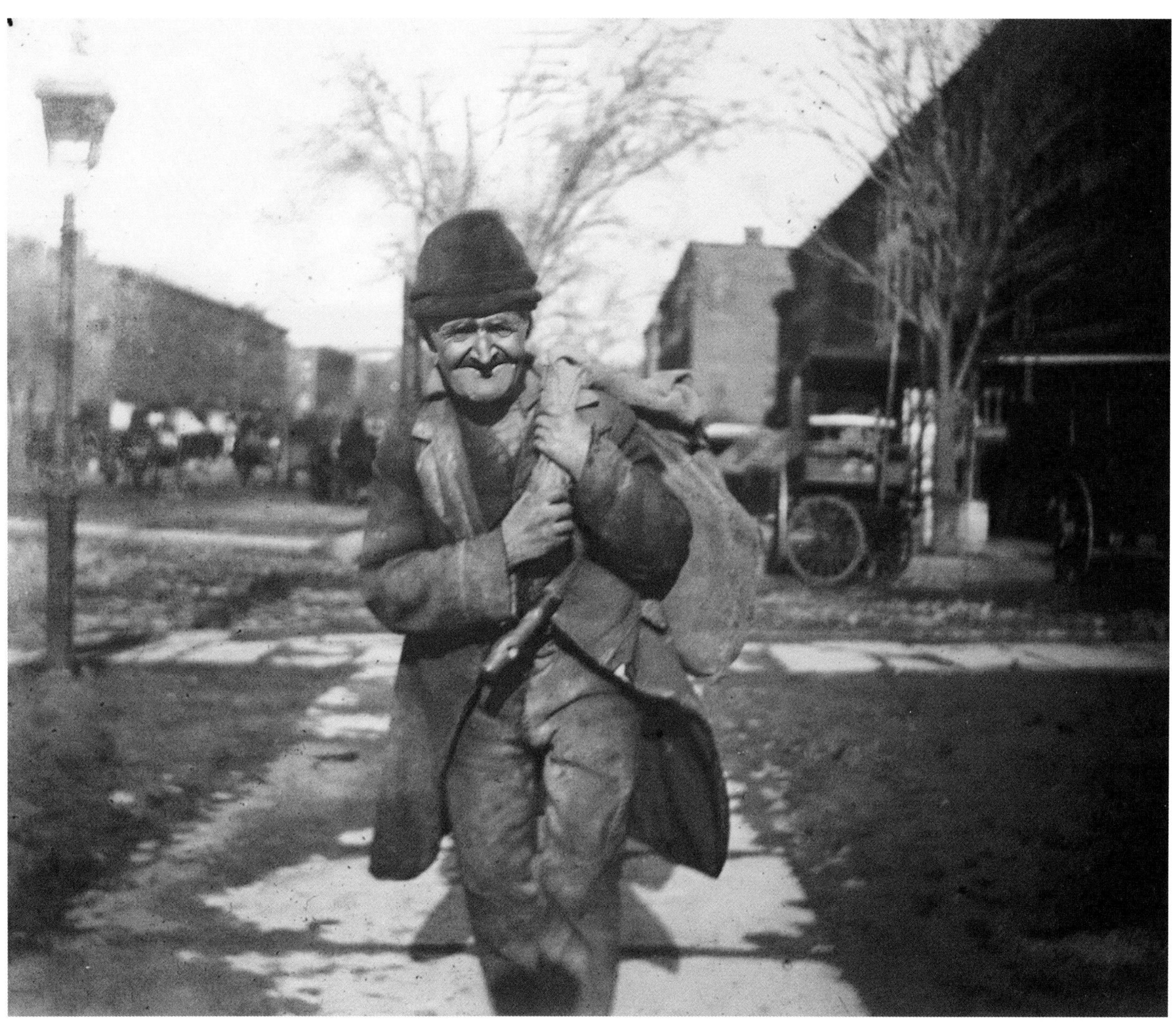

Another image of Brooklyn's rag-picker, Brooklyn, 1870s. These colorful Victorian street types, who went about on foot with sacks slung over their shoulders, hobo-like, often went by the name "ragpicker," or "rag-and-bone man." Other sobriquets were, old-clothesman, junkman, junk dealer, bone-grubber, bone-picker, chiffonnier, rag-gatherer, bag board, and totter. It was a frugal era and almost everything could be reused or repurposed, providing something of a livelihood for the less fortunate. Scraps of cloth could be turned into paper, broken glass melted down and reused. Even cat fur was sought after and could be turned into a fashionable coat or some accessory. More prosperous ragmen might have a cart pulled by a donkey or a dog. It's worth noting that Brainerd's "rag-picker" is among his very few posed portraits. He might even have been a friend. George Bradford Brainerd Photograph Collection, Brooklyn Public Library/Center for Brooklyn History.

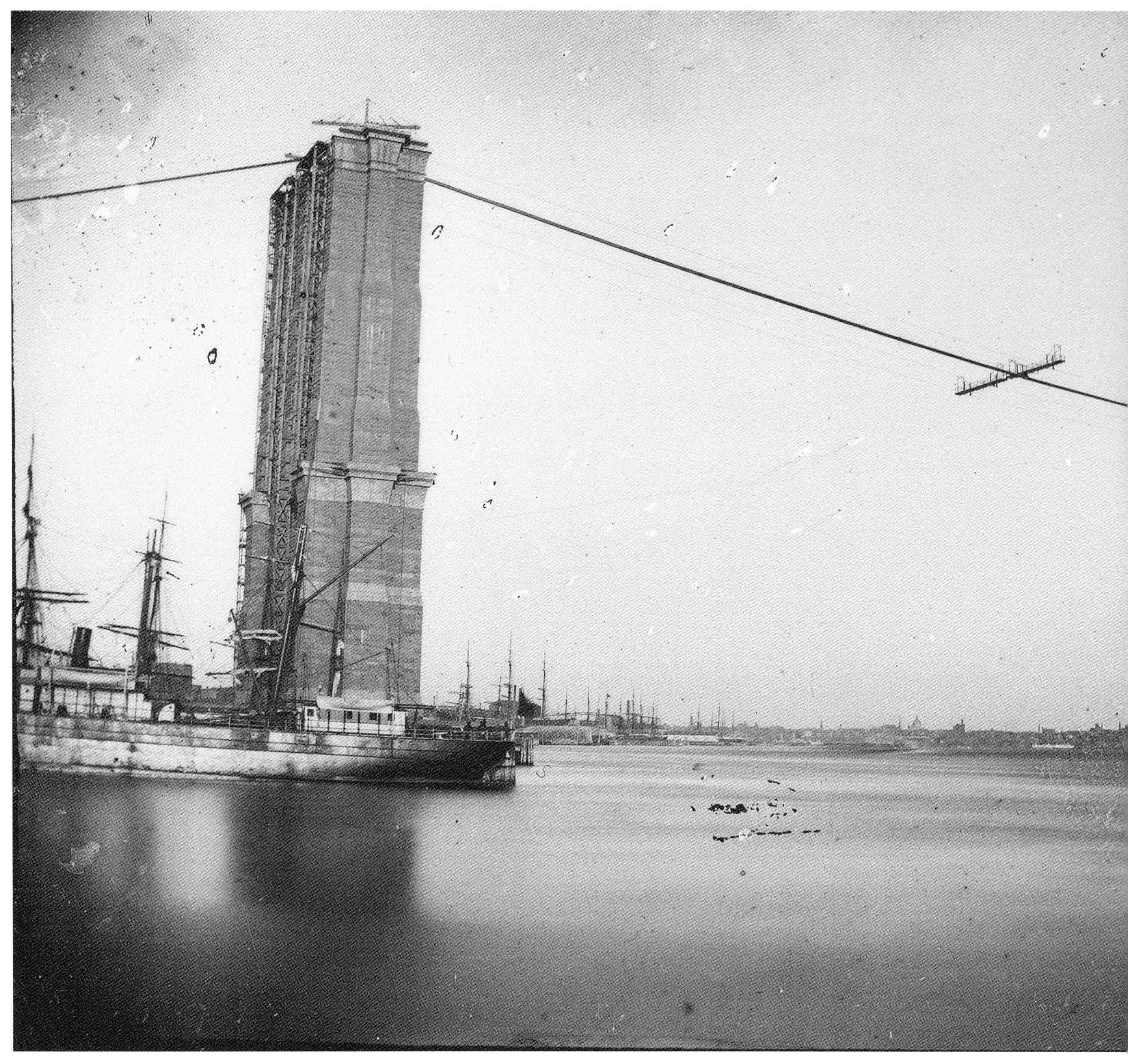

Brooklyn Bridge, 1876. One of Brainerd's most iconic images recording early construction on the Brooklyn Bridge, masterwork of engineers John Agustus and Washington Roebling. The photograph was taken just as the first steel cables, whose complex weaving process had been devised by John Roebling, were being strung from tower to tower across the East River—a milestone celebrated in all the newspapers. The bridge officially opened on May 24, 1883, with Emily Warren Roebling, wife of Washington Roebling and a key figure in the great bridge's history, taking the first ride across the great span, apparently clutching a rooster, symbol of victory. George Bradford Brainerd Photograph Collection, Brooklyn Public Library/Center for Brooklyn History.

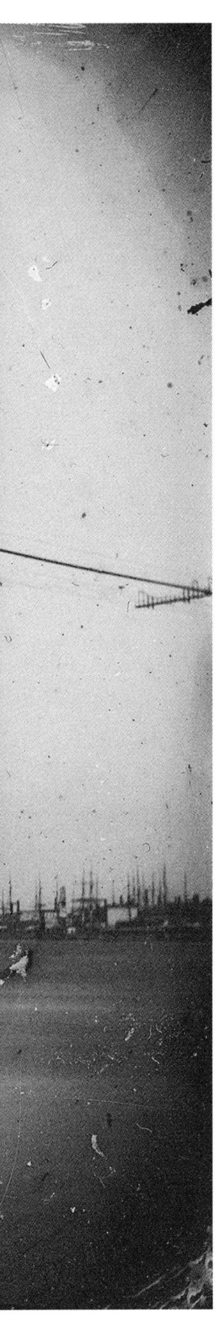

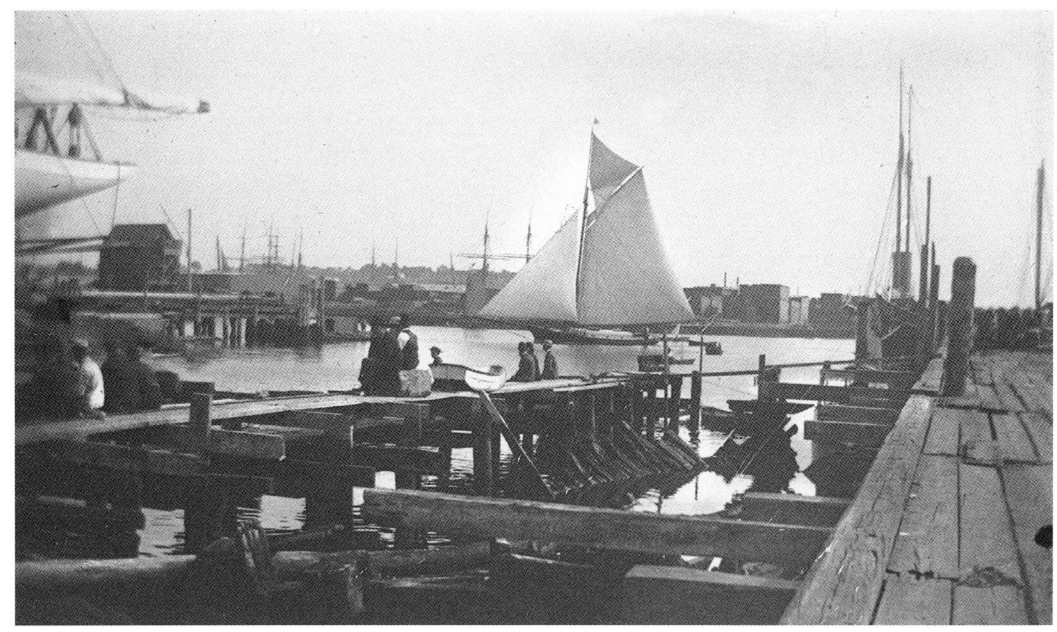

On the Waterfront

The Atlantic Docks in Brooklyn's Red Hook district were among Brainerd's most cherished subjects, probably because he spent so much time there as deputy water purveyor. The docks themselves were the brainchild of Colonel Daniel Richards, who in 1839 began to develop the Brooklyn harbor shoreline by erecting a contained set of docks, warehouses, and a basin for deep water ships. Later, William Beard and two brothers, Jeremiah P. Robinson and George Robinson, began work on a second 100-acre basin named the "Erie," as it was initially designed to process wheat coming downriver on barges and canal boats from the Erie Canal. While grain was a principal cargo, lumber, iron, coffee, raw cotton, leather, foodstuffs, and countless other products also arrived on the docks, which employed as many as 10,000 men.

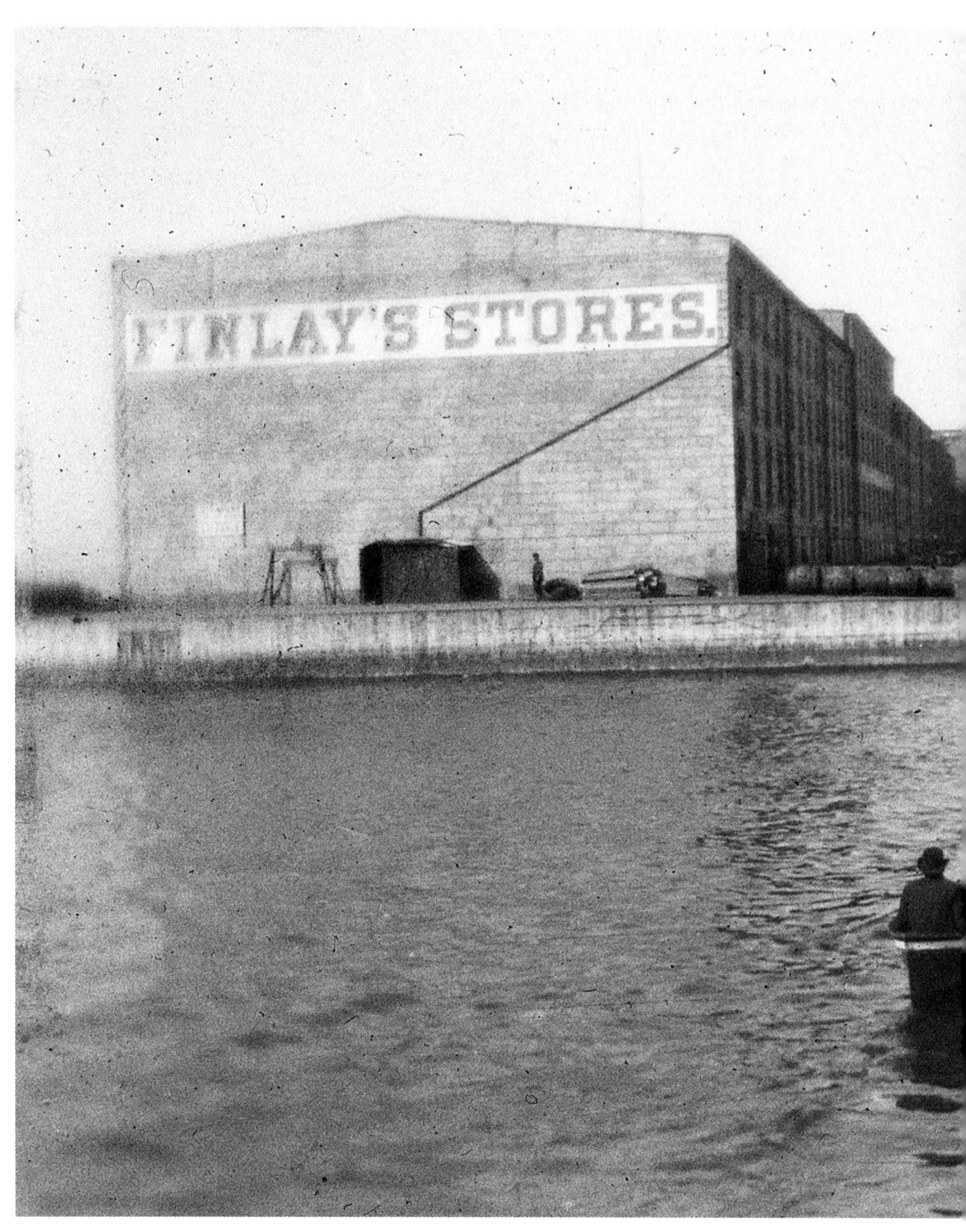

The Atlantic Docks —*Brooklyn Daily Eagle,* 1870

66 Twenty years ago, the southernmost portion of the 12th ward of this city, between Red Hook Point and the Gowanus Canal, was a complete waste of unproductive marsh lands and mud flats submerged at high tide and only partially visible at low tide. The Atlantic Docks, located in the northern section of the ward, was in a crude stage of construction and accorded and but trifling commercial patronage, and it's continued contiguous territory contained but few

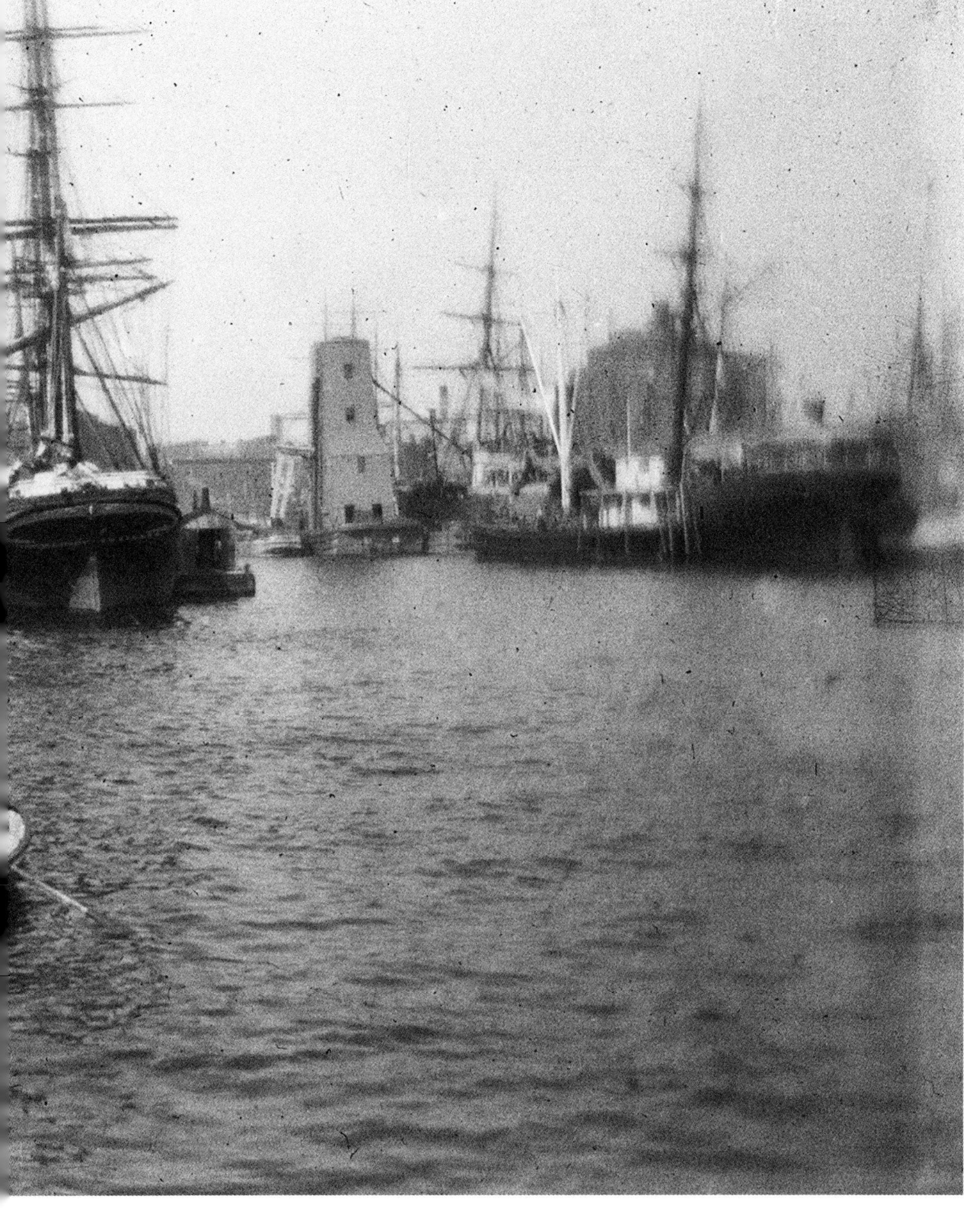

Atlantic Docks, Brooklyn, 1870s. In this sweeping image of two men in a rowing skiff heading across the great Erie Basin, we get a sense of the vastness of the harbor, which was usually crowded with ships of all types, from puffing steam tugs to huge four-masted clippers that would sail all the way to China. George Bradford Brainerd Photograph Collection, Brooklyn Public Library/ Center for Brooklyn History.

buildings and were sparsely populated. In consequence of the exposed position of the shore from the Atlantic Basin to the Gowanus Canal, a distance of nearly two miles, there was no accommodation for ships, and no vessel could have lain with safety beside a dock, even had any existed within those limits, except in the calmest weather; for with a fresh breeze from any point of the compass between northwest and southwest, sweeping a distance of eight or nine miles across the open bay, heavy waves came tumbling in upon the unprotected shore, with sufficient force to have seriously injured the strongest vessel in the merchant service."

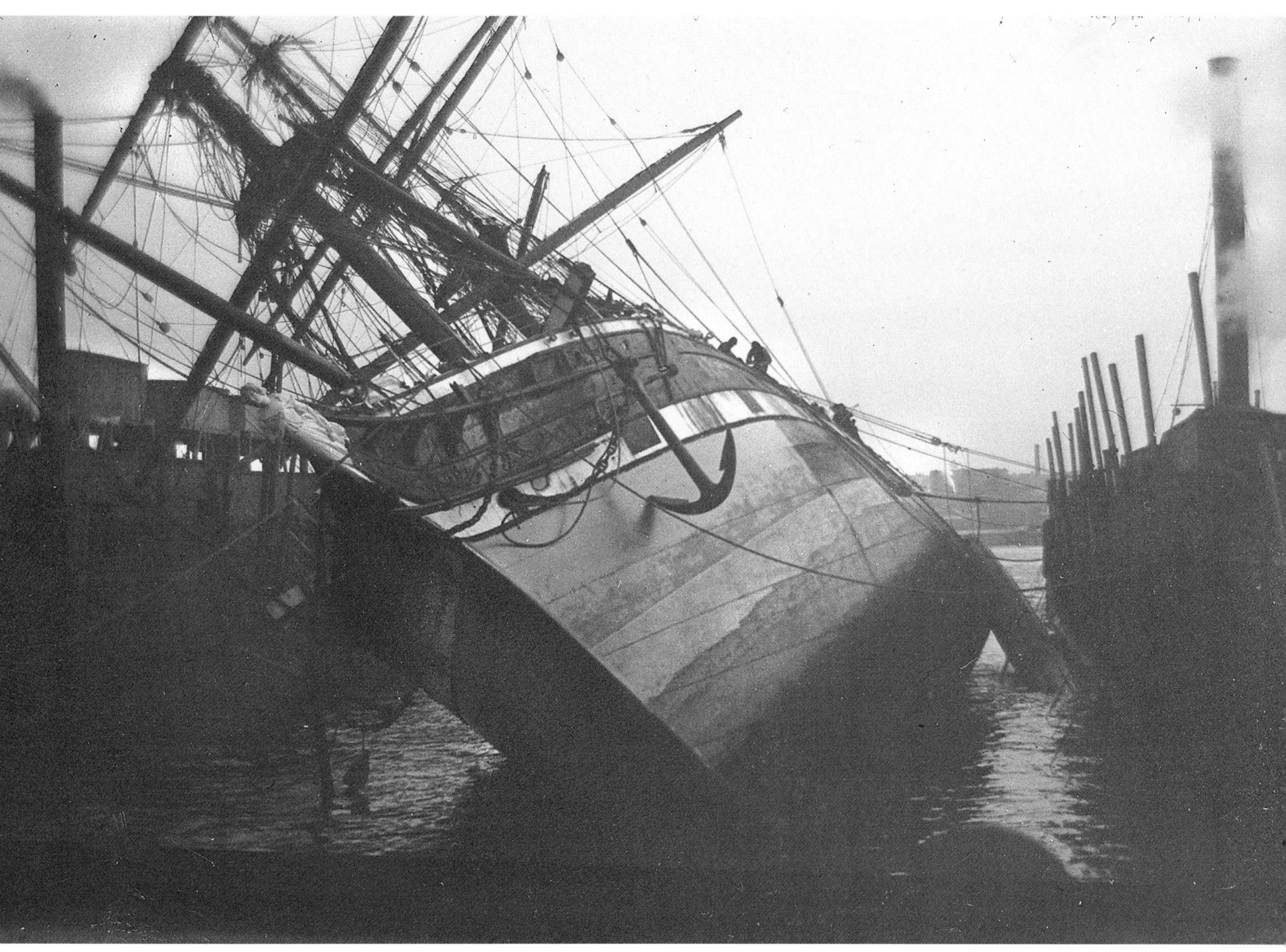

Vessel in Erie Basin Dry Dock, 1870s. The Erie Basin dry dock, completed in
1866, was built to handle some of the largest ships afloat, like the 360-foot,
3,000-ton steamer *Bristol*, flagship of the old Fall River Line, which was hauled
out of the water for repairs at Red Hook in the 1870s. It was a graving dock,
where ships are floated in and then the water is pumped out to allow work on
the hull. The dock contributed to making Red Hook the center of the shipping industry in New York and was part of Erie Basin's dry and shipping dock
infrastructure, the largest in the city. You get a sense of the immensity of the
vessel from the tiny figures seen at work on the hull. George Bradford Brainerd
Photograph Collection, Brooklyn Public Library/Center for Brooklyn History.

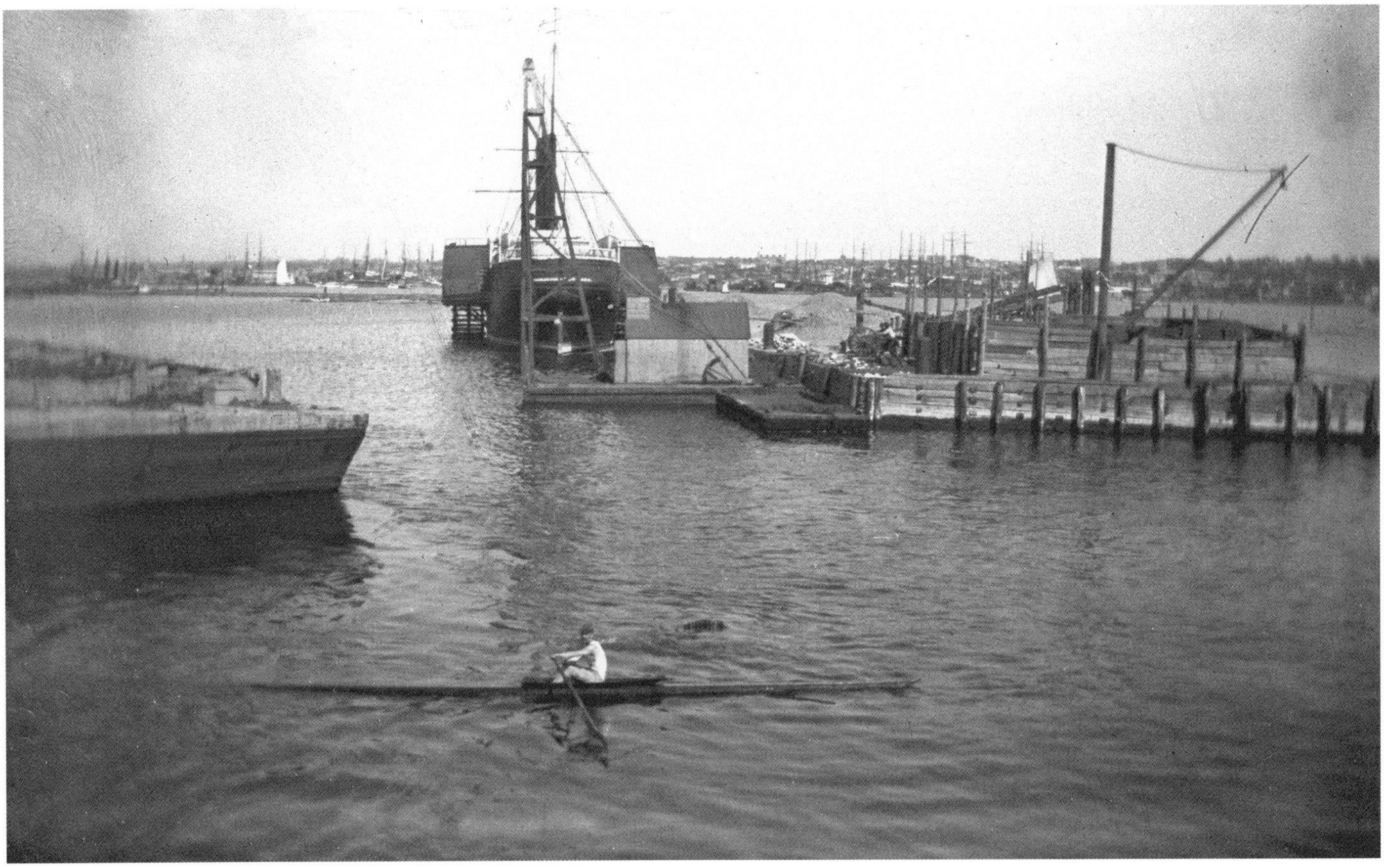

Erie Basin Boathouse, 1870s. In an image reminiscent of the American realist painter Thomas Eakins (1844–1916), Brainerd captures a rower out for an early morning run in Red Hook's Erie Basin. Brainerd's photo comes just a few years after Eakins produced his famous series of rowers on the Schuylkill River in Philadelphia. George Bradford Brainerd Photograph Collection, Brooklyn Public Library/Center for Brooklyn History.

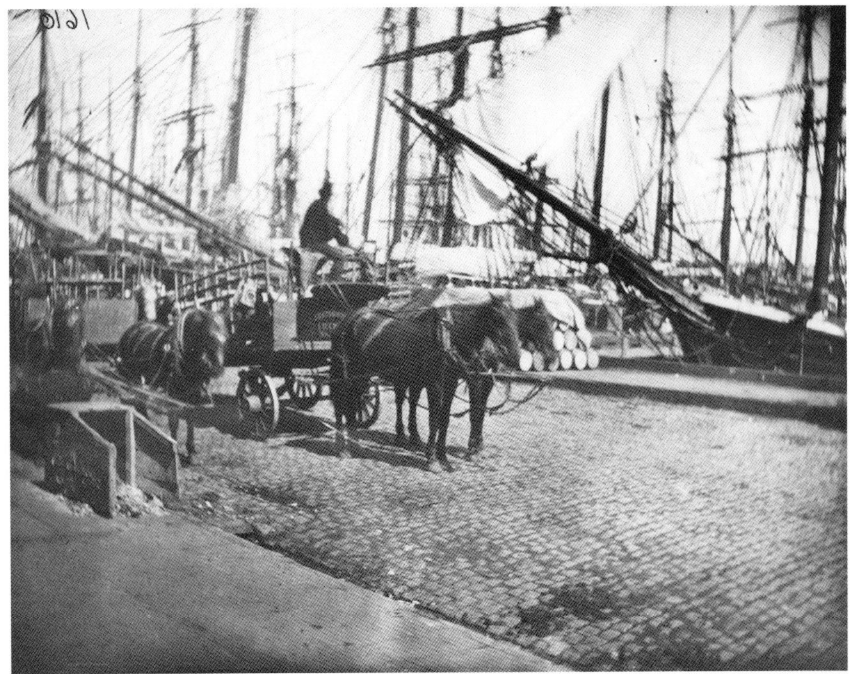

South Street, Manhattan, 1875. In this picture of clipper ships tied up at New York's South Street, with bowsprits jutting over the quay, it's evident how vessels on the New York side were compelled to anchor perpendicular to dock, which, according to Brooklyn dockworkers, made the loading and unloading of cargo more cumbersome. The docks at Red Hook, meanwhile, had been designed to allow ships to lay parallel to the wharf, which speeded up dock work. George Bradford Brainerd Photograph Collection, Brooklyn Public Library/Center for Brooklyn History.

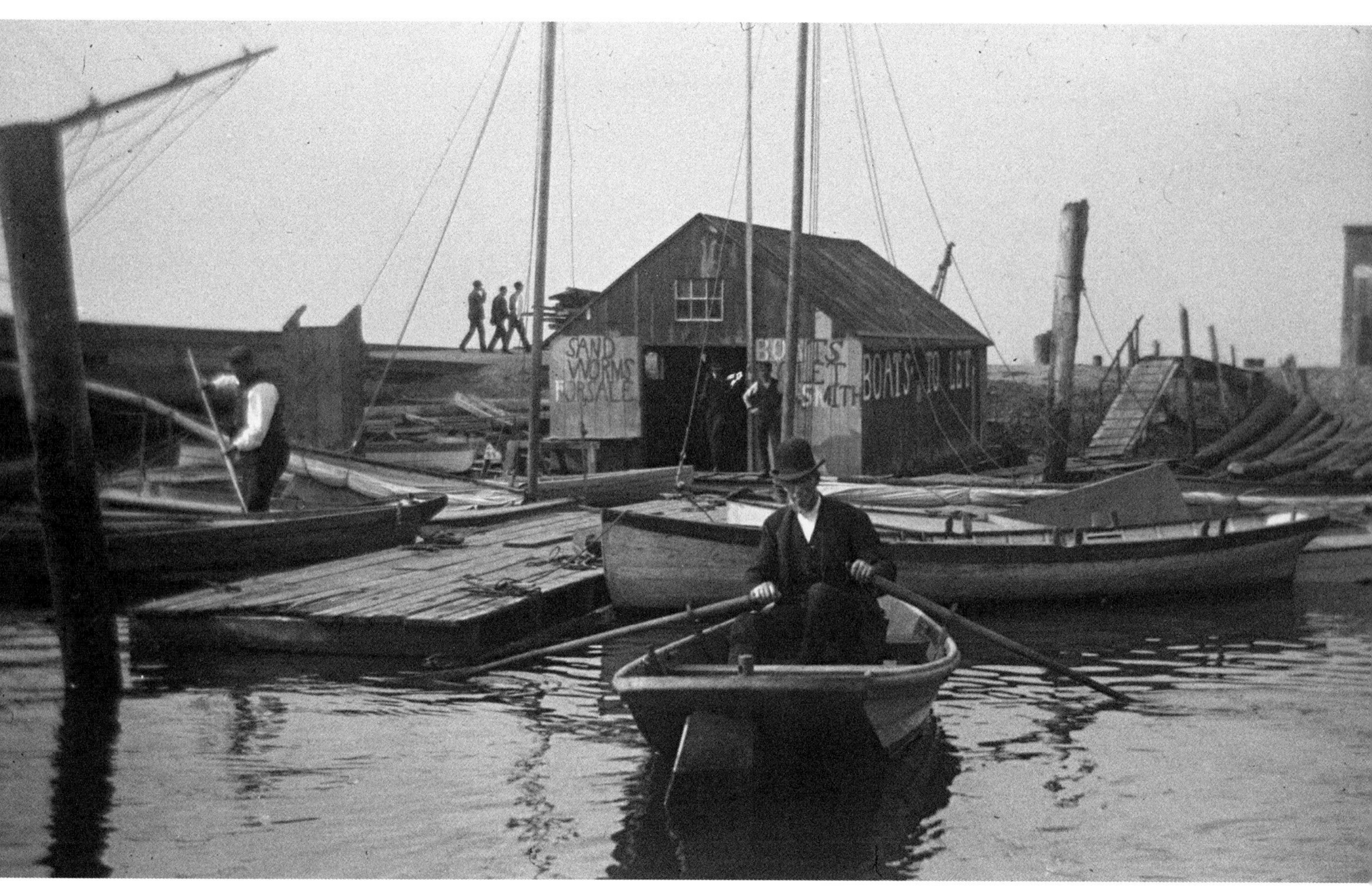

Above and right, Erie Basin Boathouse, 1870s. It wasn't all work at the Atlantic Docks, which were also a locus of fun for Brooklynites, who rented rowboats and sailboats and could also purchase bait for fishing. In the late 19th century, floating baths were built along the Brooklyn waterfront, which were hugely popular with the poor, allowing the less privileged a place in which to cool off, play, and relax. The authorities, however, usually limited the stay to only 20 minutes, enough time to get clean, not splash around. Still, boys found a way to skirt the rules, sneaking from one establishment to the next. George Bradford Brainerd Photograph Collection, Brooklyn Public Library/Center for Brooklyn History.

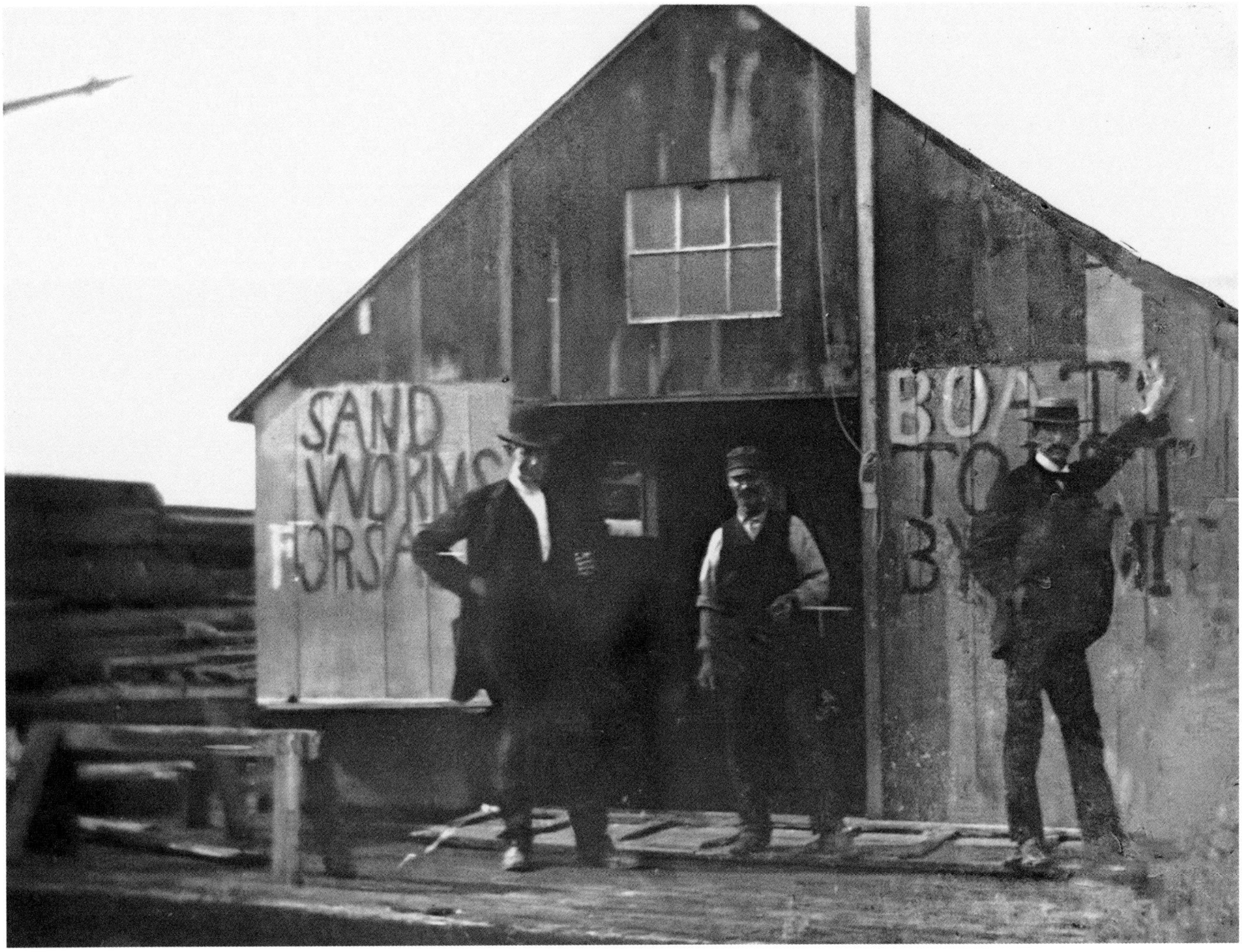

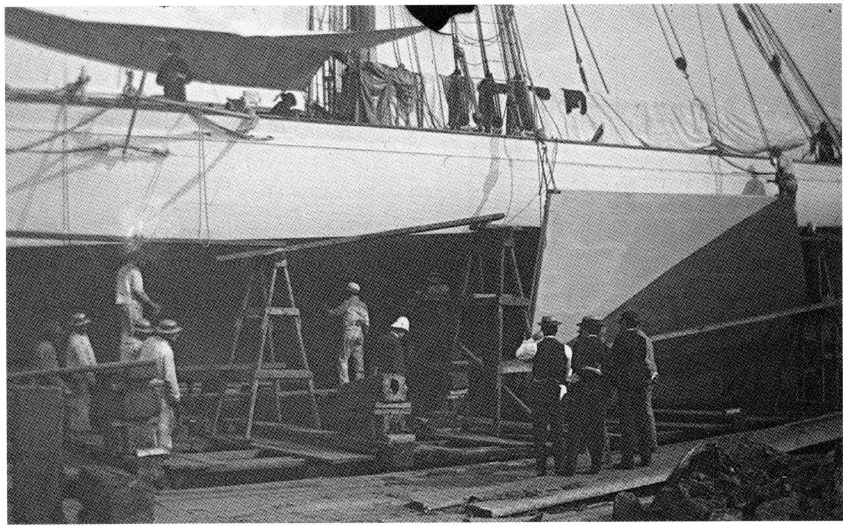

Left, sailing yacht, *Mayflower,* 1880s. The docks at Red Hook also handled pleasure craft like the glorious America's Cup sailing yacht *Mayflower,* which is pictured here getting some repairs to her hull. Designed by Edward "Ned" Burgess, *Mayflower* was the second America's Cup Defender, launched in 1886 from the yard of George Lawley & Son. Built of white oak and hard pine, the 106-foot vessel was owned by the railroad tycoon and yachtsman General Charles Jackson Paine of Boston, a former Civil War commander. George Bradford Brainerd Photograph Collection, Brooklyn Public Library/Center for Brooklyn History.

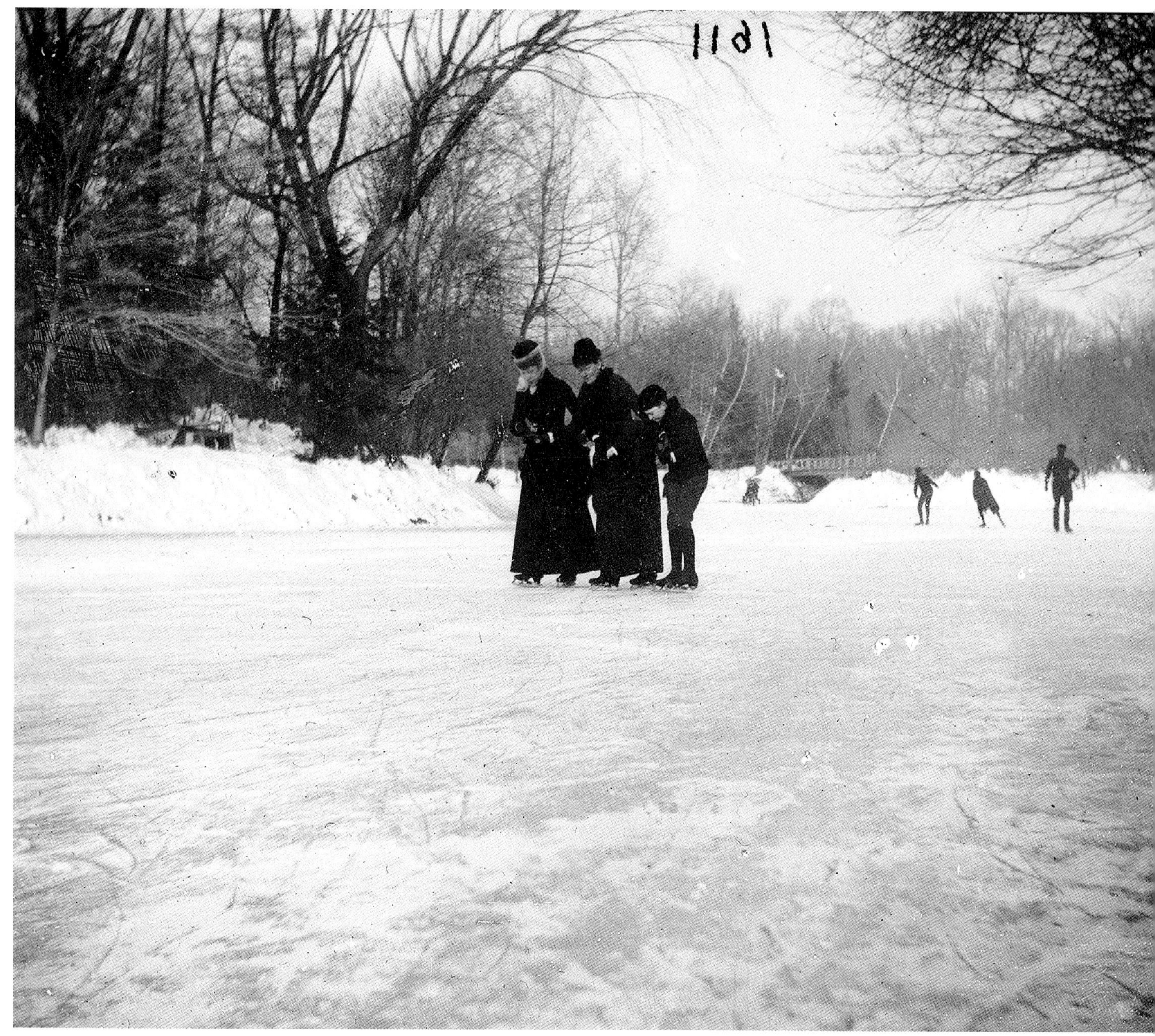

A delightful candid image of skaters in Brooklyn's Prospect Park. Is that a smile we detect from the lady in the center being helped along by family or friends? Skating, like tennis, was one of the post–Civil War amusements that permitted men and women to interact in a more relaxed manner, a change reflected in Brainerd's later photographs. George Bradford Brainerd Photograph Collection, Brooklyn Public Library/Center for Brooklyn History.

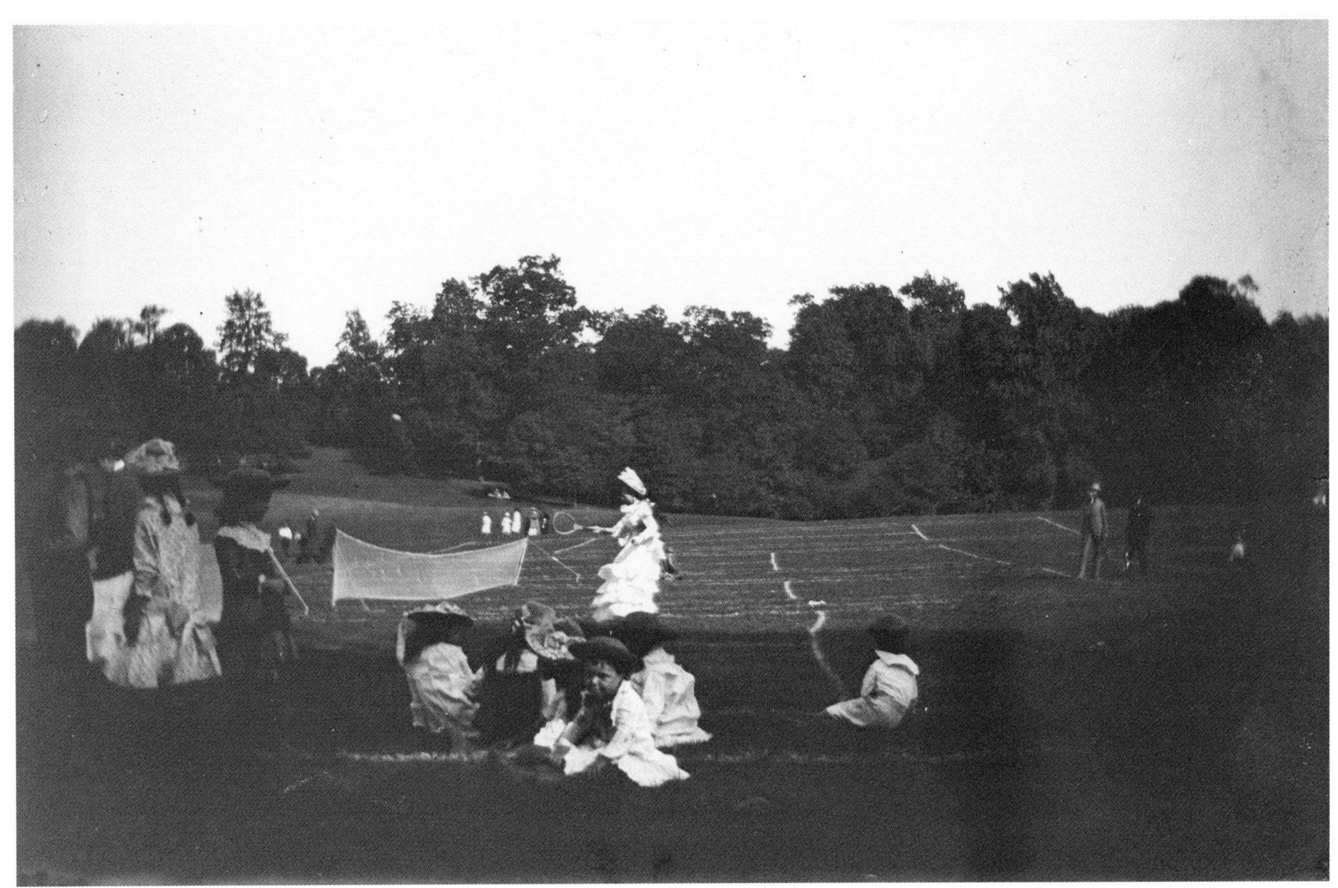

Victorians at Play

Lawn Tennis in Prospect Park, 1870s. A rare depiction of Gilded Age glamour by Brainerd, this lovely image of women playing lawn tennis in Prospect Park, all sporting the latest fashions, may be among the earliest photographs of the new sport, just imported from England. George Bradford Brainerd Photograph Collection, Brooklyn Public Library/ Center for Brooklyn History.

In the early 1850s, a hippopotamus named Obaysch became the talk of Victorian London, spawning a trade in hippo-related memorabilia and even a dance known as the Hippopotamus Polka. Obaysch, the first hippopotamus seen in Great Britain since Roman times, had been captured in 1849, when quite young, on the banks of the White Nile, and was sent over to England by the Pasha of Egypt as a present to Queen Victoria. He arrived at Southampton on May 25, 1850, and on the evening of the same day "was safely housed in an apartment prepared for him at the Zoological Gardens where he has ever since become an object

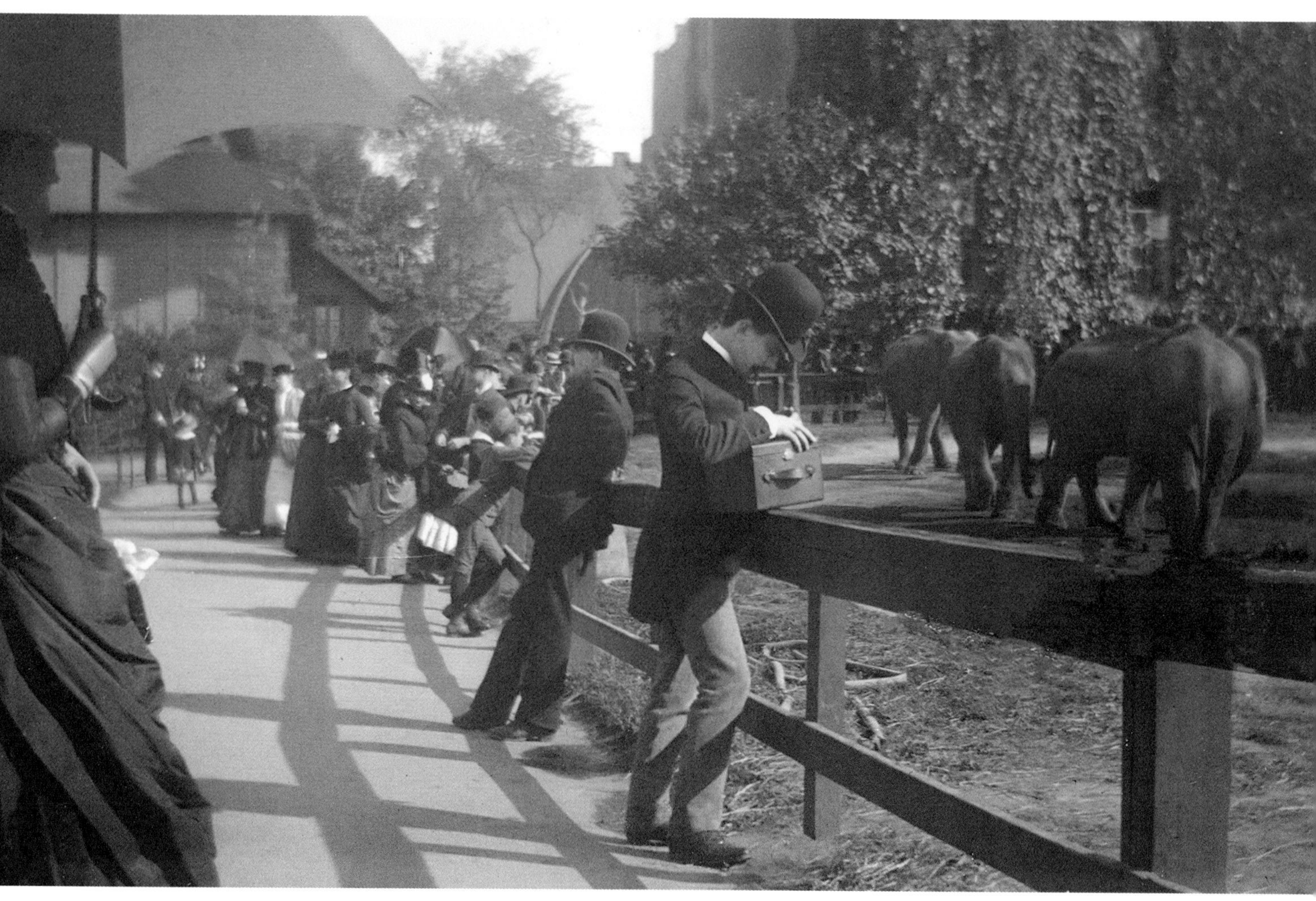

of great attraction." Dozens of articles were written about Obaysch, whom the *London Times* described as, "playful as a Newfoundland puppy." But what really sparked interest in the animal was a photograph, a stereographic slide, showing the enormous creature lounging contentedly in his cage as crowds stared wide-eyed through the bars. This iconic image was snapped in 1852 by a pioneering amateur photographer, the Count de Montizon, who would note that the picture had been taken by "instantaneous exposure." As far as we know, Montizon's was the very first "snapshot" of a zoo animal, but it certainly was not the last.

Zoological gardens, known as "menageries," were just one of the many outdoor amusements available to city

Central Park Zoo, 1885. The painter Edgar Degas was known for his keen interest in Japanese prints, with their startling asymmetrical compositions. But it was photography, more than anything, especially the "snapshot"—with its radical cropping of figures at the edge of the picture frame, and chance poses—that exerted the greatest influence on the French master. In this lovely photograph of a fashionable lady with her parasol shielding her from the harsh sun at Central Park Zoo, one can't help but be reminded of Degas or even Seurat's *A Sunday Afternoon on the Island of La Grande Jatte*. A

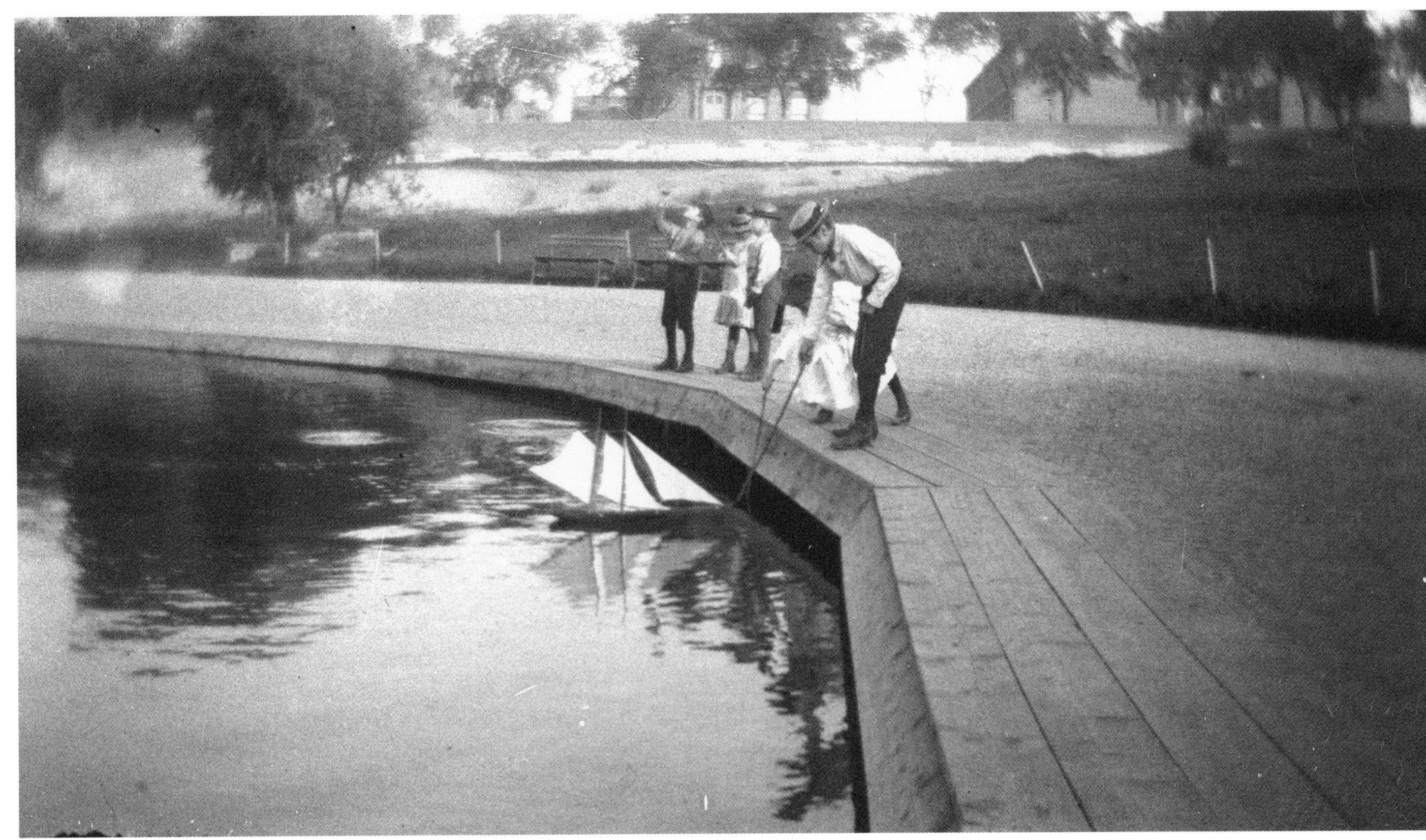

dwellers during the Victorian era. New York's Central Park and Brooklyn's Prospect Park played host to a variety of activities, including skating and sledding in the winter, along with baseball, croquet, and the fashionable new sport of lawn tennis, imported from England in 1880, in spring and summer. Boating in Central Park was also especially popular, with six boat landings built around the area known as the Lake. Then as now, the Lake covers 18 acres and was once a swamp that celebrated park designers Frederick Law Olmsted and Calvert Vaux laid out to hug the natural rock outcrops. Passenger boats were able to pick up and drop off passengers at the six landings, as well as the steps leading to the Bethesda Terrace & Fountain. The swan boats were among the more whimsical of conveyances, whisking parkgoers around the Lake in the Victorian era.

delightful touch is Brainerd's recording of a fellow "snap-shooter" aiming his apparatus toward the elephants. One wonders, though—is it the animals or the people who are on display?

Above, Central Park, 1870s. A decade before Impressionists like Seurat and Renoir were celebrating everyday life in la Belle Epoque, Brainerd was using cameras he built himself to capture such transient moments for eternity.

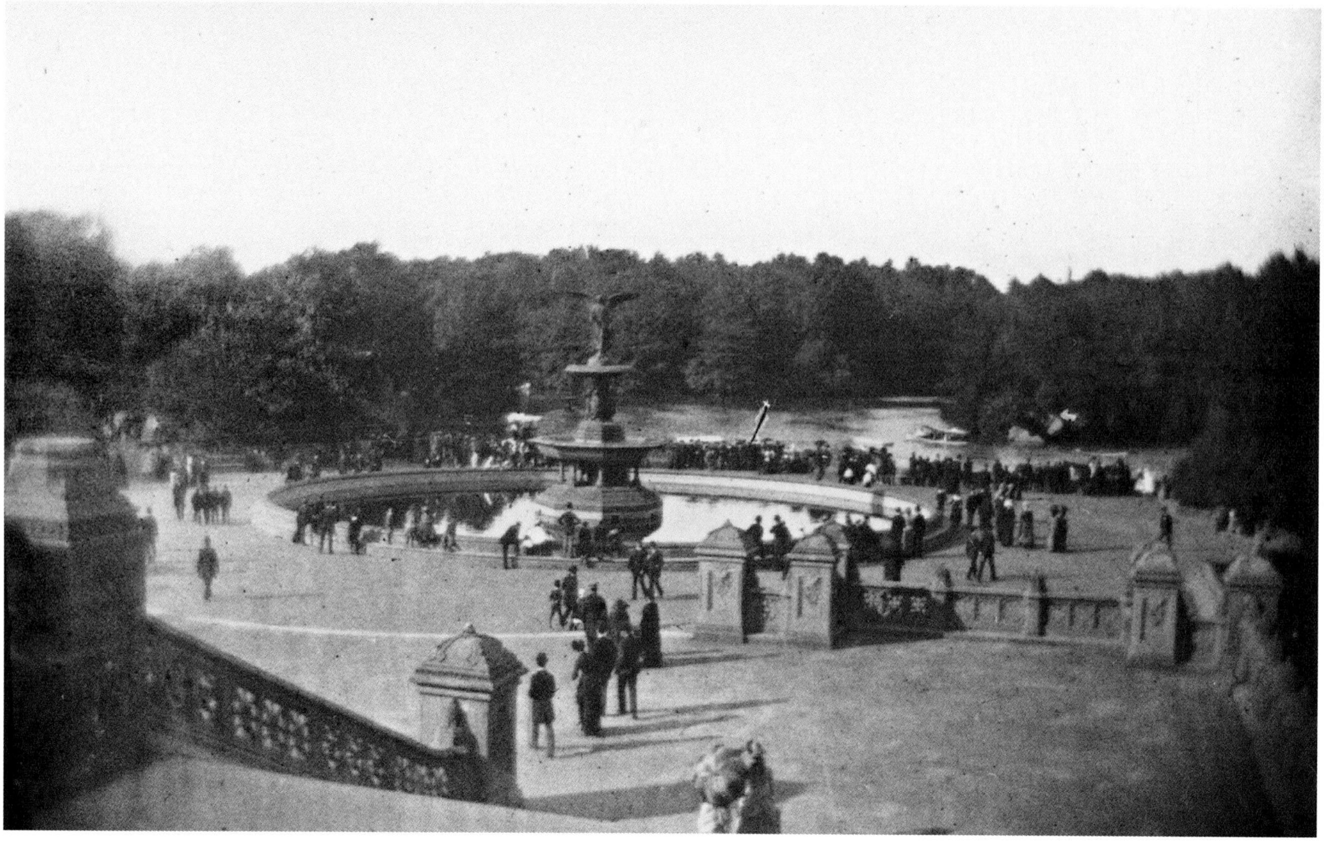

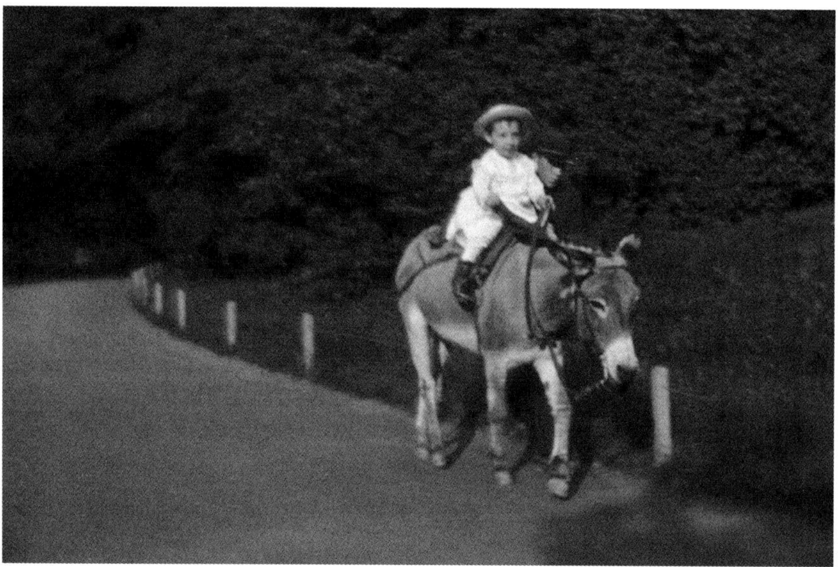

Central Park, 1870s. Bethesda Terrace and the Fountain in Central Park overlooking the Lake, was a favorite gathering place and Sunday promenade, where wealthy New Yorkers liked to congregate and show off their finery. Left, boy riding a donkey in the late 1870s. George Bradford Brainerd Photograph Collection, Brooklyn Public Library/Center for Brooklyn History.

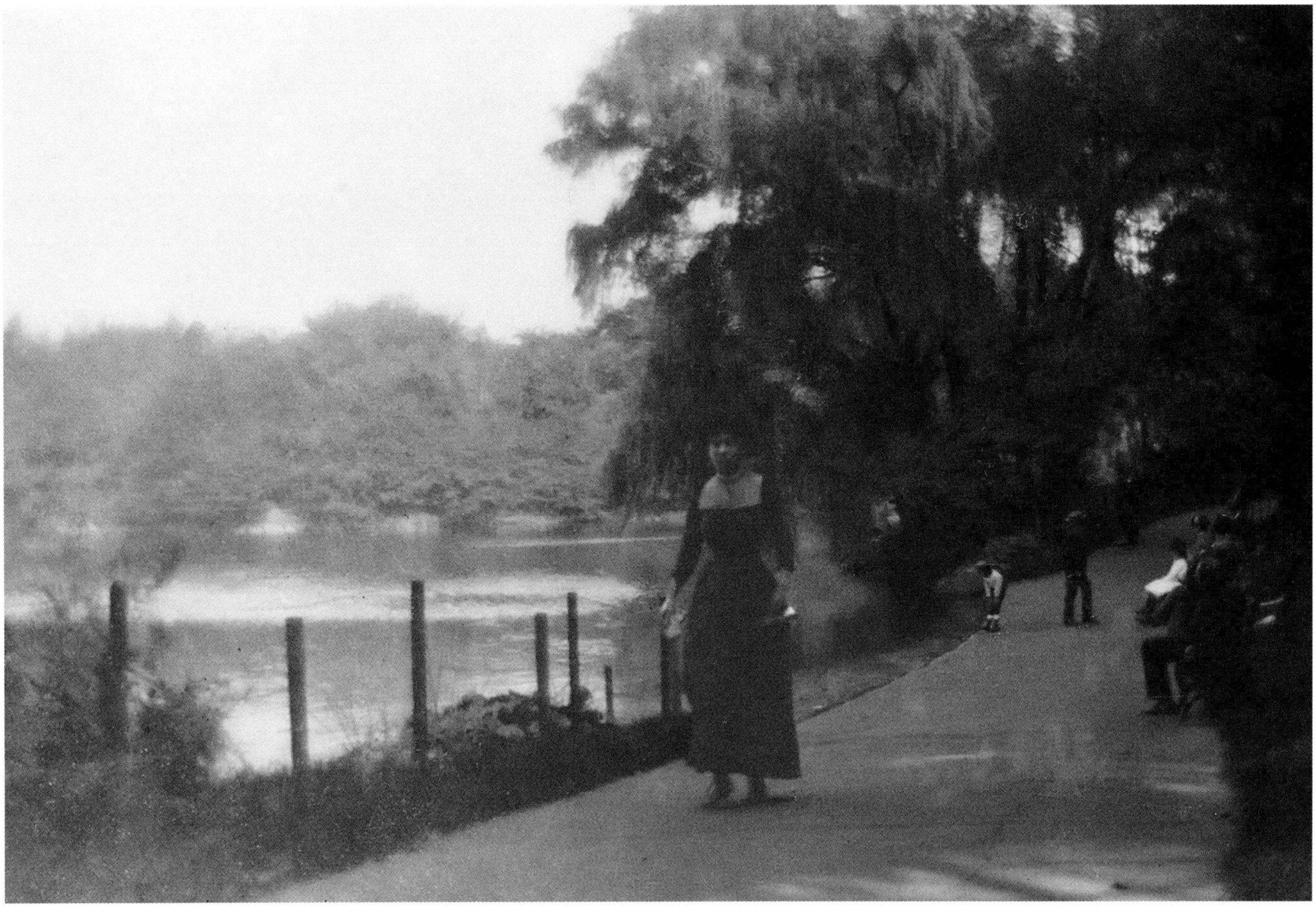

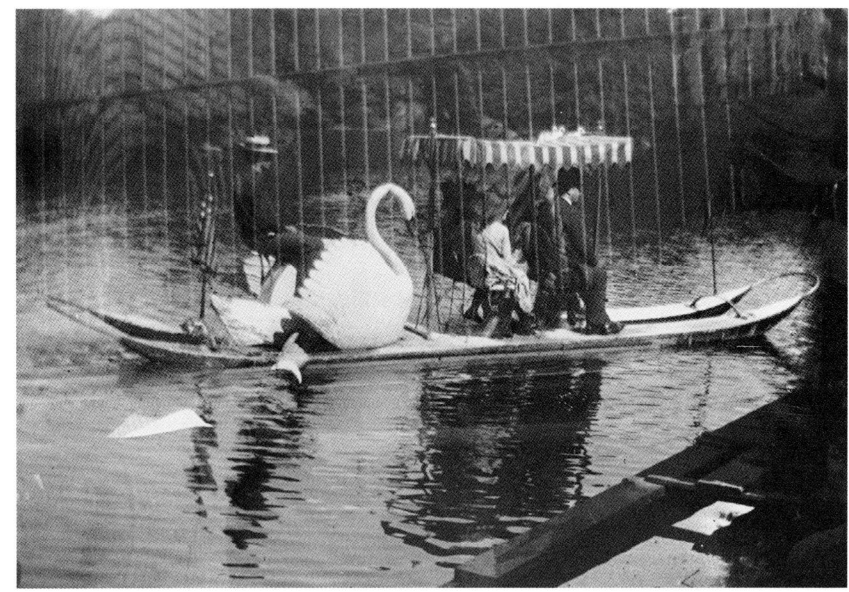

Central Park, 1870s. When Central Park was opened in the 1860s, there were six boat landings built around the area known as the Lake. The Lake, which still today covers 18 acres, was once a swamp that park designers Frederick Law Olmsted and Calvert Vaux laid out to hug the natural rock outcrops. Passenger boats were able to pick up and drop off passengers at the six landings, as well as the steps leading to the Bethesda Terrace & Fountain (at left). George Bradford Brainerd Photograph Collection, Brooklyn Public Library/Center for Brooklyn History.

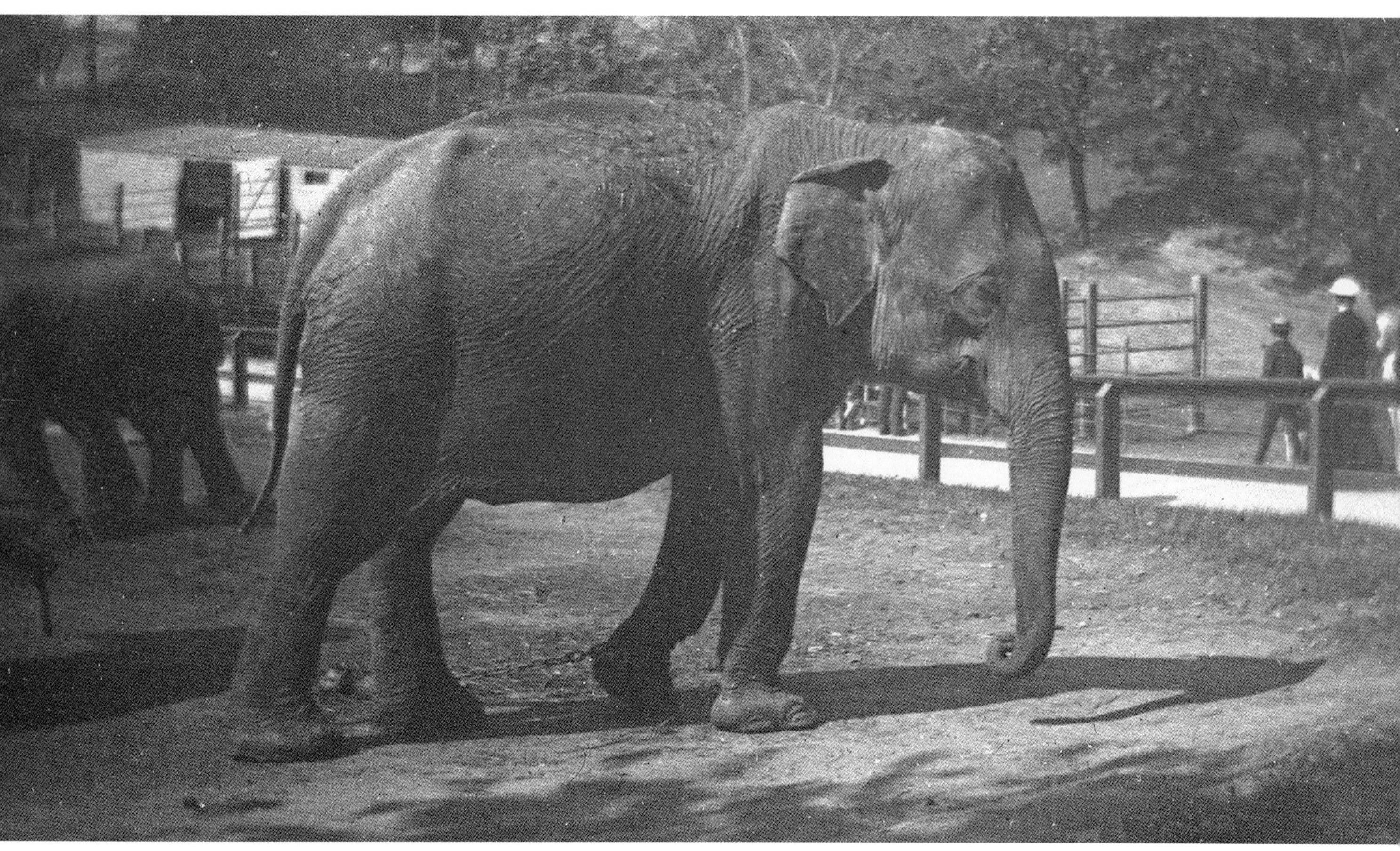

As for the Zoo itself, it's worth noting that Olmsted and Vaux had not included one in their original design, fearing the addition of various pens and animal enclosures would mar the glorious vistas they worked so hard to create. Their position, however, was overruled by the Tammany-controlled Park Commission, which, in the words of one commentator, saw a way that "public uses might be subordinated to private profit," allowing lucrative jobs and concessions to be awarded to political favorites. Though built upon Tammany graft, the Central Park Zoo proved immensely popular, with the number of visitors surging to more than 7,000 a day by 1873.

Elephant, Central Park Zoo, late 1870s. George Bradford Brainerd Photographic Collection, Brooklyn Public Library/Center for Brooklyn History.

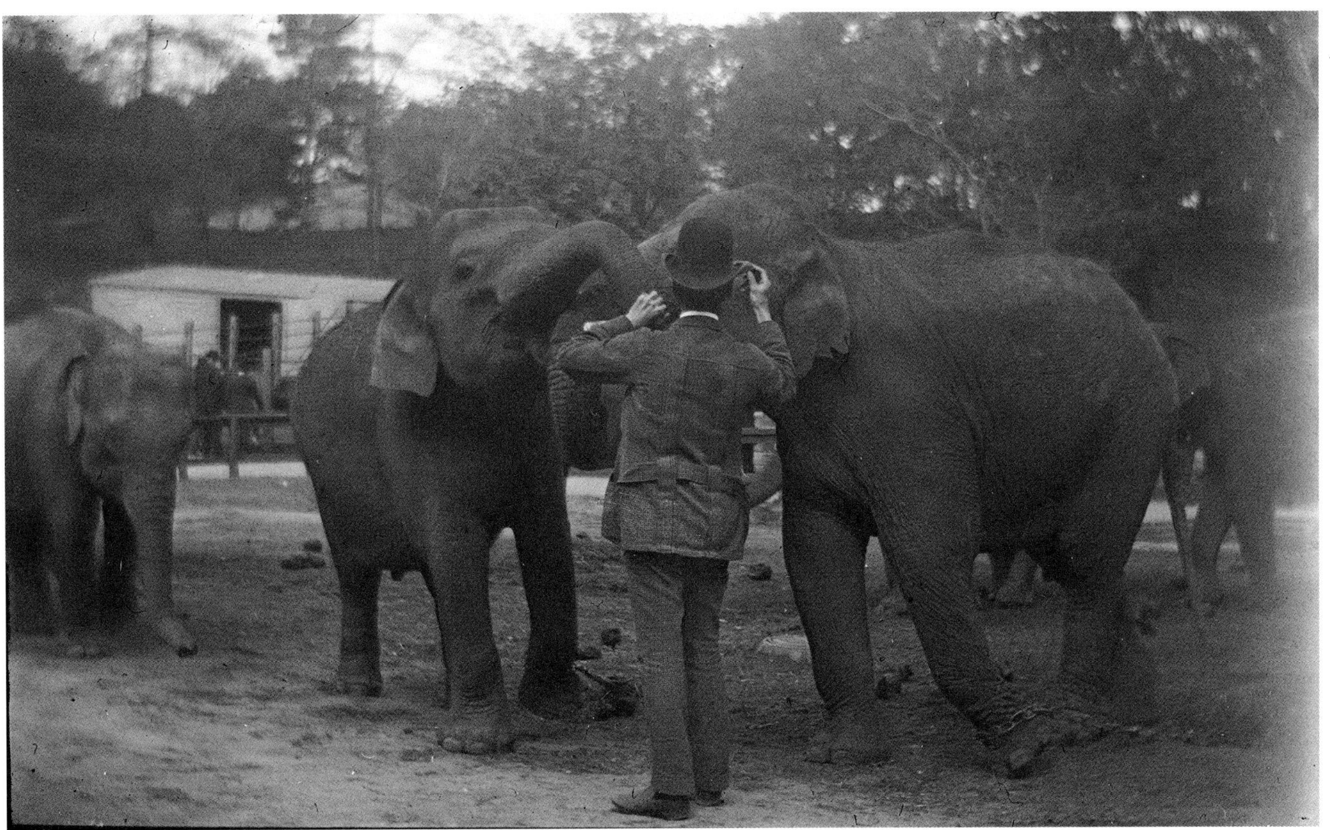

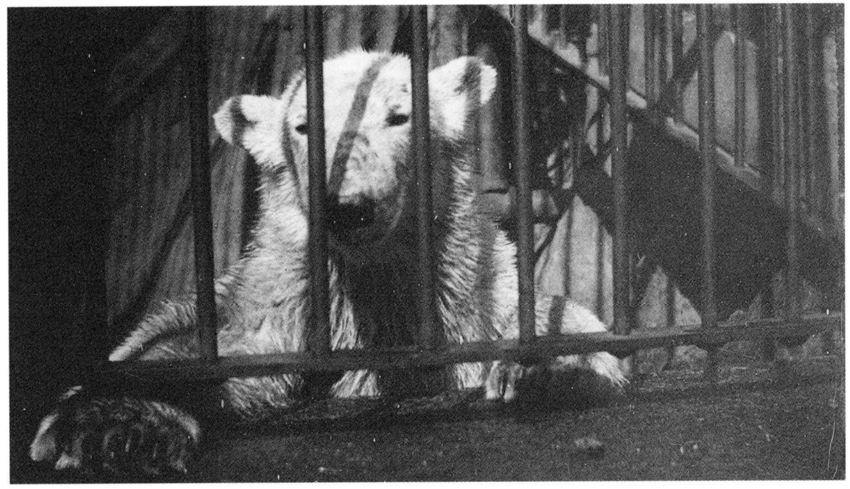

Elephants in Central Park, 1870s. George Bradford Brainerd Photograph Collection, Brooklyn Public Library/Center for Brooklyn History.

Polar bear, Central Park Zoo, 1870s. A rather pitiful image of this emblem of the North, the polar bear, whose sad fate seems to be on display in this Brainerd picture from around 1878. George Bradford Brainerd Photograph Collection, Brooklyn Public Library/Center for Brooklyn History.

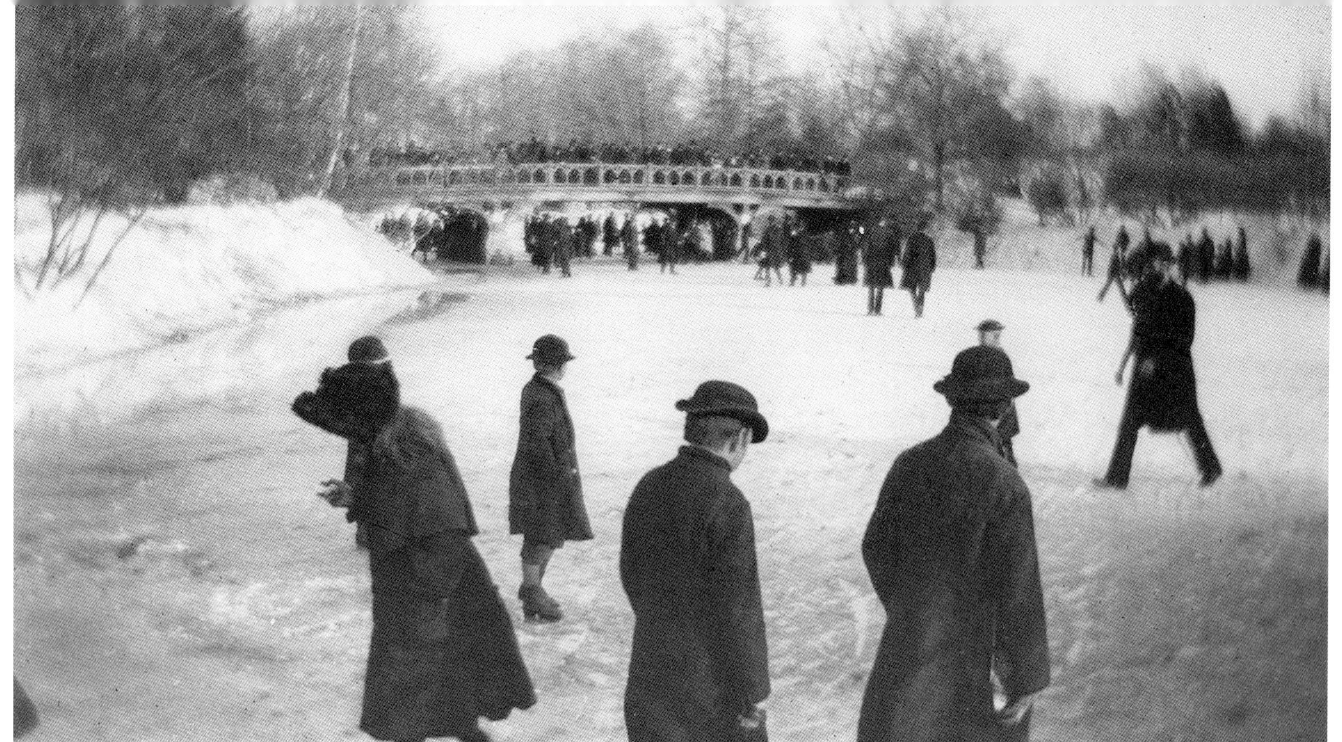

Winter Wonderland

The Skating Season —*Brooklyn Daily Eagle*, 1871

"The skating season was opened yesterday in downright earnest, and all the private ponds were well patronized. The long deprivation of this exhilarating sport made its devotees seize upon every available piece of ice with great avidity and cling to it until they had to leave the spot through exhaustion. All day the Union Pond [was located in Williamsburg] presented a very attractive appearance from the number of ladies skaters that were seen gliding hither and thither on their steel runners. In the evening the rush was kept up, and when the lamps in the pagoda and other houses were lighted, the pond presented a brilliant and picturesque appearance. The saloons too were crowded by lady visitors, the whole reminding one of the palmiest days of the Union [rink], when everybody and his sister frequented that famous resort."

Skating, Prospect Park Brooklyn, late 1870s. With his mobile cameras, George Brainerd produced some of the first pictures of the fashionable winter pastime of ice skating, which became a craze after the Civil War. Both Brooklyn's Prospect Park and New York's Central Park were hugely popular skating grounds, the city even employing a gentleman each day in the winter to check the thickness of the ice and hoist a flag in the air when it was safe to venture out. George Bradford Brainerd Photographic Collection, Brooklyn Public Library/Center for Brooklyn History.

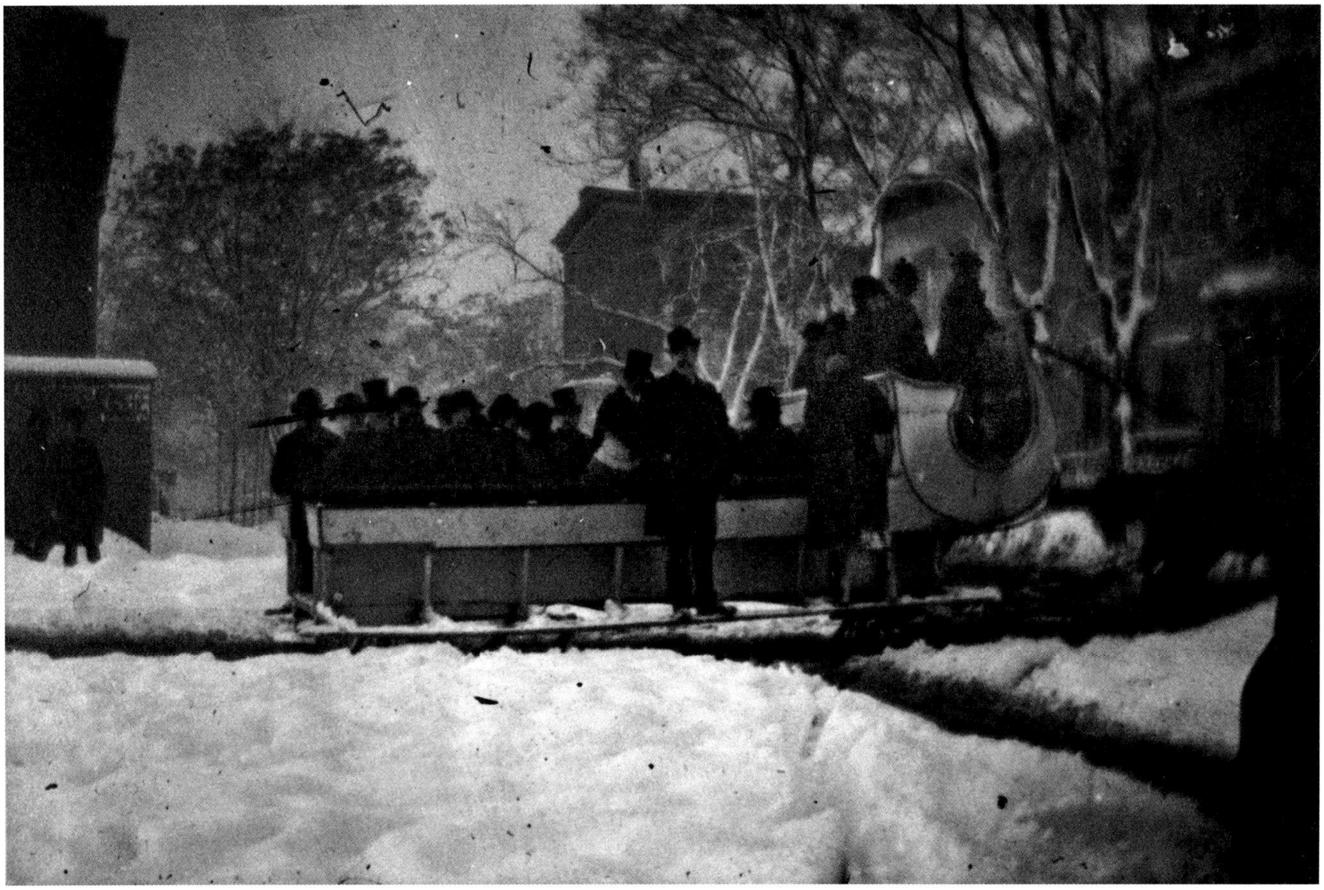

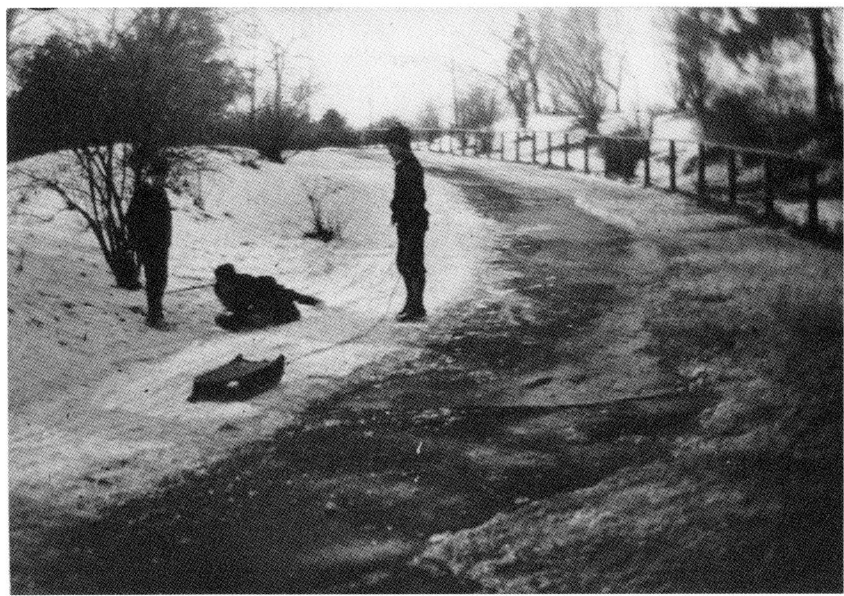

Winter pastimes like ice skating, sledding, and sleighing became favorite subjects for Brainerd, allowing the photographer to test out faster shutter speeds while capturing the timeless New England scenes beloved by Victorians. To capture motion, he adopted a modified version of the guillotine shutter, in which a vertical sliding plate, fitted behind the lens, was drawn by a string with rubber bands pulling it down again when the exposure had been made.

A dramatic high-angle view of skaters dotting the ice at Brooklyn's Prospect Park. Once again, Brainerd would have employed a handheld camera with faster dry plates to freeze motion, as he has here with a number of skaters caught mid-stride. The image dates to the late 1870s, making it a quite early example of action photography. George Bradford Brainerd Photographic Collection, Brooklyn Public Library/ Center for Brooklyn History.

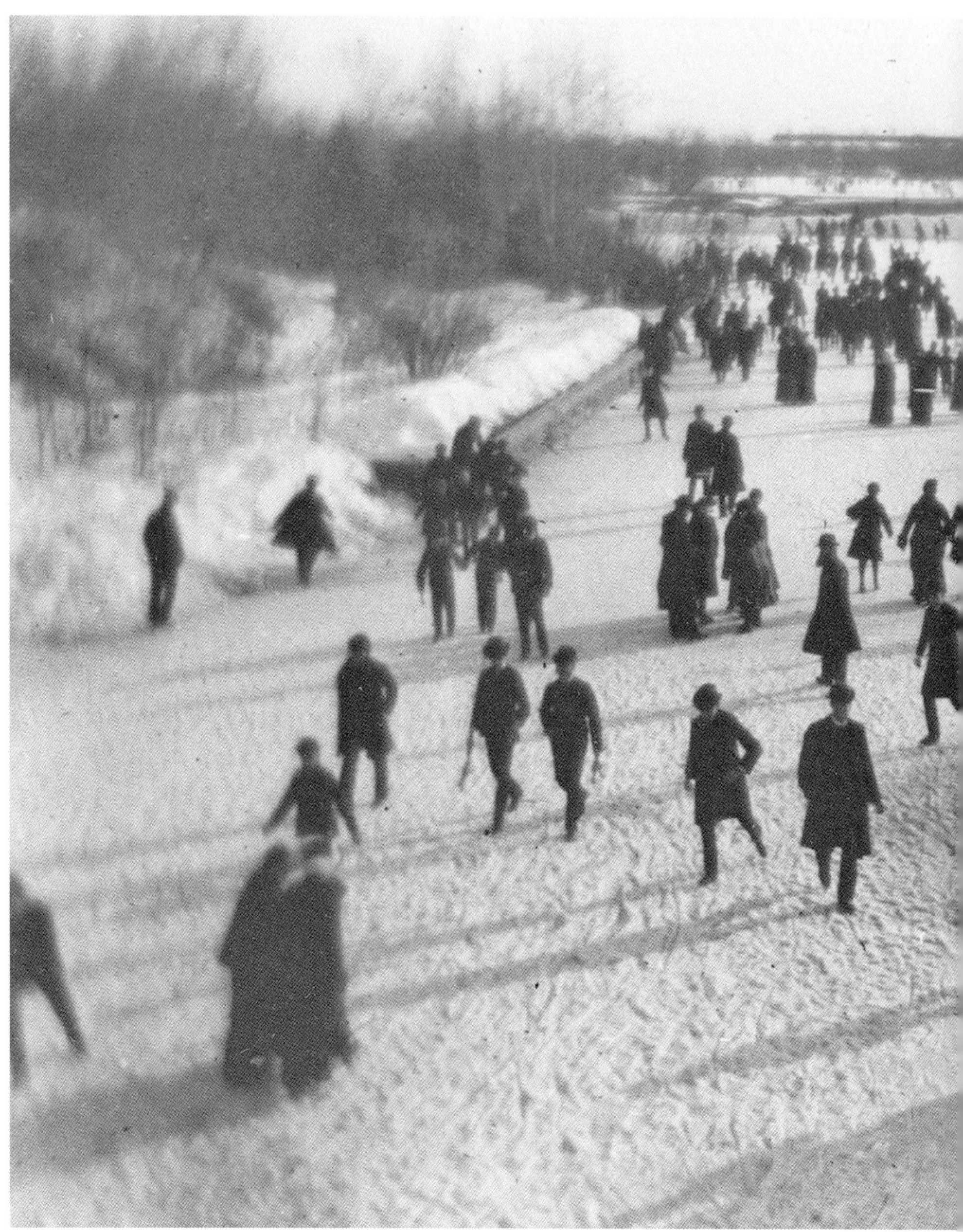

117

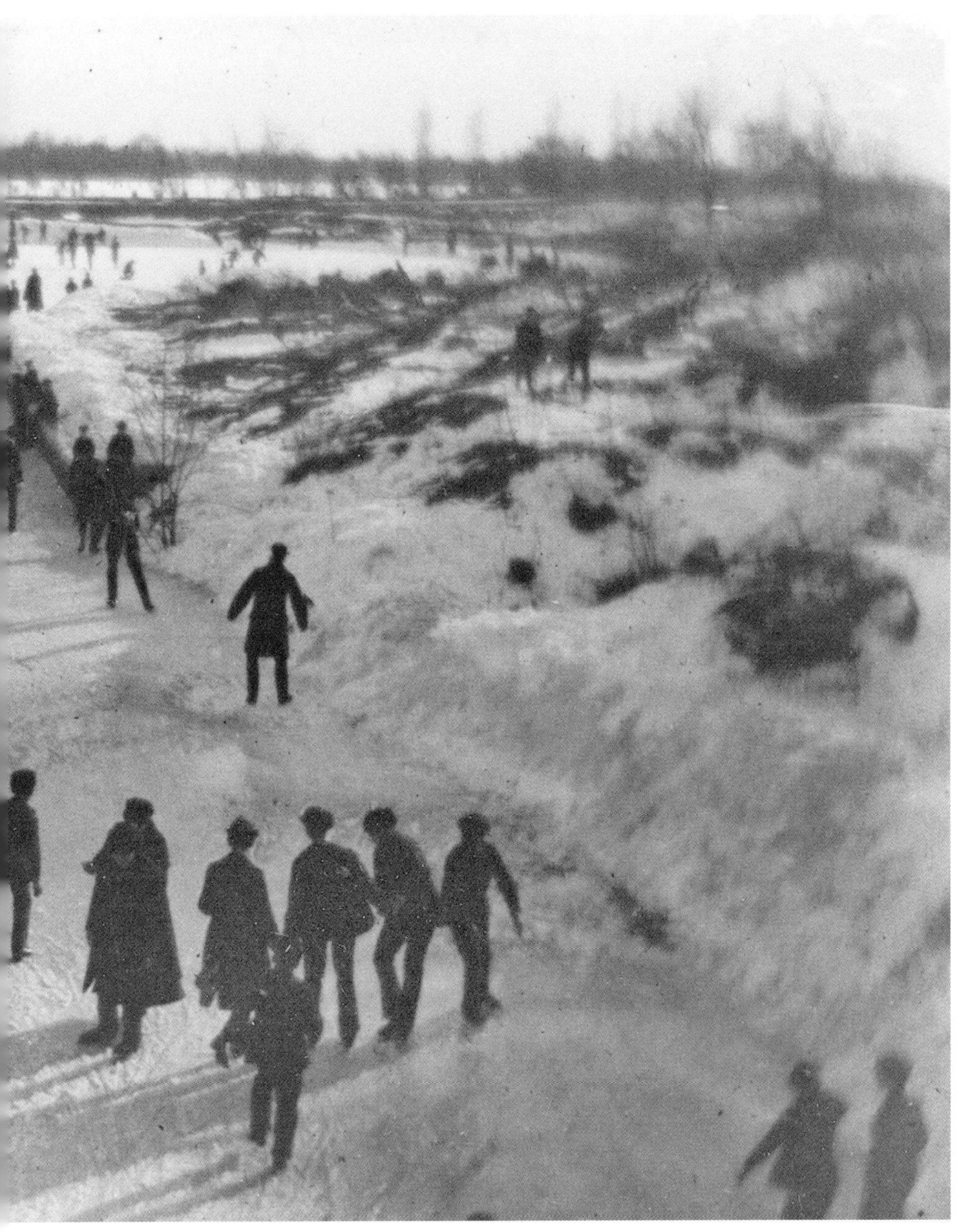

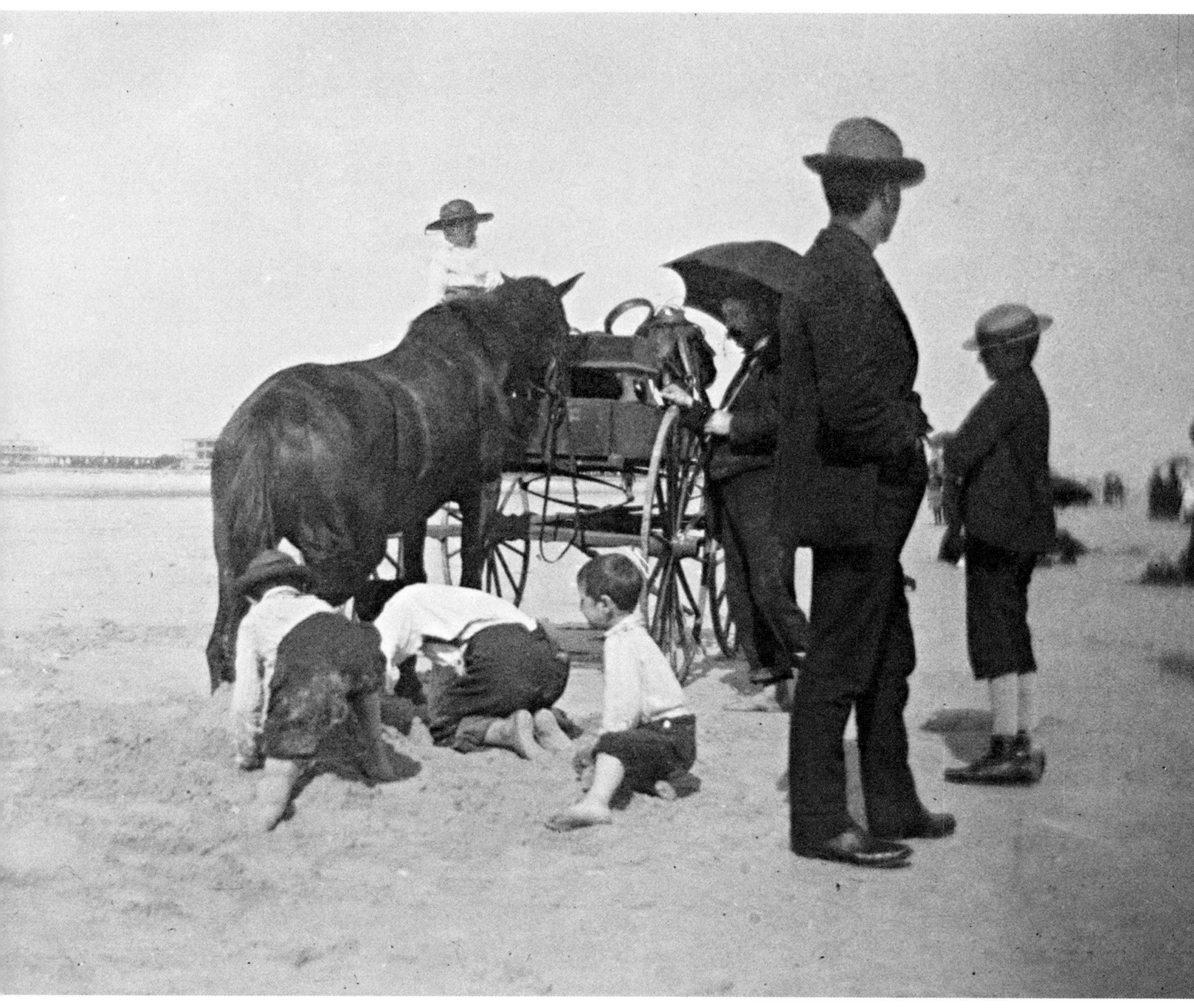

This stately image of a family with their carriage
at Coney Island recalls Degas's *A Carriage At The
Races*, evoking a leisurely air of middle-class pros-
perity with the whole family enjoying a jaunt to the
seaside. With the emergence of new money and the
advent of the weekend came opportunities for lei-
sure activities, which Brainerd was keen to record.
Coney Island was a favorite haunt with Brainerd,
who exposed dozens of plates over the years.

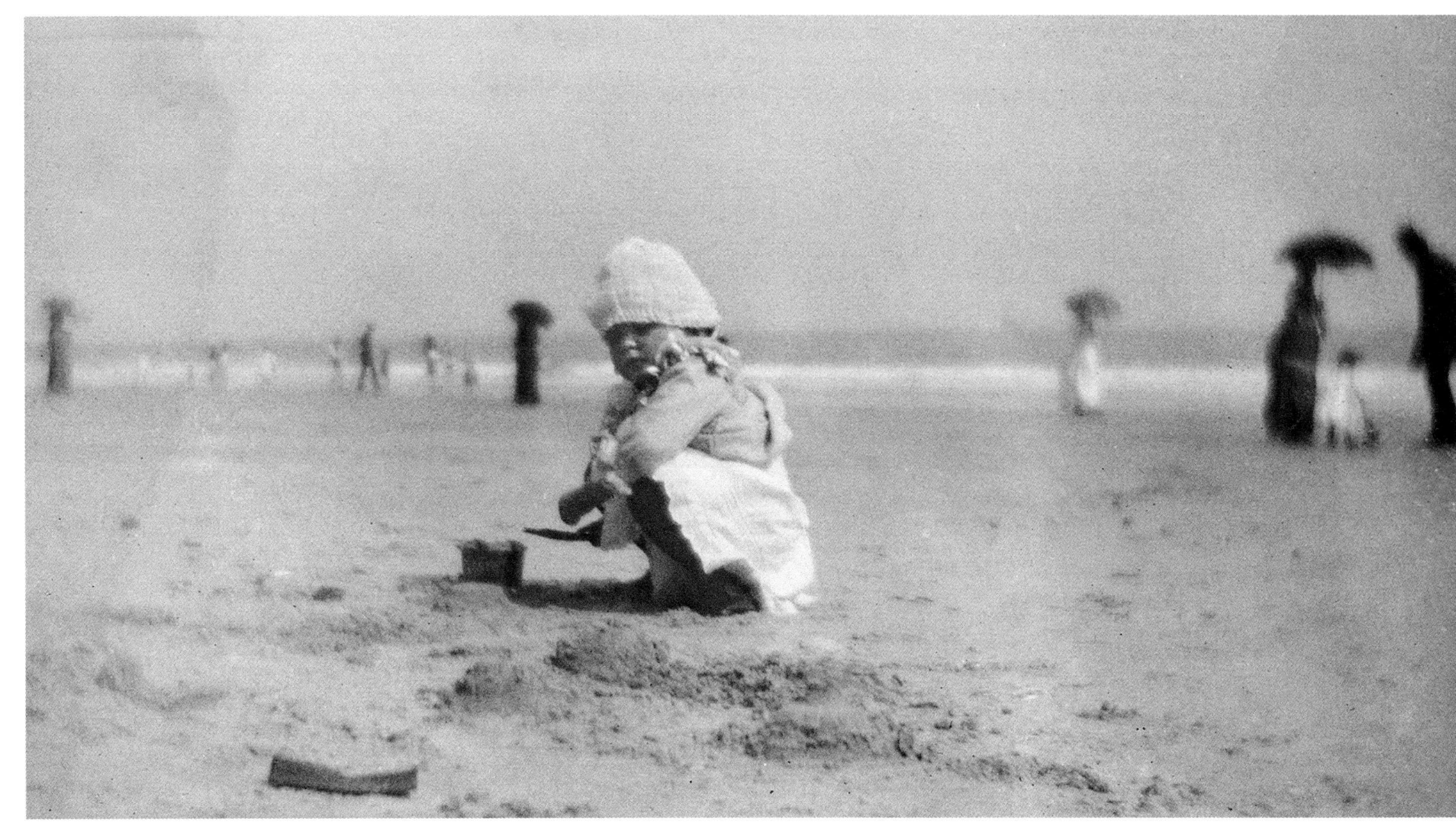

To the Seashore

I t's been said that wherever saltwater meets sand there's enjoyment. And few places have known as much plea- sure as a five-mile sweep of magnificent beach which Lenape Indians called "the land without shadows," and the Dutch named *Konijnen Eiland*, or "Rabbit Island," presum- ably from their abundance in the early days. We know the place as Coney Island. The seaside pleasure ground in south- ern Brooklyn has had various nicknames in its 175-year his- tory: "America's Playground," the "Nickel Empire," and even "Sodom By the Sea." Others have dubbed the entertainment mecca "Electric Eden" and the "Poor Man's Paradise," on whose sandy beaches half a million nearly naked bodies have been known to congregate. But whatever it goes by, the

Coney Island, late 1870s. Another of Brainerd's languorous images of the famous seaside resort anticipating in many ways the work of American Impressionist painters such as Edward Henry Potthast, who was also drawn to Coney Island but not until the early 1900s. George Bradford Brainerd Pho- tographic Collection, Brooklyn Public Library/Center for Brooklyn History.

Coney Island, 1875. A ghostly image of 19th-century beachgoers and a solitary figure in the sand. The picture was taken using wet plate apparatus with a long exposure, which accounts for the motion blur. The figure at the left in the bowler hat, probably Brainerd himself, had to stand stock-still during the minutes-long exposure, which creates a nice interplay with the figures in motion, producing a sort of proto-cinematic effect. George Bradford Brainerd Photographic Collection, Brooklyn Public Library/ Center for Brooklyn History.

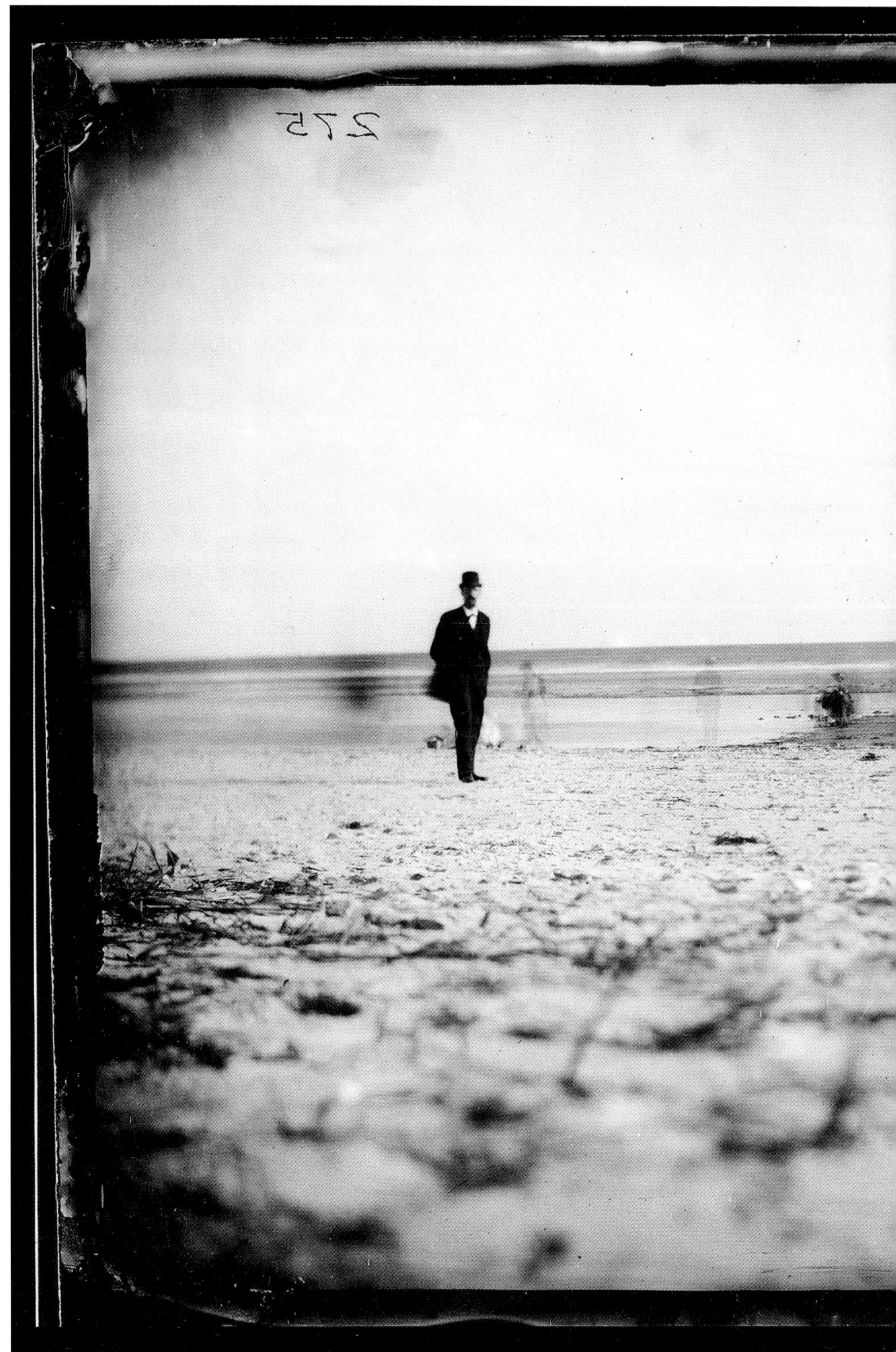

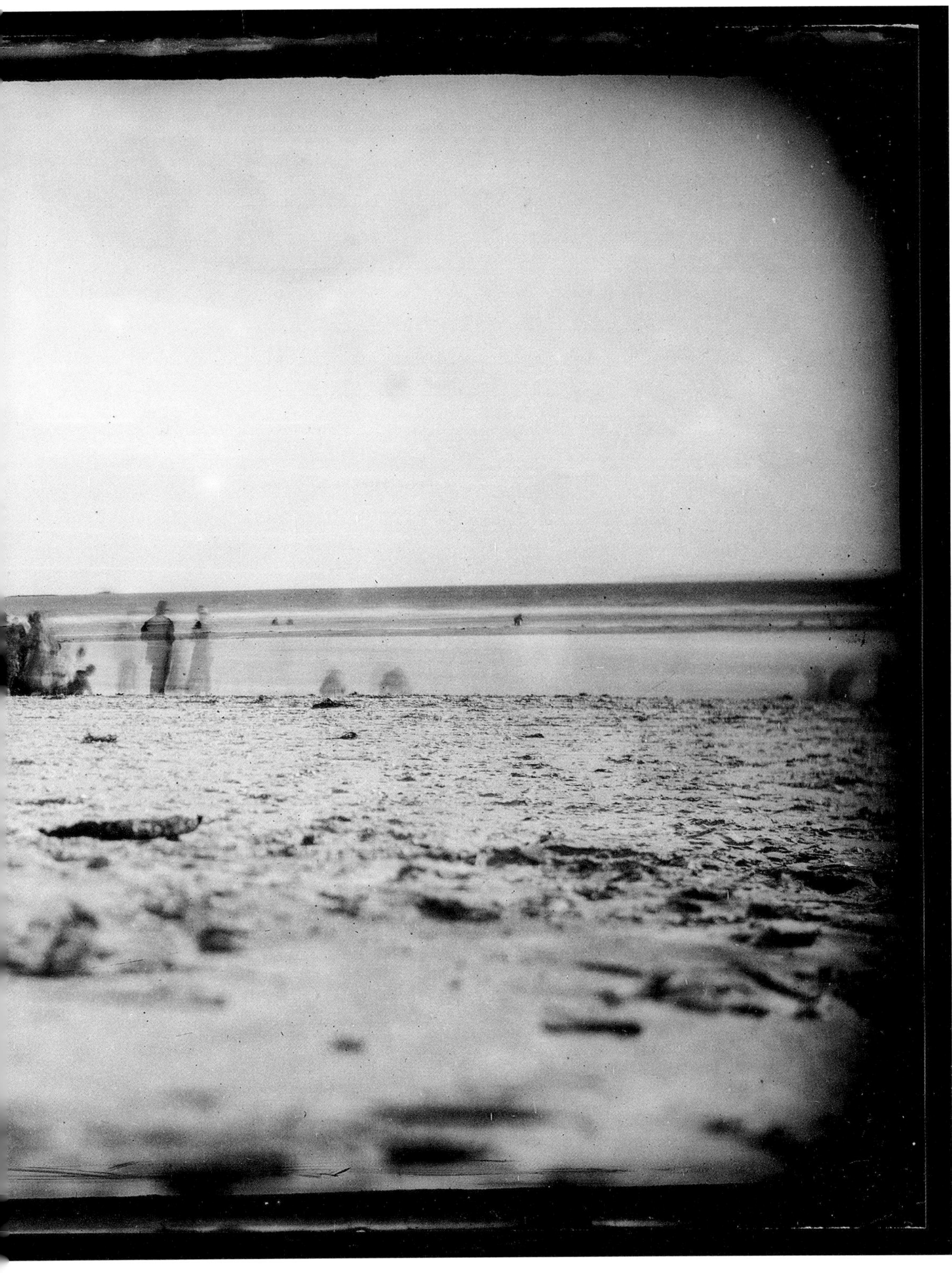

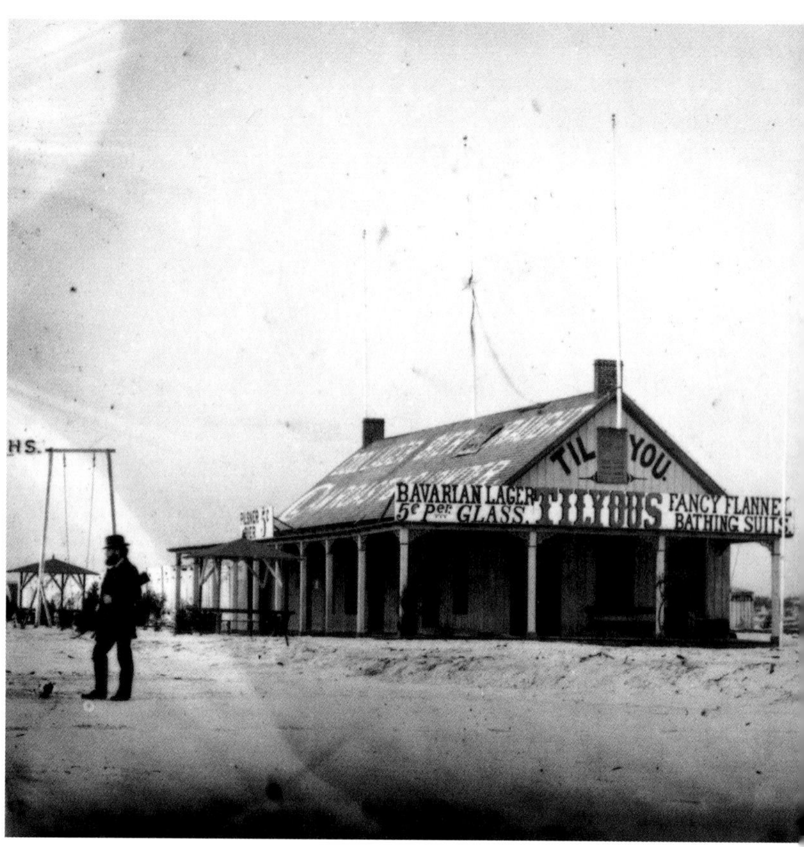

Poor Man's Paradise has aways been a picture-taker's paradise. No place in America, not even the Grand Canyon, has inspired such a rich photographic record.

In the 1870s, when Brainerd started taking pictures of the summer resort and its flocks of bathers, Coney Island was still a disreputable place, populated by muggers, gamblers, and petty thieves, Indeed, things were so out of hand, that Brooklyn police detectives, probably in exchange for a little donation, were in the habit of tipping off the three-card monte men prior to raids, prompting an exasperated *Brooklyn Eagle* to ask, "What Are the Detectives Good For?" Still, in spite of such inconveniences, a visitor to the resort in those years pronounced it worthy of an occasional visit, as long as one did not bring along a sister or a girlfriend: "On the whole, Coney Island, though shabby, third class, worn out and often frequented by hard characters, is not a bad place to visit once in a great while."

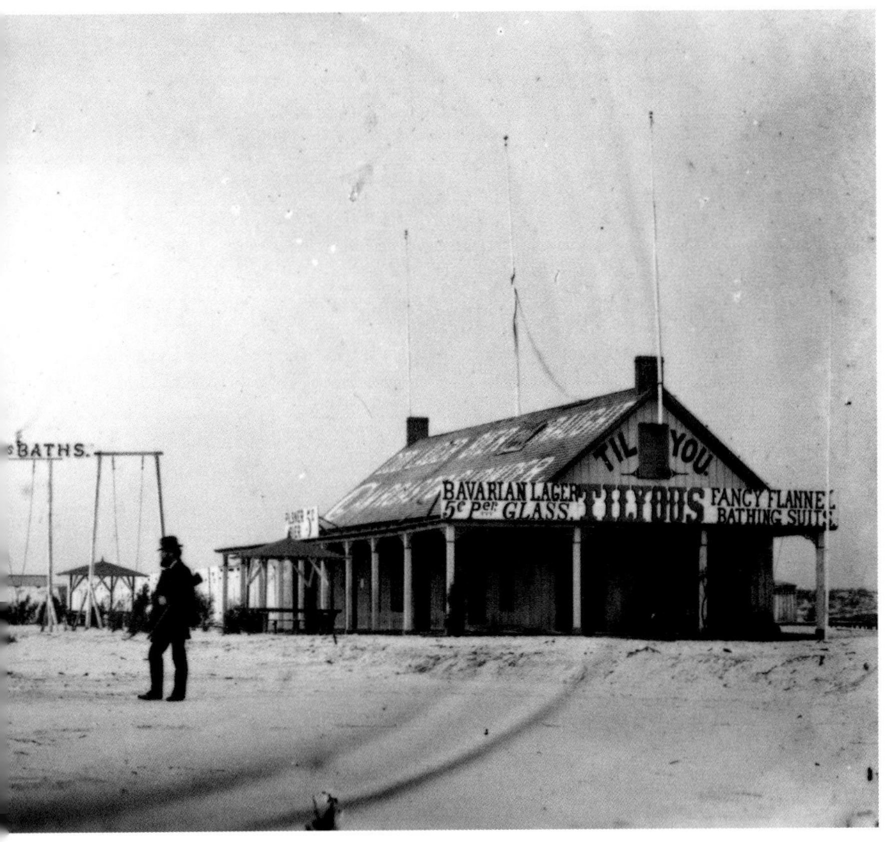

Tilyou Surf House, Coney Island, 1874. George Brainerd had been fascinated with Coney Island ever since he was a little boy, when the area was so remote Melville enjoyed its solitude as he worked to complete *Moby Dick*. About the same time, the shaggy-bearded Walt Whitman could be glimpsed ambling along the beach declaiming Shakespeare to the seagulls. Tilyou Surf House was started by the parents of George Tilyou (1862–1914), the great showman who created Coney Island's most enduring attraction, Steeple-chase Park, which opened in 1897. At the Surf House, George's father, Peter Tilyou, offered free clam chowder bowls to guests who purchased a 25-cent ticket to bathe at the Coney Island Beach. Coney Island was still a rough place in these years, which might explain the shotgun-toting gentle-man in the foreground. George Bradford Brainerd Photograph Collection, Brooklyn Public Library/Center for Brooklyn History.

Brainerd's photographs, spanning the wet- and dry-plate eras, offer a remarkable record of Coney Island's transformation, from a collection of sand dunes and bathing shacks, to its boom years after the Civil War, when a series of larger beer saloons, hotels, and bathhouses were hastily put up and great swarms of people, brought thither by trolleys and railroads, began to descend on the resort, which would soon become America's greatest amusement park. Again, we are left to wonder what Brainerd's feelings about Coney Island really were—except that it was a visual treat! And that's probably enough.

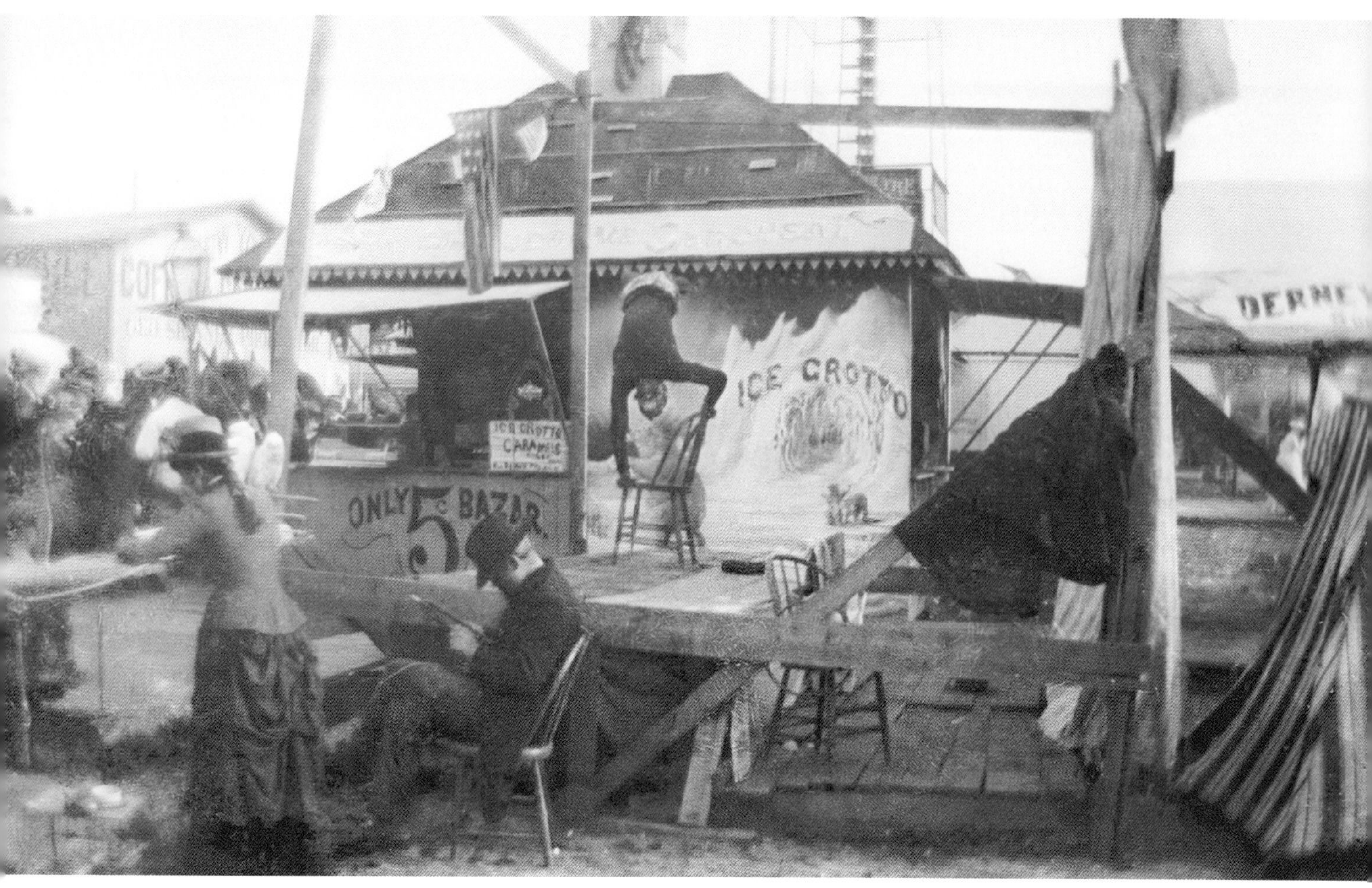

An Afternoon at Coney Island —*New York Sun*, 1860

"Coney Island was formerly in much greater repute among New Yorkers than it is at present, but of late years it has lost its reputation, and is not the place to which most people could take a sister or lady friend. The [Steamboat where you arrive] is a rickety affair, threatening to tumble down at every moment. There is no canopy, no waiting room, nothing to shelter visitors, nothing to be seen but sand, sky, water and dock. After landing . . . a broad sandy path, with wooden flat boards, conducts the visitor to the hotel, or pavilion, or drinking saloon, or clam bakery, whichever you may please to call the big, clumsy yellow wooden house standing there. A short distance beyond are the bathing houses.

Coney Island acrobat, 1870s. Brainerd's camouflaged camera allowed him to probe the seamier side of Coney Island, with its freak shows, brash beer stands, and rollicking gambling joints. Here, Brainerd's keen lens captures a legless acrobat performing a handstand on a chair—a haunting image evoking the work of the great photographer Diane Arbus. George Bradford Brainerd Photograph Collection, Brooklyn Public Library/Center for Brooklyn History.

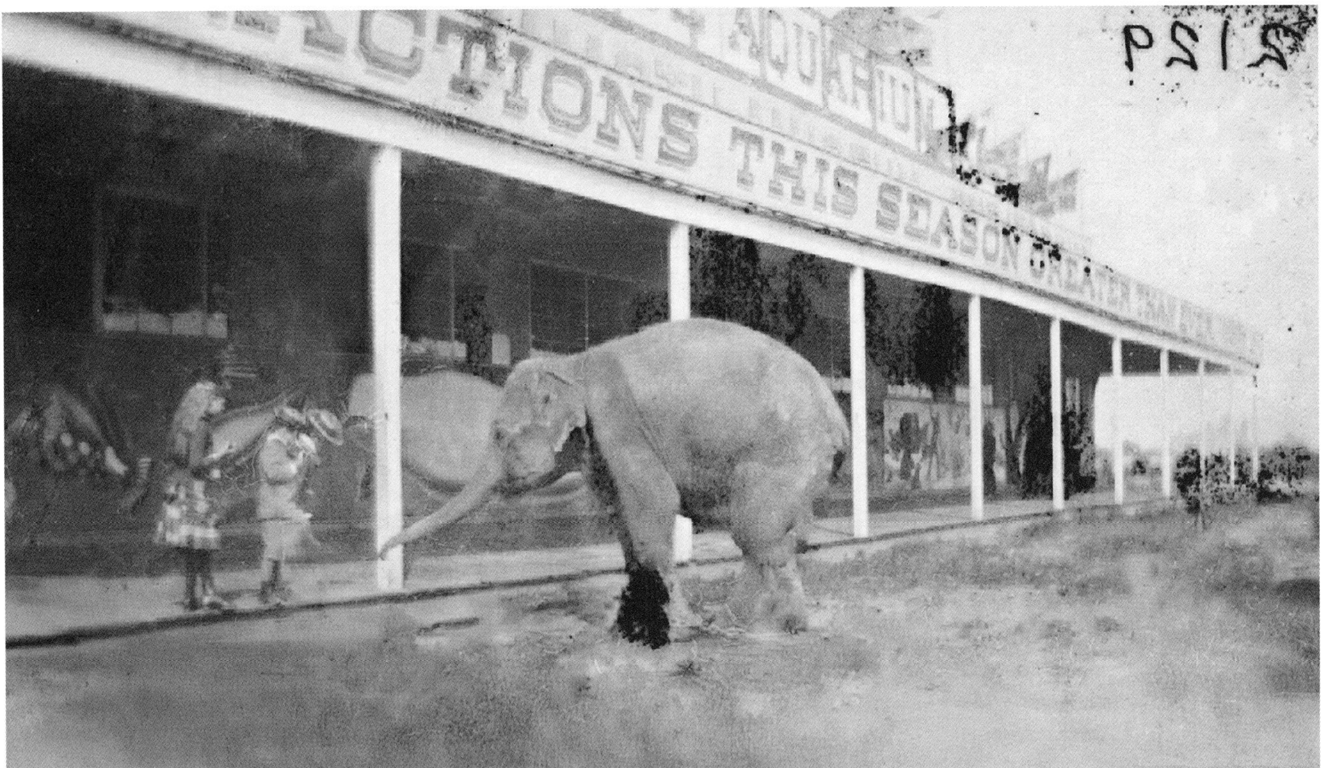

Feeding an Elephant, Coney Island, 1870s. George Bradford Brainerd Photograph Collection, Brooklyn Public Library/Center for Brooklyn History.

"These bathing houses are unutterably shabby and forlorn. They stand in rows forming a quadrangle, the area of which is covered with sand, agreeably diversified with noxious weeds, bits of superannuated tinware, fragments of old hats and the remains of a cat or two. You pay 18 cents for the use of a bathing costume, consisting of blue overalls without buttons, but tied with strings of blue shirt and a shockingly bad straw hat, frayed around the rim till the straw stands around the head . . . like a halo of prickly glory. With these treasures, you retire to one of the bathing houses, which is scarcely big enough to turn around in. . . . The lock is most probably broken, and you are obliged to fasten the door with your cravat. In this magnificent saloon the transformation takes place, and you emerge a very shabby, uncouth barefooted wretch.

"You feel exceedingly mean as you scuffle over the sand to the water's edge, eyed by numerous strangers who daily congregate at this locality. Plunging about in the surf are vast numbers of ugly monsters, dripping with wet, and with

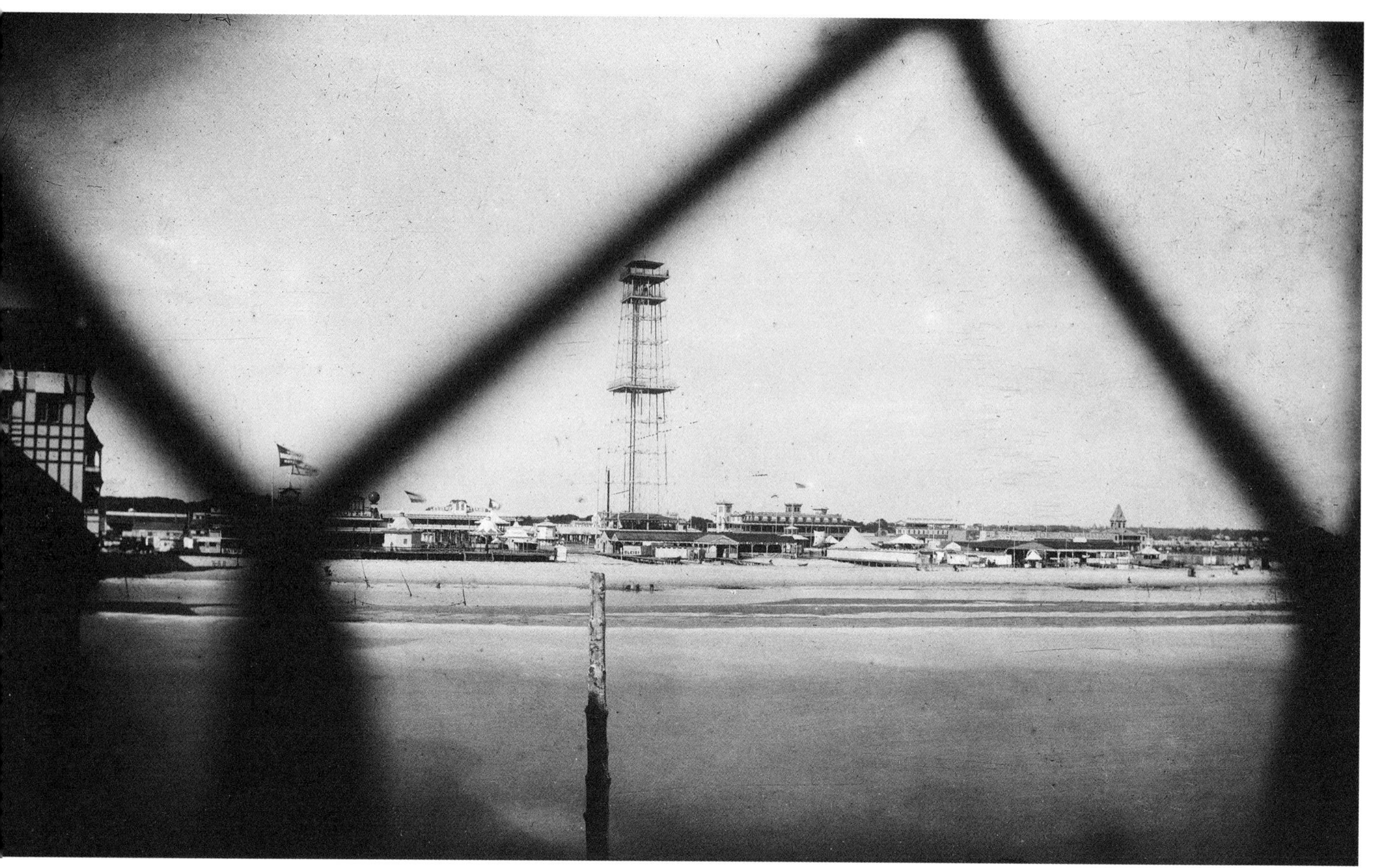

their clothes clinging tight to their bodies. You joined them. They leap about in the surf; They let the great breakers roll over them; They gambol, they play, they make themselves supremely ridiculous, and at last skulk over the sand back to the shabbily constructed bathing houses, donned their own garments and mixed with the crowd on the beach."

Beyond the Breakers —*Brooklyn Daily Eagle*, 1872

"On Wednesday last Mr. James Cassidy of New York, visited Coney Island, and went in bathing. He ventured beyond the breakers and was carried a mile or two from the beach. His perilous condition was earnestly watched by his friends onshore for more than an hour, when the Steamboat *Americacus* hove insight and rescued the almost exhausted man. He was taken on board, covered with blankets, and landed in New York."

View of Culver's Tower Coney Island, 1879. In 1876, following the close of the Philadelphia Centennial Exhibition, railroad entrepreneur Andrew Culver purchased one of the main attractions, Sawyer's Observation Tower, and re-erected it at Culver Plaza South on Coney Island. Often called the Iron Tower, the Steel Tower, or the Iron Observatory, the steel structure stood a dizzying 300-feet high. Two steam elevators carried visitors to a platform at the top where telescopes gave a 40-mile panoramic view. George Bradford Brainerd Photograph Collection, Brooklyn Public Library/Center for Brooklyn History.

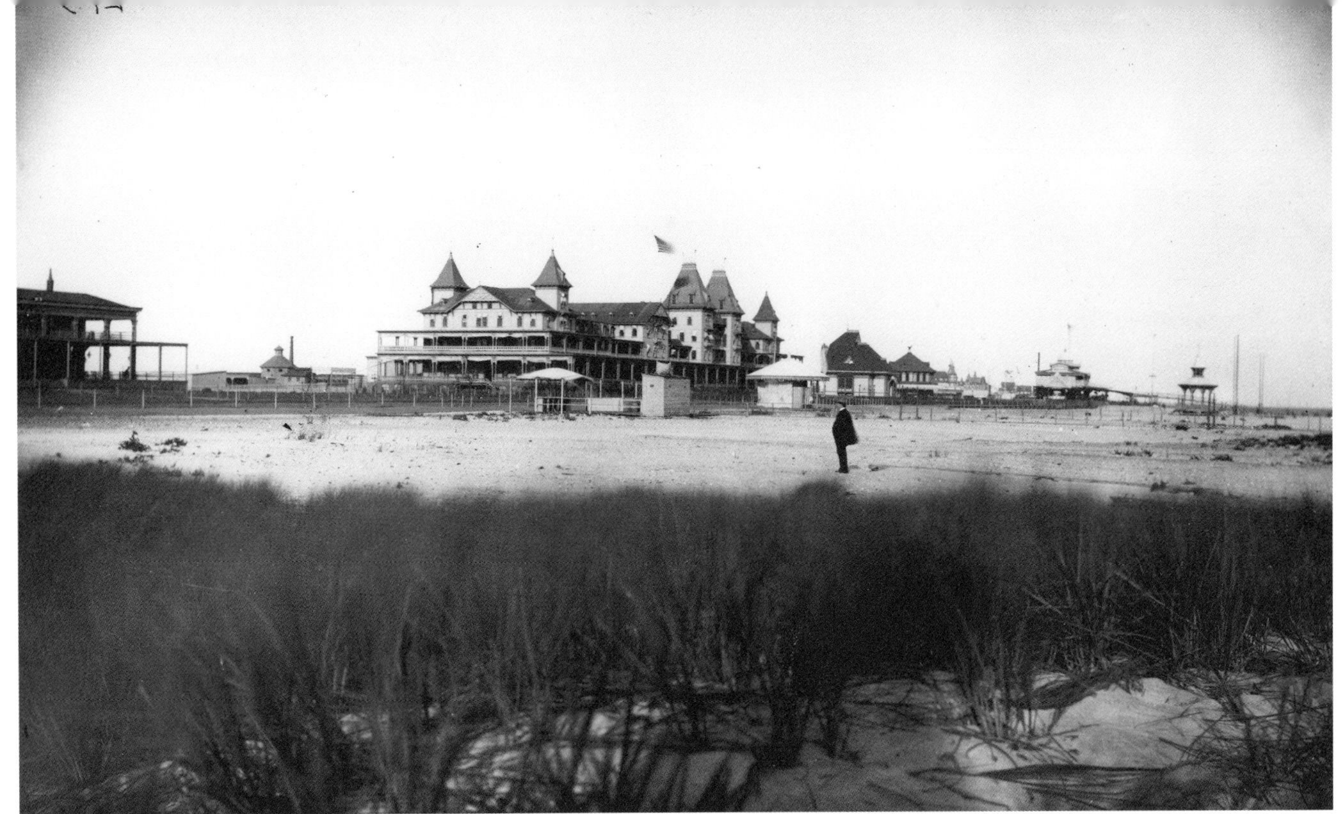

Above, the turreted Brighton Beach Hotel circa 1878 looms above the dunes on Brighton Beach, just east of Coney Island proper. In contrast to Coney Island, which attracted mostly working-class visitors, Brighton Beach catered to middle- and upper-middle-class families, with a sumptuous hotel, music hall, and even a horse-racing track. Below, one of the great early attractions to Coney Island, the so-called Elephantine Colossus, which towered 122 feet above Surf Avenue from 1885 to 1896. The seven-story structure, designed by James V. Lafferty, boasted a grand hall and a museum as well as a telescope from which visitors got a bird's-eye view of the sprawling amusement park. George Bradford Brainerd Photographic Collection, Brooklyn Public Library/Center for Brooklyn History.

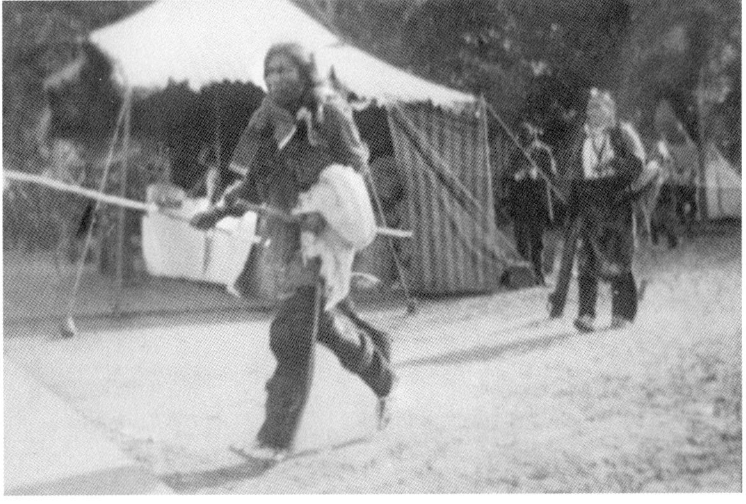

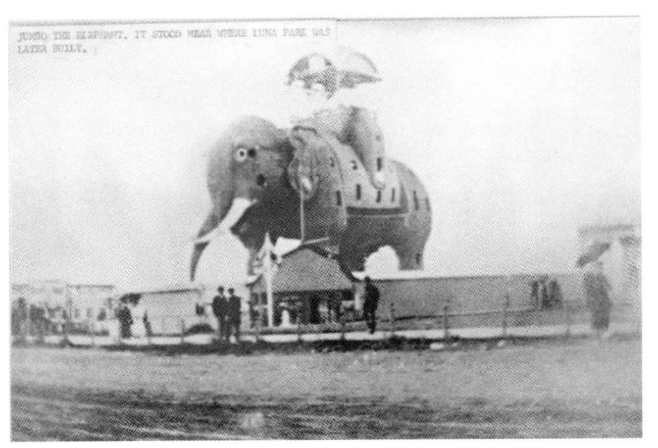

Native American performers, Coney Island 1870s. While ex-cavalrymen like George Armstrong Custer were rounding up American Indians on the Great Plains, showmen like P. T. Barnum were profiting from their uprooted condition, enlisting Native acts to whoop it up under the Big Top. Coney Island impresarios also brought in aboriginals such as purported headhunters to thrill crowds, hence this American Indian, which Brainerd photographed at Coney Island around 1878 running with a spear.

127

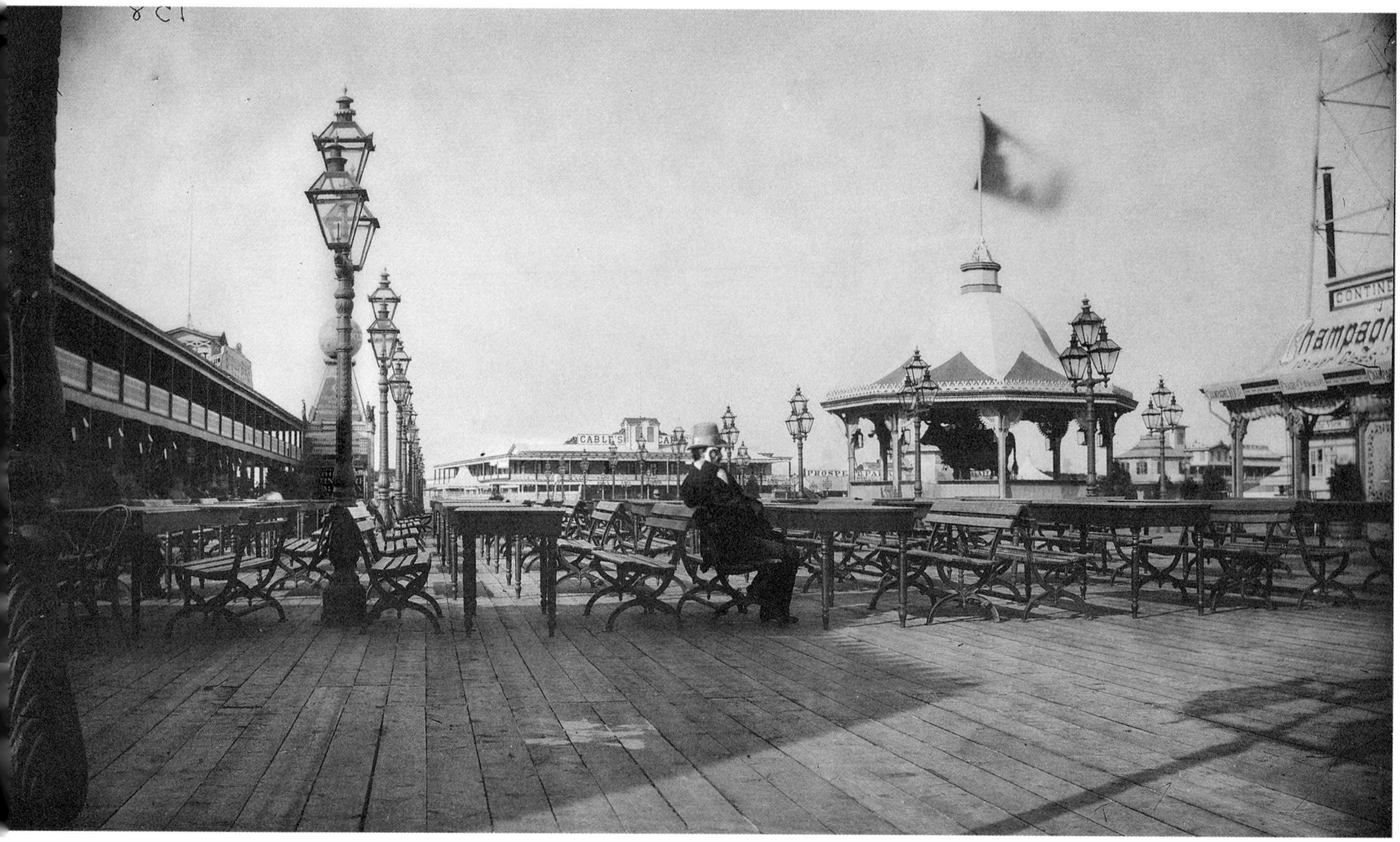

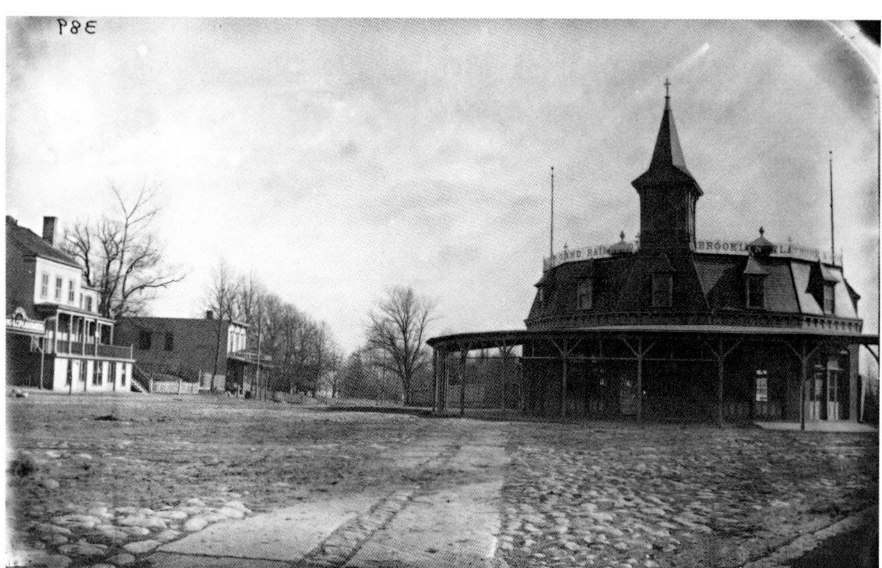

Left, Coney Island Railroad Station, 1870s. Andrew R. Culver, president of the Prospect Park and Coney Island Railroad, built a steam railway to West Brighton, the Culver Line, in the 1860s. For 35 cents, one could ride the Prospect Park & Coney Island Railroad to the Culver Depot terminal at Surf Avenue. Above, the so-called "Iron Cow," along the Boardwalk. George Bradford Brainerd Photograph Collection, Brooklyn Public Library/Center for Brooklyn History.

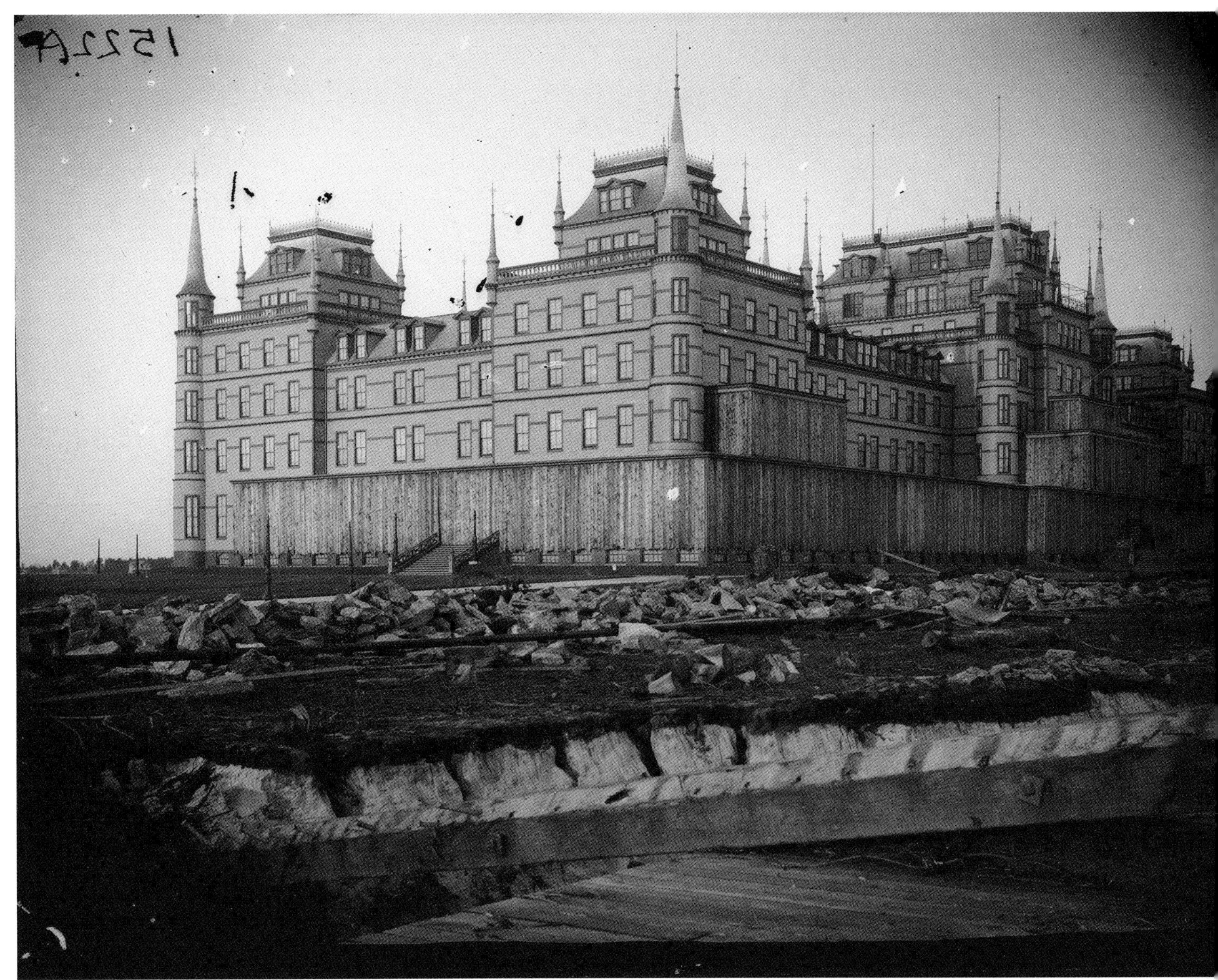

Oriental Hotel, Brighton Beach, 1877. While Coney Island was cultivating its unsavory reputation as the haunt of muggers, petty thieves, and gamblers, nearby Manhattan and Brighton Beach were going in the other direction, with cany developers like William Engeman and Austin Corbin putting up lavish hotels catering to New York's carriage trade. The most celebrated of these resorts were the Brighton Beach Hotel, the Manhattan Beach Hotel, and Oriental Hotel, the Oriental being the most lavish of the three. Built by Corbin in 1878, the Oriental was the haunt of the super-rich, who enjoyed steam-powered elevators whisking them between seven floors, and a restaurant that could accommodate 20,000 diners a day. Of course, this being the Gilded Age, all this magnificence was the scheme of a crook, a colorful one for sure. Austin Corbin, a banking and railroad tycoon, made a fortune in the post–Civil War South running an Arkansas cotton plantation using convict labor. When that plan fizzled, he worked out a deal with an Italian prince to bring over Italian immigrants, who like the enslaved Africans before them, were more or less Corbin's chattel, forced to toil in his cotton fields. Corbin's bigoted, racist views came to the fore in Brooklyn when he announced that "Jews" were barred from the Oriental Hotel, a policy that was widely condemned, but didn't stop Corbin from continuing to rake in millions. He eventually retired to a 22,000-acre New Hampshire estate that would host such luminaries as Theodore Roosevelt and the Prince of Whales. George Bradford Brainerd Photograph Collection, Brooklyn Public Library/Center for Brooklyn History.

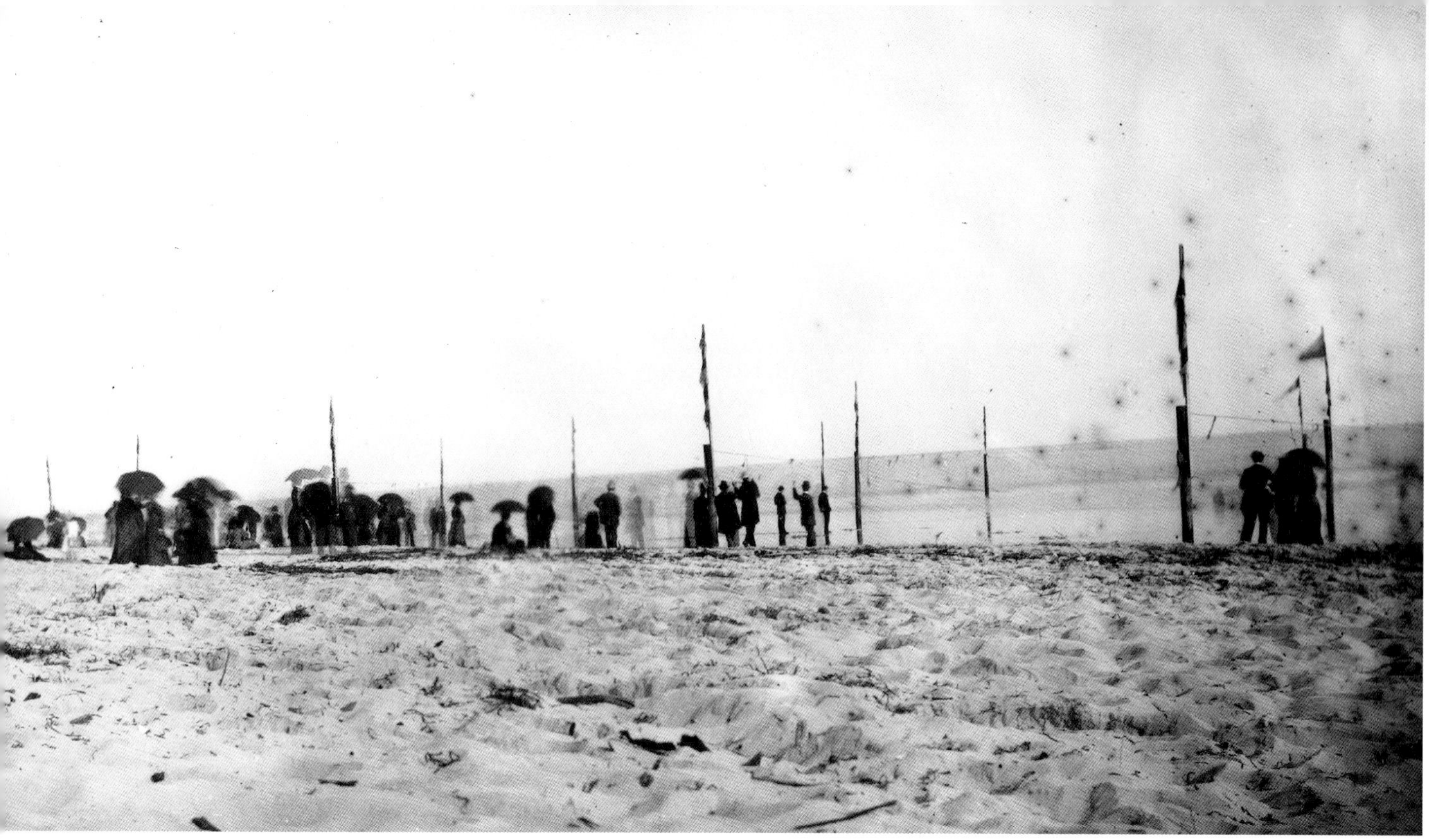

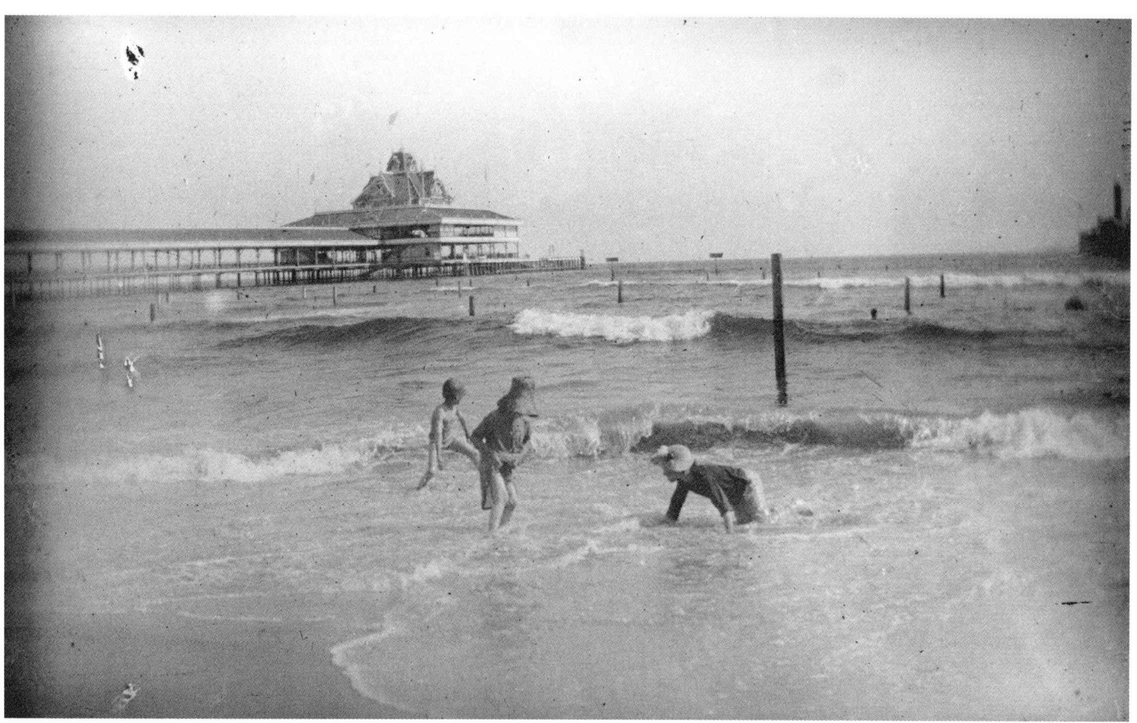

These two photographs by Brainerd, the first from the 1870s and second from the 1880s, chronicle the evolution of the seaside vacation culture, with beachgoers in the early days donning street clothes and promenading along on shore like a Parisian boulevard. By the mid-1880s, however, families were splashing in the waves much like today, the only difference being Victorian swimwear, which was rather more elaborate for modesty's sake. Coney Island beach, 1884. George Bradford Brainerd Photographic Collection, Brooklyn Public Library/Center for Brooklyn History.

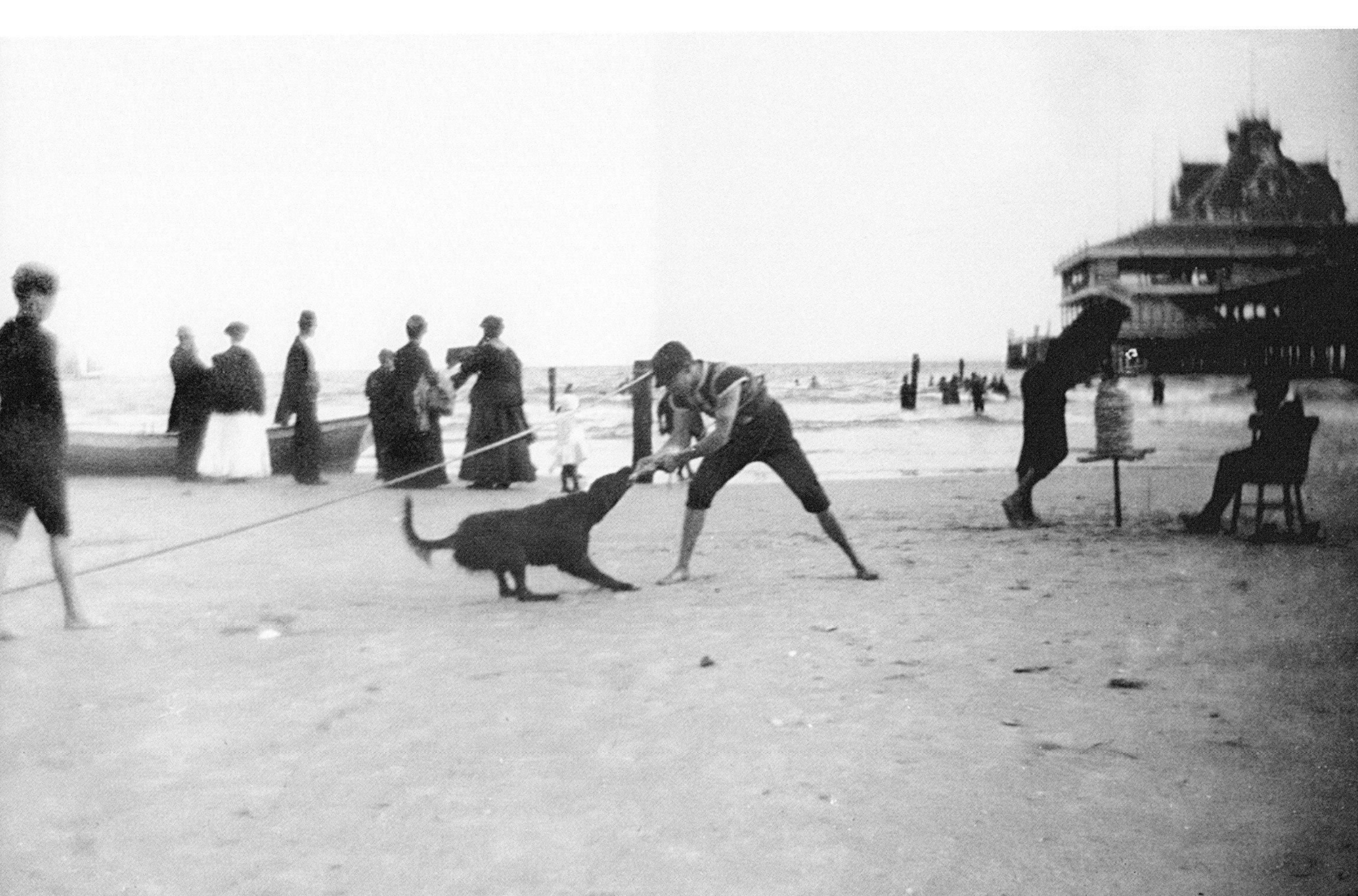

Boy and dog, Coney Island, 1870s. This photograph again shows Brainerd's attention to composition while capturing the leisurely atmosphere at Coney Island—the playful tug-of-war with a dog contrasting with the languid manner of bathers. George Bradford Brainerd Photograph Collection, Brooklyn Public Library/Center for Brooklyn History.

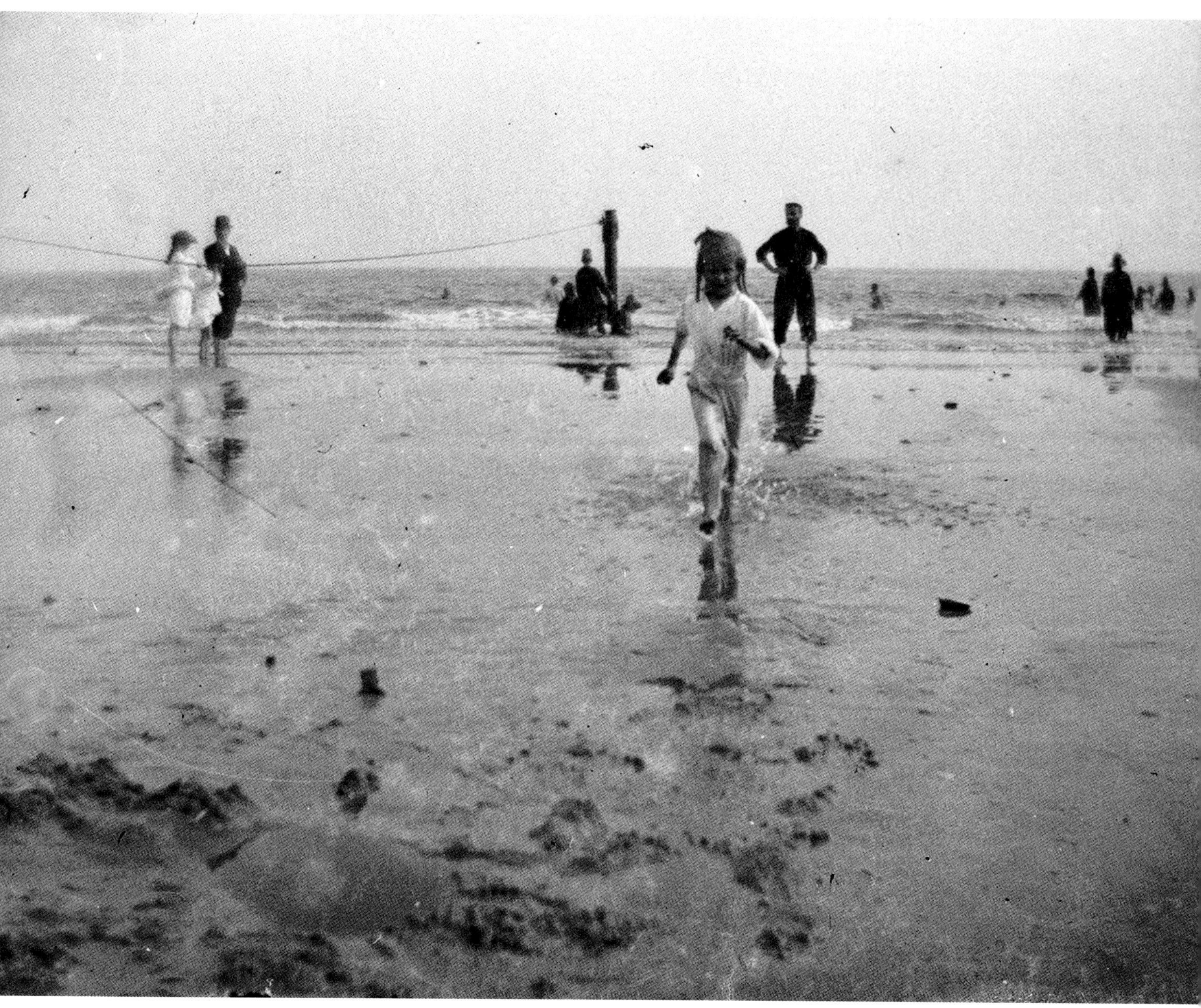

Coney Island beach, 1884. George Bradford
Brainerd Photographic Collection, Brooklyn
Public Library/Center for Brooklyn History.

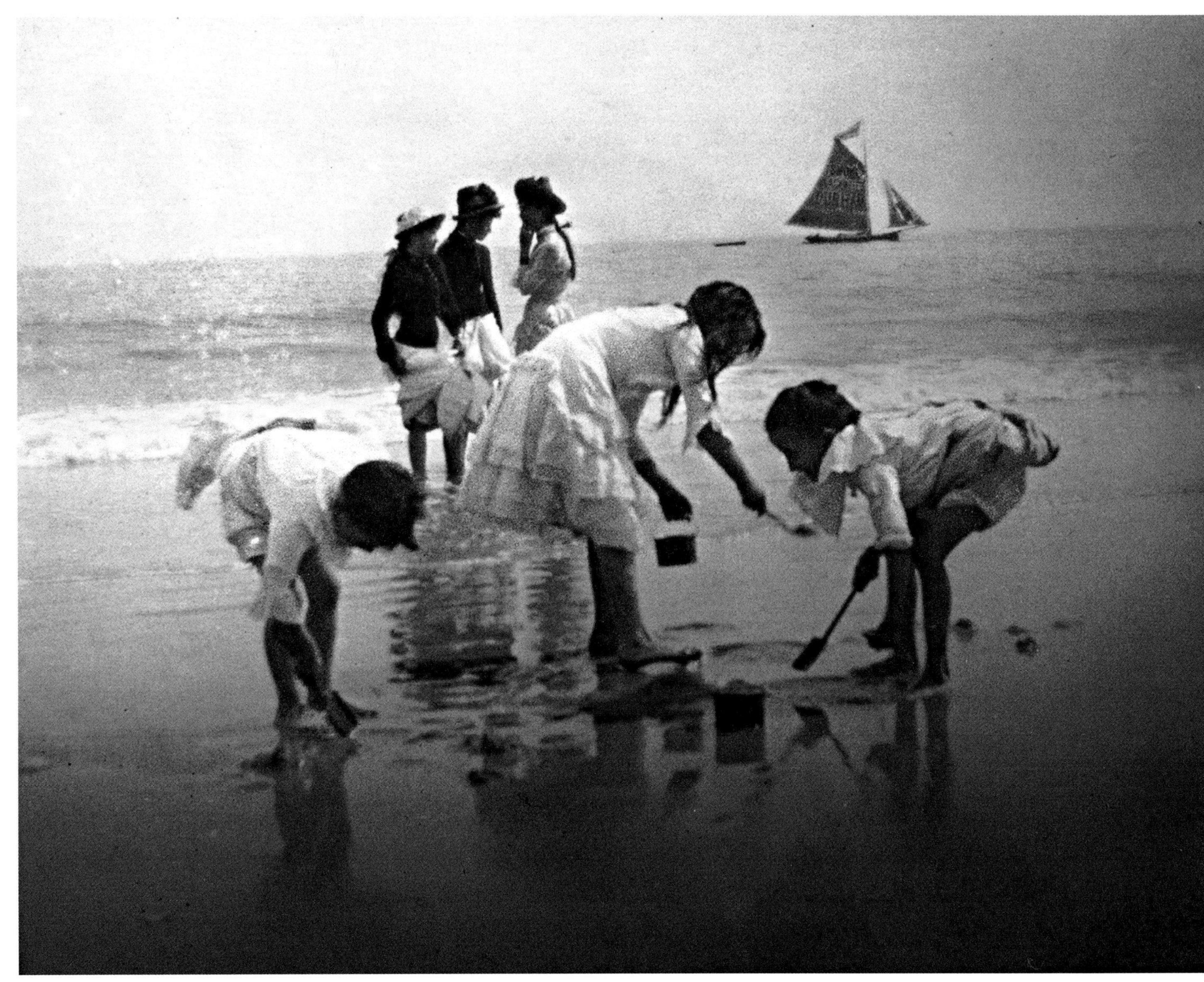

Girls playing on the beach, Coney Island, 1877. The beach was a particularly recurrent theme
with the French Impressionist, who, thanks to the invention of portable paint tubes, could bring
their easels outdoors and paint *en plein air.* Brainerd may have had Manet in mind when he
made this enchanting photograph of girls in their beach frocks with a solitary sailboat on the hori-
zon. No American painter, however, at this early date, had captured the America seashore with
such emotional power as George Brainerd, the amateur photographer from Brooklyn. George
Bradford Brainerd Photograph Collection, Brooklyn Public Library/Center for Brooklyn History.

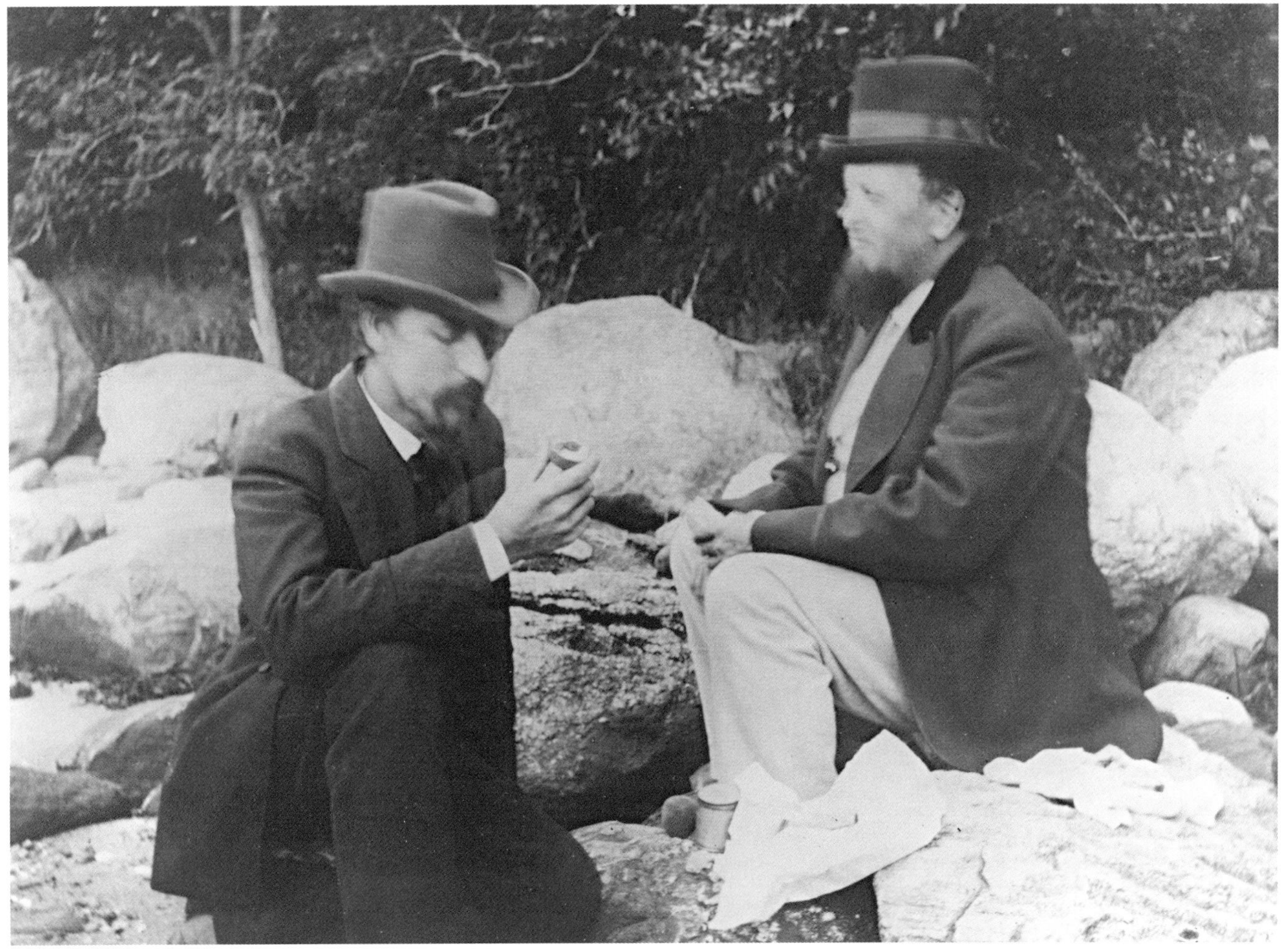

When I think about my childhood, I see pictures.

—Joan Scavetta Hesselberg

I'm indebted to many people for making this book possible. I want to particularly thank Tom Piezzo, former director of the Brainerd Memorial Library, in Haddam, Connecticut, who first introduced me to the work of George Bradford Brainerd, through the library's collection of Brainerd's Connecticut River photographs, taken between 1878 and 1885. Tom wanted to exhibit a few of these, many of which were local scenes, and asked me to prepare a

A dapper George Brainerd (left) takes a break to enjoy a peach during a photography outing on Long Island. His companion is probably Wallace Goold Levison, another amateur picture-taker from Brooklyn with whom Brainerd enjoyed a close friendship. After Brainerd's death, Levison wound up with a number of Brainerd's photographic plates, which are now mistakenly attributed to Levison, though a majority are Brainerd's, or, at least, were taken with cameras he devised and built. Indeed, Levison never claimed to be a photographer, but a chemist.

brief biography of Brainerd, who was born in 1845 in the Haddam Neck section of town, a descendant of one of the town's founders. Tom also located a copy of Julie C. Moffat's 1996 New York University master's thesis on Brainerd, where I was intrigued by the statement, "The definitive work on George Brainerd has yet to be done." I took this as a challenge, though I've only scratched the surface on the work of this pioneering 19th-century photographer, whose contribution to the medium is largely unrecognized.

The George Bradford Brainerd collection, consisting of nearly 2,000 glass plates, is jointly held by The Brooklyn Museum and The Brooklyn Public Library. I'm grateful to both institutions for their valuable assistance. I especially want to thank Alice Griffin, archivist at BPL's Center for Brooklyn History, for her generous assistance in obtaining high-resolution digital images of the Brainerd plates, many of which are printed here for the first time. I also wish to thank Stephanie Crawford, archivist with the Brooklyn Museum, who was able to locate an unpublished manuscript with a sketch on Brainerd, containing fascinating tidbits about Brainerd's work with the Brooklyn Water Department, as well as some details regarding his early photography, including the fact that he experimented successfully with coffee as an emulsion for dry plates instead of the standard gelatin used in candy making. Others to whom I am grateful are my publicist, Maria Weinberger, who read early drafts of the book and provided many valuable suggestions, as well as Jenny Heath Law, librarian at Brainerd Library, who helped secure several key documents relating to Brainerd's only patent for an early "Detective" model camera.

I do not know how I'll ever be able to thank my former colleague at Shore Line Newspapers in Guilford, Connecticut, photographer Kim Tyler, who, along with her partner, Cary Pollick, worked tirelessly to ensure Brainerd's glass negatives looked as sharp and crisp as when they were first exposed in the 1870s and 1880s. The delicate emulsions of more than a few of the plates had been damaged, some, it seemed, beyond repair. But Kim, through the magic of digital technology, was able to restore them to their former glory. For that, and a dozen other technical issues Kim was able to solve, I am eternally grateful.

I wanted this book to be a visual treat. I think it is, which is mostly due to the efforts of Meredith Dias, senior production editor at Globe, and her team. Many thanks also to my editor, Rick Rinehart, not only for believing in this project from the start, but also for his steady hand in shepherding the work from the idea stage to the final printed book.

Often, as I worked on this book, I paused to look at a little box camera I have on a shelf in my office—a classic Kodak Brownie, or Kodak No. 2, this one in red leatherette, which once sold for only $1, making "instant" photography accessible to nearly everyone. The Brownie belonged to my mom, a first-generation Italian American from Astoria in Queens, Joan Scavetta Hesselberg, who at this writing is 94 years young. Mom was what was described in the early days of the snapshot as a "camera fiend," taking her little red Brownie everywhere, even on a trip she made to Mexico with her girlfriends after World War II. "We drove through the desert at night," Mom often says of her adventure. "We were so scared, we thought there were bandits hiding in the bushes!" Today, half a dozen scrapbooks at the bottom of her clothes closet attest to her diligence as a "snapshooter" and provide a visual diary of her childhood in Queens as well as a record of her many travels. The pictures are a treasure. No one would call them art, but they tell a story. "When a photo of a person looks deep into your spirit and tells you a thousand stories," wrote Sameh Elsayed, "stories from your past even before you existed, then the photo is way above any description." Thank you, Mom, for your love of stories—it is to you I dedicate this book.